Life-Span Communication

LEA'S COMMUNICATION SERIES
Jennings Bryant/Dolf Zillmann, General Editors

Selected Titles in Applied Communications
(Teresa L. Thompson, Advisory Editor) include:

Braithwaite/Thompson • Handbook of Communication and People With Disabilities

Hornik • Public Health Communication: Evidence for Behavior Change

Hummert/Nussbaum • Aging, Communication and Health: Linking Research and Practice for Successful Aging

Nussbaum/Coupland • Handbook of Communication and Aging Research, Second Edition

Nussbaum/Pecchioni/Robinson/Thompson • Communication and Aging, Second Edition

Ray • Communication and Disenfranchisement: Social Health Issues and Implications

Socha/Diggs • Communication, Race, and Family: Exploring Communication in Black, White, and Biracial Families

Whaley • Explaining Illness: Research, Theory, and Strategy

Williams/Nussbaum • Intergenerational Communication Across the Life Span

For a complete list of LEA titles, please contact Lawrence Erlbaum Associates, Publishers, at www.erlbaum.com.

Life-Span Communication

Loretta L. Pecchioni
Lousiana State University

Kevin B. Wright
University of Oklahoma

Jon F. Nussbaum
Pennsylvania State University

LAWRENCE ERLBAUM ASSOCIATES, PUBLISHERS
2005   Mahwah, New Jersey   London

This book was typeset in 11/13 pt. Goudy Roman, Bold, and Italic.
The heads were typeset in Americana, Americana Bold, and Americana Bold Italic

Lawrence Erlbaum Associates, Inc., Publishers
10 Industrial Avenue
Mahwah, New Jersey 07430
www.erlbaum.com

Cover design by Kathryn Houghtaling Lacey

Library of Congress Cataloging-in-Publication Data

Life-span communication / [edited by] Loretta L. Pecchioni, Kevin B. Wright,
    Jon F. Nussbaum.—2nd ed.
        p.   cm.—(LEA's communication series)
    Includes bibliographical references and index.
    ISBN 0-8058-4111-3 (case : alk. paper)—ISBN 0-8058-4112-1 (pbk. : alk. paper)
        1. Interpersonal communication.   2. Communication—Psychological aspects.
    3. Developmental psychology.   I. Pecchioni, Loretta L. II. Wright, Kevin B.
    III. Nussbaum, Jon F. IV. Series.

    BF637.C45L53   2005
    153.6—dc22   2005007213

Books published by Lawrence Erlbaum Associates are printed on
acid-free paper, and their bindings are chosen for strength and
durability.

Printed in the United States of America
10 9 8 7 6 5 4 3 2 1

To
Joe and Loretta
Carrie
Mary Ann, Molly, Kara, and Emily

Contents in Brief

Contents

III: RELATIONAL CONTEXTS

Preface

Human beings naturally grow and develop, learning from their experiences and redefining the meaning of events as they reflect on the past in light of new events. Because we are inherently social creatures, we are also communicative creatures. Communication allows us to share our inner thoughts with others. Sharing our lives is at the heart of human existence. This text examines the role of communication in our lives as we age, from our earliest years to the end of our lives.

The first chapter lays the foundation with an overview of the theoretical and methodological issues related to studying communication across the life span and provides a more detailed preview of the later sections. The second section discusses the foundations of communication—cognitive processes and language. Next, we examine communication in relational contexts and selected communication competencies reflecting change as we grow and develop. This in-depth examination of interpersonal processes is followed by a review of communication in leisure and the media as it relates to the life-span perspective. The last chapter returns to our earlier discussion of theoretical and methodological issues, providing a summary of the issues discussed throughout the book and discussing the implications the life-span perspective has for future research.

Examining communication dynamics as they change across the life span is at the heart of my research concerns. Learning about the numerous ways in which individuals adapt to their changing circumstances and renegotiate their relationships is fascinating to me. I was first introduced to these issues during my graduate career, thanks to Jon Nussbaum. However, his groundbreaking text, *Life-span Communication: Normative Processes* (1989), is now out of date, and a tremendous increase in research related to these issues called for an update. Thus, this book was conceived to address the growth in research related to life-span issues. As we discussed the update, I suggested the current format, which departs considerably from the first text. These changes are notable for those of you familiar with the original. Any problems you have with the current organization are my responsibility.

I want to thank my coauthors for their considerable contributions to the text. Not only did Jon Nussbaum serve as an inspiration for this update, he wrote significant portions of the text. Kevin Wright breathed new life into the project when it was stalled, and his writing contributions are significant. Any problems with the structure, flow, and style of the text, however, are also my responsibility. I also want to thank the staff at Lawrence Erlbaum Associates for their support and patience during this project. Linda Bathgate has always been supportive and understanding, even when I missed deadlines, and Karin Wittig Bates has been incredibly helpful in moving the text through the publication process.

Working on this book has been both a joy and a struggle for me. As a consequence, I have learned more than I expected. Now that it is in your hands, I hope that you, the readers, will find something in it that is of use in your personal lives, if not in your professional ones.

—*Loretta L. Pecchioni*
November 2004

Life-Span Communication

I

Introduction and Overview: Theoretical and Methodological Issues of Communication Across the Life Span

1

Life-Span Communication:
Perspective and
Methodology

This chapter is organized to introduce the Life-Span Communication perspective and how this unique and fascinating way of understanding human interaction can be captured in social scientific investigations. Attempts to understand and explain how human behavior may change across the life span have become quite popular in our sister disciplines of psychology, sociology, and human development (see Bigner, 1994; Hareven, 1978; Mosher, Youngman, & Day, 1999; Schwebel, Maher, & Fagley, 1990; Smith, 1996; and, Stevenson, 1994). A few pioneering communication scholars, borrowing heavily from the efforts in these complementary disciplines, began to speculate several decades ago that a life span approach may be a useful metaperspective in our attempt to capture the complexities of human communication at different points during our lives (Knapp, 1978; Nussbaum, 1989).

Life span developmental psychologists have typically been interested in how cognitive processes, such as intelligence or memory, develop and change across the life span. Sociologists interested in life span or life course (the more common term in sociology) changes have typically

3

concentrated their investigations on the changing demographic structure of various cultures, societies, or relationships and how these population changes relate to social policy. Communication scholars, using life-span theories, methodologies, and research findings generated by these social scientists, have begun to investigate language, cognition, communication skills, relationships, and many other topics typically addressed in the discipline of communication from a life-span perspective.

A brief but thorough description of what we mean by the life-span perspective is outlined in this chapter. Several assertions of the life-span perspective are presented to highlight the unique qualities of considering human behavior from this perspective. Next, we introduce Life-Span Communication, and several propositions are presented to merge the assertions of the life-span perspective into the study of communication. Next, we discuss various methodologies that have been developed to capture change across the life span. Then, we conclude the chapter with a preview of the rest of the book, providing an overarching framework for the more detailed discussion of issues that follows.

THE LIFE-SPAN PERSPECTIVE

The basic premise of any life-span approach to understanding and describing human behavior is that the potential for human development extends throughout the entirety of our life span. Development refers to the changes that occur with the accumulation of time. This simple statement is rather controversial. A great many developmental scholars hold quite strongly on to the writings and beliefs of Piaget (1954; 1959, 1972) and others that the early years of existence (up to about the age of 12) is the period of our life in which the most important and interesting developmental phenomena occur. Changes that occur after 12 years are not considered to be significant or to exist at all or to represent decline rather than development. To this day, the majority of research in the subdiscipline of psychology called developmental psychology is the study of childhood. Quite to the contrary, life-span scholars do not consider any one period of our life span, the first 12 years of our lives or the last 12 years of our lives, to hold supremacy in regulating the nature of development (Baltes, Smith, & Studinger, 1992). Although all serious developmental scholars do agree that rates of development vary across the life span and that certain characteristics of human behavior may experience critical developmental periods, it is best to recognize that one of the fundamental assumptions of the life-span perspective is that important and interesting events occur throughout the entirety of our lives. Therefore, it is important not to limit our investigations of human behavior to the first 12 or so years of life but to extend our theories and studies of human behavior to encompass all of our lives.

Baltes, Reese, and Nesselroade (1988) defined life-span developmental psychology as "the description, explanation, and modification (optimization) of intraindividual change in behavior across the life span, and with interindividual differences (and similarities) in intraindividual change" (p. 4). Life-span developmental psychologists attempt to create a body of knowledge centered on what behavioral development looks like, where this development comes from and why development occurs, and how development can be altered to improve our lives.

Five assertions of the life-span perspective, as put forth by Baltes (1987), are helpful in understanding this perspective and can aid in our attempt to champion this perspective for communication students and scholars:

- positive development occurs throughout the life span,
- diversity and pluralism occur in the changes throughout life,
- development is best viewed as a gain–loss dynamic,
- inter- and intra-individual diversity exists as we progress through the life span, and
- a person–environment interaction cannot be ignored in our explanations of development.

The first assertion is that life-span scholars reject commonly held notions that, as we age past the childhood years, we are in a constant state of decline. This assertion is directly related to the notion referred to previously that positive development can only occur in childhood. Our ability to think; to perform numerous physical activities; to see, hear, touch, and smell; or to perform the great majority of human activities is often considered to reach an apex very early in our lives. This misconception that "aging equals decline" stems from focusing on maturation as a physical process; therefore, with physical maturity, all development stops. This bias has infested investigations as well as investigators, resulting in poorly designed studies that accentuate the process of decline throughout the life span and ignore any positive development. As social creatures, socioemotional development can and does continue throughout the life span. In the communication discipline, researchers have only recently considered that our ability to communicate effectively or to manage interpersonal conflict may actually increase or, at the very least, change as we age. A major focus of this book is to point out not only that our ability to communicate competently may increase as we age, but that communication scholars and students should begin to question and look for these positive developments across the life span as well as possible declines.

2   A second assertion emerging from the life-span perspective is that "considerable diversity and pluralism is found in the directionality of changes that constitute development. The direction of change varies by behavior" (Baltes, Smith, & Studinger, 1992, p. 25). Development is not a simple linear process or trend that moves at the same speed and in the same positive or negative manner throughout the life span. To make matters even more complex, different human abilities do not develop in perfect sync and may be differentially influenced by environmental factors outside of the genetic script (which will be discussed more fully in assertion five). Our physical capabilities often outpace our mental and emotional abilities early in life. Later in life, our physical capabilities may decline as our mental and emotional abilities remain sound. The domain of interpersonal competencies that depend on a complex interaction of cognitive, language, and general communication skills, as well as the skills of those with whom we interact, may develop quite separately and can lead to a rather complex, multidirectional understanding of our ability to interact with some level of effectiveness.

3   A third assertion, related to the first two previously discussed, is that development is best viewed as a gain–loss dynamic. Certain abilities do decline across the life span. As will be pointed out in later chapters, numerous cognitive abilities and physical skills do show a steady and slow decline with increasing age. Other cognitive and physical abilities, however, show a very nice positive increase across the life span. One of the more important and interesting messages of this book is the central role that communication plays in our ability to maintain stability across numerous areas of decline and to accentuate the areas of positive growth across the life span. Most people successfully adapt to changes in their physical, social, and emotional lives. One of the most obvious means with which to maintain positive development, in spite of physical decline, is through the use of new technologies. If one is losing his or her ability to hear and thus to maintain supportive relationships, a hearing aid can correct for certain hearing loss. The use of technology helps to maintain a high level of social integration. In some ways, the more intriguing communicative effects may be found in our ability to become more competent as a relational partner as we age. As we discuss in more detail later in this chapter, our experiences with various communication occurrences inform our future

behavior. Thus, it is reasonable to assume that a positive learning curve related to development may serve our health, financial, and social support needs quite well across the life span. More detailed examples of these issues will be more fully discussed in future chapters.

The fourth assertion from the life-span perspective reminds us that there is much intra- and inter-individual diversity as we develop throughout the life span. Perhaps the important point to keep in mind is the fact that different cohorts of individuals may think and behave differently from one another. Differences across groups of individuals at various ages are called cohort effects. Comparing a group of 20-year-olds with a group of 60-year-olds and finding significant differences in some variable of interest does not necessarily mean that these differences have anything to do with age. Individuals of differing ages may think or behave differently because they have lived through different historical or cultural times. An individual who lived through an economic depression as a child may store paper products in volume as an adult. An individual whose childhood was during a time of great economic excess may never consider storing paper products at any time in his or her life. These differing behaviors may have nothing to do with age-related differences between 70-year-olds and teenagers, but may have everything to do with the effect of history. Communication students and scholars must be aware that changes can occur within an individual as he or she ages and that these changes may exhibit a large amount of variability across different individuals. At the same time, all differences found in thinking or behavior between individuals of differing ages may not be because of age.

In addition, individuals who on the surface have the same experience may actually have very different meanings for that experience. For example, Rutter and Rutter (1993) discussed the fallacy of simply asking if an individual is married or not. The experience of marriage may be quite different depending on when a person gets married, who his or her partner is, the quality of their relationship, the changes that occur within their relationship, their larger social network, and the cultural milieu of their times. The experience of marriage may even differ for an individual because a second marriage is impacted by the experience of a first marriage.

A final assertion of the life-span perspective concerns the notion that the person and the environment reciprocally influence one another. At the start of this century, popular belief is that the gene is the deterministic cause and best explanation of all human behavior. This assumption has led numerous scientists and popular writers to act as if cracking the human genetic code will put to rest all of our previous attempts to understand everything that is human. As with every other previous "best explanation," those individuals who wanted the human genome project to provide a complete understanding of human behavior have certainly been disappointed. With the mapping of the human genome and advances in genetic screening, scientists have developed a better understanding of the complex nature of genes and their interactions with each other, their impact across the life span, and how they are impacted by the environment. This final assertion of the life-span perspective underlines the necessity to incorporate the interaction of person and environment into our understanding of human perception and behavior. The interaction of the person and the environment can create a reality much beyond the sole influence or additive influence of person and environment acting independently. Communication researchers are especially "burdened" with a responsibility to incorporate individual influences, such as cognition, social cognition, language, and communication skills, and environmental influences, such as culture, existing relationships, and the physical environment, into our explanations of interpersonal communication.

Environmental constraints that we often cannot control as we age can significantly affect our development. Psychologists and sociologists have long pointed to the environment as having a significant impact on our perceptions and behavior. Communication scholars also have much to discuss about the possible effects of environmental influences, such as culture, historical times, and social networks, on each of our communicative behaviors and relational lives. These environmental influences are often not predictable nor do they affect each of us in the same way. Although many reports of twins who share the same genetic code and usually the same environmental influences indicate that the twins usually behave the same way, in reality, the twins are far from identical in each domain of human behavior and perception. Each of us, whether we are a twin or not, is greatly affected by the changing, dynamic patterns of interaction that occur within our families as new brothers or sisters are added to the mix or within our social networks as friendships are developed or changed. The direction and intensity of our numerous relationships are far from linear and predictable as we progress throughout our lives. Although this complexity may seemingly make any understanding of communication impossible, an understanding of the diversity inherent in development should help us to capture the reality of our interactive lives and the meanings people assign to their life experiences.

An important factor in the individual–environment mutual influence is the reality that our environment is not limited to the physical aspects of our world, but also consists of our social environment. As a consequence, the meanings that individuals and their social networks assign to these events depend on their timing and sequencing. Many life events are considered to have "normative" periods for their occurrence. Most people in the United States become a parent for the first time during their 20s or early 30s. Having a child at the age of 14 is considered to be "non-normative" and, therefore, may be assigned very different meanings compared with that child being born when the parents are in their 20s. The sequencing of events may also impact the meanings that are assigned. Although social standards have changed in recent years, many people still argue that a couple should marry first and then have children. Because humans are active organisms, making sense of the world around them and making choices about plans of action, the meanings that are assigned to events are affected by our prior history and our plans for the future.

These five assertions serve as a foundation with which to understand what it "takes" to begin to think as a life-span developmentalist. Change should be viewed as a constant in our lives and as a factor that must be traced across time. Development occurs at any point in our life span; however, the rate of change may vary, but is certainly not limited to the first few years of our existence. Gains and losses in various human abilities occur throughout our life spans with a remarkable amount of variability, both within and between individuals. The changes that we experience do not occur in a linear fashion, but are highly complex. Differences found between cohorts of different aged individuals should not be automatically attributed to age. Finally, the interaction between the person and the environment must be accounted for in any developmental explanation of human perception and behavior.

LIFE-SPAN COMMUNICATION

A major objective of this book is to merge the life-span perspective that has a solid foundation in psychology and sociology into our understanding of human communication. In many ways, the various constructs or phenomena that social scientists outside of the communication discipline investigate can appear rather simple when compared with the act of human communication. At the very least, communication scholars must incorporate the content of life-span developmental psychology (intelligence, memory, language, etc.), and the content of sociology (demography, culture, society, social policy, etc.) into any acceptable explanation of human interaction. We believe that a basic understanding of human interaction cannot be complete unless the life-span perspective is incorporated into our current theories of human communication.

A modification of the definition of life-span developmental psychology as stated earlier may be a good starting place from which to introduce Life-Span Communication: *Life-Span Communication deals with the description, explanation, and modification of the communication process across the life span.* Life-Span Communication scholars and students are interested in what a developing process of communication looks like, where the communication process develops and why it develops, and how the communication process can be altered to create an optimal context for living.

We set forth the following five propositions to highlight how a life-span perspective can enhance our understanding of human communication, and, at the same time, can open up new lines of inquiry, ultimately producing new questions that cannot be answered without a solid foundation in the life-span perspective. We propose that:

- the nature of communication is fundamentally developmental,
- a complete understanding of human communication is dependent on multiple levels of knowledge that occur simultaneously,
- change can be quantitative and qualitative,
- life-span communication scholars and students can incorporate all current theories of communication into this perspective as long as the theories are testable and the results are useful, and
- unique methodologies are required to capture communication change across the life span.

Our first proposition is that the nature of human communication is fundamentally developmental. Whether communication is thought of as primarily a skill to be mastered so that meanings can be transferred effectively and efficiently or whether communication is a process through which meanings are co-constructed in interactions, communication is not a single, time-irrelevant object. Communication requires time to be developed, time to be transmitted, time to be interpreted, and time to be reflected on. The process of any single, nonverbal communicative event may be very brief. On the other hand, a relationship that emerges in the process of communication may continuously develop throughout the entire life span. In either case, communication is best viewed as a flow of events across time rather than a static occurrence. Thinking of communication as developmental implies that communicative events are continuously unfolding and impacted by a wide range of individual characteristics and factors as well as previous experiences of those involved in the event.

As the communication process unfolds within human interaction, changes occur on numerous levels that may be manifested in different ways at various points in the life span. Later chapters in this book concentrate on the necessary cognitive, language, and communicative competency abilities that are required in any one particular communicative act. These abilities are not only constantly in need of adaptation within any one conversation, but these abilities also change as a function of a life span of interactive experiences. The cognitive abilities and language skills that served an individual well in his or her interactions at age 10 may be totally inappropriate during interactions at age 50. An individual's capacity to communicate must continuously develop for that individual to master his or her environment and to interact effectively throughout the transitions, adaptations, and new challenges that arise over the life span.

Related to this proposition that communication is developmental is the idea that any communicative event or series of events is made clearer when studied as a progression of events rather than as an isolated event. By this we mean that a communicative event is often given meaning by the communicative events that have occurred previously. A richer understanding of communication can be achieved by studying how the communication emerged in a conversation or a relationship over time. Thus, communication is both affected by and creates our social worlds, with the individuals involved actively being influenced by and influencing their environment. Put simply, past experiences shape current experiences.

A second proposition that we put forward is that a complete understanding of human communication is dependent on multiple levels of knowledge that occur simultaneously. Life-Span Communication scholars and students need to be aware of the influence of individual characteristics, relationship characteristics, societal characteristics, and cultural characteristics within each communicative act. For instance, communicative change can occur at the individual level by learning a new strategy with which to persuade someone to go out for an evening. Communicative change can also occur at a societal level because of a tragic historical event similar to the World Trade Center terrorist attack. Often, communication researchers have attempted to understand human interaction by controlling or eliminating all possible influences on the interaction except the one factor that is of interest to the researcher. This control of one particular communicative perception or behavior permits the researcher to systematically observe the direct effect or influence that one variable may have on another variable. Although this very acceptable experimental technique has served social scientists well over the years, any attempt to remove all possible levels of influence from an explanation of communication may mask the most significant and most interesting components of the communication process. Therefore, life-span communication scholars who are searching for change across time need to look for their explanations of change in numerous places simultaneously. This search is made even more difficult because of the possible interaction between the levels of influence. We are not saying that experimental methods are not useful for communication research. We do want to make it clear, however, that life-span communication scholars need to be aware of the multiple influences that affect each communicative act and to be prepared to expand their investigations to capture all possible contributors to change. The effectiveness of any individual message to persuade may depend on much more than the characteristics of the message (a common topic in communication research). Any particular message is delivered with a particular style, in a particular relationship, between individuals of a certain age, within diverse cultures. The different factors that need to be addressed certainly create a much more complex problem for life-span communication researchers.

The third proposition that guides life-span communication is that change can be quantitative or qualitative. The type of life-span change that has most often been investigated in all social science is quantitative change. Researchers have found that intelligence scores, memory indices, and number of close friends do change across our life span. These changes are reflected in statistically significant differences between reported scores at various points in the life span. The changes in these scores have led researchers to conclude that our intelligence may be declining with age or that our ability to remember events at age 80 is not as good as it was at age 30 or that our social network is much smaller in our old age than it was when we were a young adult. These changes represent very important pieces of information for us as we attempt to understand human behavior.

These quantitative changes, however, only represent a difference in degree, not a difference in nature or kind. Qualitative change across the life span would indicate a fundamental departure in the meaning of an event or a relationship. For a researcher interested in intelligence, a quantitative change may be a change across time from a score of 100 to a score of 105. A qualitative change would be some indication that this change in scores represents that this individual has become meaningfully smarter. That 5-point quantitative increase has actually changed the way this individual processes information and has in essence created a different person. For a researcher interested in social support, a quantitative change would indicate the number of individuals in the support network. From a more qualitative perspective, a researcher would examine the relative quality of that support and changes in ability to access the support network when a life crisis occurs.

Communication researchers have investigated numerous phenomena in much the same way as the researcher interested in intelligence mentioned previously noticed the quantitative change in intelligence scores. A quantitative difference score has become the "gold standard" for acceptable results in the social sciences. Life-Span Communication scholars should not be satisfied with the discovery of quantitative change without further investigation into whether that change has resulted in a fundamental, qualitative change in the nature of the phenomenon under investigation. In the chapters concerning relationship development later in this book, the work of several notable communication scholars who have posited that relationships develop through time is reviewed. These researchers have noted that, as a relationship develops, the participants in that relationship may spend more time together, self-disclose on more intimate topics, and touch each other more often and in different locations on the body. Each of these behaviors can be measured quantitatively, and it can be shown that the frequency of these particular behaviors increase with time. A qualitative change in the dynamics of this relationship may be closely related to the pure increase in behavioral frequency that reflects a change in the nature of the relationship itself. The participants may indicate that they have moved from an intimate friend relationship to an intimate romantic relationship. The change in the relational definition from friendship to romantic partners is, for all practical purposes, a different relationship. How did this happen? What events led to this relational redefinition? Has the relational redefinition changed the way the behaviors are perceived? This qualitative change in the very nature of the relationship should be a fundamental concern for those interested in life-span communication.

A fourth proposition posited is that Life-Span communication scholars and students can incorporate all current theories of communication into this perspective as long as the theories are testable and the results are useful. This particular proposition asks those individuals interested in communication across the life span to be inclusive of theory rather than exclusive. Whether a theory is derived from a positivistic tradition or from a constructivist perspective, each theory should be viewed as a possible attempt to help build our knowledge base concerning human communication. At the very same time, the authors of this book are disappointed in the failure of the great majority of communication theories to incorporate any notion of development in their particular explanations of communication. Suggesting that communication as a developmental phenomenon has been systematically ignored in the discipline is not an understatement. This lack of interest among communication theorists has not only led to the need for this particular book, but has created a research climate in which developmental change across the life span in the discipline of communication has not enjoyed the rich history of pertinent findings as our sister disciplines.

The scant attention given to Life-Span Communication in communication theory has not only ignored change across individual communicative events or across the life span (see proposition #1 discussed earlier), but has led to reporting that a finding based on a sample of college students supports a particular theory, which is then generalized to support all communication regardless of one's point in the life span. Research findings that list specific communicative competencies in an interactive situation common for college sophomores have been intentionally or unintentionally generalized to represent communicative competencies across all age groups. Rarely do you read in the discussion section of any journal article published in communication that these results, supporting a particular theory, should not be generalized beyond this sample of college students. In effect, any results from any sample that support the communication theory under consideration is taken as evidence that all humans behave in an age-neutral manner. This "overgeneralization" of research findings well beyond a particular sample of college students reflects an implicit acknowledgement that individuals, their communicative perceptions and behaviors, and the relationships within which they participate do not change across the life span. Life-Span Communication scholars and students need to incorporate the fundamentally sound information presented in these communication theories into our life-span perspective. This book is one attempt to accomplish this goal of moving communication theory toward serious consideration of life-span development.

5   Our final proposition is that unique research methodologies are required to capture communication change across the life span. Because of the details related to research design, this proposition is discussed in more detail in the next section of this chapter. For now, we want to point out

that the traditional research methodologies being taught to undergraduate and graduate students in the social sciences—survey methods and experimentation—are not necessarily sensitive to documenting change across time. This statement is true for both quantitative research methodologies and qualitative methodologies, such as discourse analysis and ethnomethodology. However, a remarkable and very active group of social scientists has been designing and implementing unique research methods that are designed to capture the complexity of change across the life span (see Cohen & Reese, 1994; Kiel & Elliot, 1996; Nesselroade & Reese, 1973). These researchers and the methods they have constructed have progressed from simple designs that document behavioral change in one subject at two distinct times, to very sophisticated, multivariate, structural equation and nonlinear models. At the time that this book is being written, the methodologies that have been constructed specifically to capture change are rarely being developed, used, or in any way understood by the great majority of communication scholars. This fact can be directly attributed to the previously noted proposition #4, which points out that most of the theories published by communication scholars have ignored life-span development. Regardless, the study of communication change across the life span necessitates an understanding of research methodology that enables the observation of change. Because of the important nature of this proposition and the number of issues related to research design, we provide a more thorough discussion of the most popular of these methodologies and emerging new approaches in the next section of this chapter. We hope that communication researchers and students will become familiar with the strengths and weaknesses of these methodologies so that we can better test and understand Life-Span Communication.

CAPTURING COMMUNICATION CHANGE ACROSS THE LIFE SPAN

The ability to design and to conduct an empirical investigation that captures communicative change across the life span is a rather complex task. One challenge is defining the level of analysis. Most life-span research in psychology has focused on the individual, whereas life-course research in sociology has focused on groups of individuals or cohorts. Communication scholars may be interested in changes at the individual, relational, social, or cultural levels. Of course, as we argued earlier, focusing on any one level cannot ignore the changes that are occurring on the other levels as well. Thus, the individual may be the focus of study, but the historical place and time of these individuals must also be examined to fully understand the changes that occur and the meanings that are assigned to those changes. Several research methods have been designed and used to capture change across the individual's life span, and these methods may be used at other levels of analysis as well. The primary methods include the cross-sectional method, the longitudinal method, and various mixed methods.

methods used

The majority of life-span developmental research conducted by social scientists has tested inter-individual change with the use of various cross-sectional age-comparative designs. The cross-sectional method compares different age groups observed at one point in time. Nunnally (1973) wrote that there are two reasons for performing a cross-sectional investigation: "The first is simply to survey differences in people of different ages at one point in time on some attribute of current intellectual or applied interest" (p. 90). The second reason to use a cross-sectional investigation is to "estimate, or at least provide hints about, developmental sequences that could be obtained only from longitudinal studies" (Nunnally, 1973, p. 91). To use this method appropriately, researchers must: (1) obtain comparable samples at different age levels, and (2) ensure that the measures mean the same thing at different age levels.

Cross Sectional

Cross-sectional designs have been used in the discipline of communication and are a favorite design in investigations conducted by the authors of this book. The method is relatively simple and inexpensive. However, it is widely recognized that cross-sectional designs suffer from a complete confound of age with cohort effects. In other words, a study can be conducted to determine whether communication skills deteriorate over the life span. A sample of 22-year-olds are surveyed and compared with a sample of 72-year-olds on a measure of communication skill competence. If significant differences are uncovered that indicate a higher score in competency skills for younger adults than older adults, there is no reason to believe that the reported difference is because of age. The difference may be the result of differing lifestyles, motivations, eating habits, or instrumentation bias that favors one group over the other, although most researchers would desperately want to conclude that these results offer proof that skills do decline with increasing age. The cross-sectional design, however, is not a method with which to capture age-related changes, although the cross-sectional design may capture age differences.

The longitudinal method follows the same object, person, relationship, or culture through all time or age levels with repeated observations. To capture the change in communicative competency skills across the life span, a large sample of 20-year-olds would be tested at time one and re-tested every 5 years or so until these subjects turned 70. Nunnally (1973) listed three advantages that longitudinal studies have over cross-sectional studies. First, longitudinal studies permit a direct analysis of age changes without the contamination from cohort effects. Second, longitudinal designs may have less severe problems with respect to sampling of subjects. Attrition in the sample is the major sampling problem in a longitudinal study. The loss of subjects between measurement occasions is serious, and much effort on the part of the investigators is required to minimize attrition. Third, longitudinal designs have the major advantage over the cross-sectional method of allowing the researcher to employ more powerful statistical methods.

Several criticisms of longitudinal designs have also been addressed in the literature (Nunnally, 1973; Schaie & Hofer, 2001). The disadvantages of longitudinal designs are similar to the disadvantages of all quasiexperiments, as outlined by Campbell and Stanley (1963). Threats to internal validity, such as maturation, historical effects, reactivity, instrumentation, statistical regression, experimental mortality, and selection, are serious. Schaie and Hofer (2001) report, however, that the magnitude and significance of these threats to internal validity can be estimated and appropriate corrections applied in the study.

Schaie (1965) proposed a "General Developmental Model," which combines many of the positive aspects of cross-sectional methods with longitudinal methods. He labeled the three strategies of data collection the cross-sequential, cohort-sequential, and time-sequential methods. In practice, the sequential designs simultaneously use cross-sectional and longitudinal methods. The study of communicative competency would begin much like the cross-sectional design, with samples of individuals of differing ages being measured for communicative competency skills at time 1. Twenty-year-olds, 25-year-olds, 30-year-olds, etc., would be tested at time 1. Five years later, a new group of 20-year-olds would be tested, as well as all the previously tested samples, who are now 5 years older. Schaie and Baltes (1975) conclude that the sequential designs are extremely useful for the generation of descriptive data. In addition, Schaie (1996) has used these sequential designs in his own longitudinal study of intellectual development.

The revolution in our attempts to uncover change across the life span has shifted from the method and design process to complex statistical analyses. Rudinger and Rietz (2001) presented a very compelling case for social scientists interested in studying change within time-bound processes to consider linear structural equation modeling (SEM). SEM moves away from testing mean differences toward the analysis of variances and covariance matrices. "Most of the conceptual problems associated with longitudinal aging research are solvable with SEM" (Rudinger & Rietz, 2001, p. 47). Numerous statisticians and psychometricians are advancing our understanding of SEM and soon should solve the rather complex statistical–mathematical issues that currently prevent SEM from being widely accepted in the social sciences (McArdle, 1998; McArdle & Nesselroade, 1994).

Another emerging approach that is gaining converts is a related group of theories variously called chaos theory, complexity theory, or the new science (Byrne, 1998; Mathews, White, & Long, 1999; Waldrop, 1992). Physicists and biologists first developed this set of theories, based in General Systems Theory, to explain nonlinear dynamics, which are especially prevalent when living organisms are the focus of study. This approach has been used to study the weather, economic conditions, traffic flow, the tipping points that move neighboring communities from peace to war, and abuse dynamics in families. The basic tenets that this set of theories hold in common include the dynamic nature of change, which is a nonlinear process, and the complex nature of the mutual influence of elements of different levels of systems as they interact with each other. Researchers applying these theories often combine both quantitative and qualitative methods in an attempt to identify and understand the numerous factors that influence a phenomenon and the mutual influences that these various factors have on each other, as well as the meanings the individuals involved assign to these events and their reactions to them. The nonlinear mathematics used in modeling these systems is not taught in most schools, even to individuals majoring in math, so it should be no surprise that communication scholars have scant understanding of these models and their use. However, many researchers using these methods find it informative to identify key factors influencing the phenomenon under study and patterns of related behavior that lead to similar outcomes. For example, any family that has experienced abusive behavior demonstrates a complex set of behaviors; however, most families with abuse can be placed into a relatively small set of categories and then appropriate interventions can be developed to address the most critical factors that lead to this type of dysfunction.

Communication scholars and students do not have ready access to these methodologies and designs in our departments. The neglect of developmental processes in communication theory has led to a neglect of developmental methodologies. However, across most campuses, social scientists have been investigating phenomena from a life-span perspective and have been simultaneously developing methods to test for change. Schaie (1988) wrote quite convincingly that methodological innovations "can directly produce paradigm shifts either by permitting the direct investigation of phenomena that were not previously specifiable by a theoretical model or by providing methods that allow investigation at different levels of conceptual specification" (p. 53). The theory and study of communication as life-span phenomena can benefit greatly by the use of these methodologies.

APPLYING THE LIFE-SPAN APPROACH TO OUR UNDERSTANDING OF COMMUNICATION

In this first part of this book, we lay out the basic assumptions of the life-span approach and its implications for communication. With this foundation, we are now ready to discuss in detail a number of communicative behaviors and how those behaviors change as we age. The rest of this book provides that detail and is divided into several sections that tie together the most closely related issues. These phenomena, however, do not occur in isolation. For example, our ability to manage interpersonal conflict is impacted by the nature of the relationship within which the conflict occurs, our abilities to think through our arguments and use language effectively, and larger social influences that help define how we should manage conflict situations. Therefore, as you read the following chapters, keep in mind the underlying issues that connect these communicative events to each other.

In part II, we focus on the foundations of communication—language and cognition—and their relationships to each other and to communicative processes. Part III focuses on relational contexts—family, marriage, and friends—and how relationships are formed, are maintained, and change over the life span. Part IV focuses on a number of communicative phenomena, including the development of our identity and the roles we play, the giving and receiving of social support, managing our health, and negotiating conflict as each of these phenomena play out in relationships. Although we focus to some extent on how individuals manage these communicative events, remember that these individuals are acting in concert with others, and the social nature of these interactions impacts the nature of our experience of these phenomena. Part V focuses on the media, leisure, and entertainment. Although the media are used as a source of leisure and entertainment, they also influence our development. Therefore, this section examines the various functions the media play in our lives, as well as other types of leisure and entertainment. In the final section of the book, we return to the life-span perspective, revisit its implications for the study of human communication, and propose a research agenda for addressing the oversight that has occurred by ignoring the role of development throughout our communicative lives.

Before proceeding to the detailed review of communicative issues, a few caveats are in order about the research that is reported in the following chapters. As noted earlier, the design of research to capture change is a difficult task and has not been the focus of many of the studies reported in this book. First, when studying children, one of the research challenges lies in discovering how children develop skills because they can enact behaviors before they can be reflective regarding them (Dunn & Slomkowski, 1992). That is, children develop knowledge first at the level of action and then on the plane of reflective thought. Because of the difficulties in examining what children understand about their actions, the research remains unclear as to whether and how communicative experiences foster development. Second, an issue related to the first lies in the form in which data are collected. Comparisons between age groups may reflect the difference inherent in observational versus self-report data, especially when the data on young children primarily come from observation and the data on adolescents primarily come from self-reports (Hartup, 1992). Comparative studies consistently reveal differences in the type of data collected and the results found between observation and self-report data (Metts, Sprecher, & Cupach, 1991; Sillars, 1991). These differences may become exacerbated when making age comparisons if the sources of data differ. A third issue is that different studies may define the same phenomenon differently (Hartup, 1992). For example, when studying interpersonal conflict, one study may ask participants how often they have conflicts with a particular person, whereas another may ask how often they have disagreements, arguments, spats, quarrels, etc. Inherently, these different definitions create differences in responses and make direct comparisons between studies problematic. Finally, most of the research reported here was not conducted from a life-span perspective. One research project may have focused on one age group who responded in a laboratory setting, and these findings were then compared with another study that was conducted in a more natural setting over a 6-month period. Although these comparisons across studies begin to provide some picture of how individuals and relationships change over time, they typically are not designed to capture the true meaning of change. A few studies are cross-sectional, a few are short longitudinal (up to 2 years), but even more rare are studies that are cross-sequential, which captures both individual and cohort changes over an extended period. With these caveats in mind, however, it does seem reasonable to state that, over time, individuals change in their communicative skills, abilities, and preferences; relational partners change their preferences for communicative behaviors; and society changes its expectations for appropriate and effective behavior.

SUMMARY

Life-span investigators study changes that occur with the accumulation of time. The fundamental goals of the life-span perspective are to describe, explain, and ultimately optimize living across the entirety of the life span. Five assertions of the life-span perspective are posited: positive development occurs throughout the life span; much diversity and pluralism occurs in the changes throughout life; development is best viewed as a gain–loss dynamic; much inter- and intra-individual diversity exists as we progress through the life span; and a person–environment interaction cannot be ignored in our explanations of development. These five assertions should serve to inform our understanding of Life-Span Communication, defined as the description, explanation, and modification of the communication process across the life span. Five propositions highlight how a life-span perspective can enhance our understanding of human communication: The nature of communication is fundamentally developmental; a complete understanding of human communication is dependent on multiple levels of knowledge that occur simultaneously; change can be quantitative and qualitative; life-span communication scholars and students can incorporate all current theories of communication into this perspective as long as the theories are testable and the results are useful; and unique methodologies are required to capture communication change across the life span. Developmental research theorists and methodologists have constructed cross-sectional, longitudinal, and various mixed methods in their attempt to design investigations that capture changes across the life span. These new methodologies and statistical techniques can aid communication scholars in creating and testing their own notions of life-span change.

II

Foundations of Communication: Cognitive Processing and Language

The first part of this book reviewed the basic concepts related to life-span communication. The second part lays the foundation for later parts by examining cognitive processing and language acquisition across the life span. Cognitive processing refers to the storage, retrieval, and use of knowledge. Language refers to the symbol codes we use for labeling objects and concepts and sharing information with others. Both are vital to the communicative processes that are reviewed in later parts of this book. Communication refers to the organized, standardized, culturally patterned system of behavior that sustains, regulates, and makes possible human relationships (Scheflen, 1972, 1974). Thus, the ability to communicate effectively and appropriately requires the cognitive structuring of the world, labeling of objects in the world in ways that those around us understand, and understanding the nuances of social interaction. Communication is an inherently social activity that allows people to share information and coordinate activities.

As will be discussed in more detail in the next two chapters, cognitive processing and language development are interrelated, but independent, processes. Communication provides the context in which language and cognition develop (Haslett & Samter, 1997). The interrelationships among social relationships, cognition, and language are complex, but social interaction is fundamental for learning, cognition, and language. Because infants need support from others to survive, they are compelled to interact with others. Therefore, we are driven to learn language and to make sense of our world and to adapt to ongoing changes that occur in life.

People often think of language use as communication; however, communication entails more than knowledge and use of language. Jacobs (1994) reframed the study of language away from "the technical structural interests of sentence grammarians" (p. 225) to the use of the term discourse to describe an effort to study the uses of language or the structure of language in interaction. In this perspective, communication requires the development of varied strategies for achieving goals; learning what is appropriate and effective in various contexts; understanding the nature of conversation with its complex set of rules related to turn taking, topic management, and face management for both the self and the other; and understanding that, although conversation is rule-driven, these rules may be violated, intentionally and successfully (Haslett & Samter, 1997). Therefore, both linguistic and mental skills must be sufficiently developed to assess situations and to adjust to the demands of the situation.

Keeping this view of communication or discourse in mind, this part lays the foundation for examining communicative competence by examining the building blocks of cognition and language. Later parts will focus on the ever-changing dynamics of discourse as related to communication competence and the skills required to build and maintain relationships across the life span.

2

Cognitive Processes

Cognition, or cognitive processes, relates to how people acquire and organize knowledge, including the representation, storage, use, and retrieval of that knowledge (Haslett & Sampter, 1997). As noted in the introduction to this part, cognitive development, language acquisition, and development of communicative skills are interrelated, but not equivalent, processes. In this chapter, we focus on cognitive processing, its development across the life span, and its connection to language and communication. Nussbaum, Hummert, Williams, and Harwood (1996) clearly connected cognitive processes to our understanding of interactive behavior. Cognition impacts our acquisition of language and communicative skills by providing the framework for acquiring knowledge and then accessing and using that knowledge during interaction, as well as assigning meaning to those interactions.

Cognition is generally recognized as the study of how people acquire knowledge (Haslett & Samter, 1997). If the knowledge that is being acquired concerns the interface of human thought processes and human interaction, then researchers have classified these specific cognitive processes into the domain of social cognition (Knapp & Miller, 1994). Haslett and Samter (1997) also linked these advances in cognitive abilities to a child's ability to communicate effectively. A normal child's ability to store, process, and retrieve information increases with age, ultimately leading to increases in the ability to use language appropriately and communicate effectively. Thus, cognition has social consequences for the individual's self-perception and esteem as well as the assessment by others of that person's abilities. Although distinguishing between cognition and social cognition may be useful for some social scientists, we suggest that all internal thought processes that involve the storage, use, and retrieval of knowledge probably play some role in our ability to communicate effectively with another human being.

Cognitive processing, however, is not just a matter of speed, but includes many different domains, such as intelligence, memory, problem solving, decision making, everyday coping, and social intelligence, each of which may be multifaceted as well. For example, intelligence does not consist of a single factor, but consists of several domains, including processing speed, information processing, working memory, memory structures, and semantic knowledge (Schaie, 1996). Because of the multidimensional nature of intelligence, an individual may perform well in one area and poorly in another (Rutter & Rutter, 1993). These different dimensions of intelligence reflect different types of knowledge. For example, one division of an individual's cognitive processing is into the categories of fluid and crystallized intelligence. Fluid intelligence includes skills and abilities that are unrelated to education and experience, such as abstract reasoning, response time, and mathematics. Assessing fluid abilities requires tests of mental manipulation of abstract symbols, such as figural analogues, series completions, and classification problems (Rutter & Rutter, 1993). Fluid intelligence peaks in early adulthood, but declines in fluid intelligence may be slowed through physical and mental activity (Nussbaum, Pecchioni, Robinson, & Thompson, 2000). By contrast, crystallized intelligence is acquired through education and personal experience, such as vocabulary, verbal skills, and comprehension skills. Assessing crystallized intelligence requires tests of vocabulary, comprehension, and information (Rutter & Rutter, 1993). These skills remain relatively stable well into old age (Nussbaum et al., 2000).

Not only is human intelligence and cognitive processing a complex set of skills, but developmental studies show that different skills are acquired through different means at different ages. For example, in the first year, perceptual patterns generate development in cognitive abilities. Later in life, however, verbal patterns have greater influence than do visual patterns (Rutter & Rutter, 1993). Therefore, not only do individuals choose different strategies with age, but they continue to develop in their thinking and problem-solving abilities across the life span (Smith & Baltes, 1990).

The empirical evidence shows that our cognitive abilities change quite dramatically across the life span. During the first few years of life, we experience tremendous gains. During the middle and later years, we may experience considerable or relatively little change in our cognitive processing abilities. These changes are the result of a complex interplay of each individual's physical, psychological, and socioemotional development (Rutter & Rutter, 1993). As individuals mature, they may experience a regression in some "mature" behaviors as other mature behaviors are acquired, depending on the particular experiences and timing of events in the individual's life. These changes may also be influenced by pathologies, such as mental retardation or dementia; however, aging does not necessarily lead to serious declines in cognitive processing. Our overall physical health is a better predictor of our mental health in older age than is chronological age (Rutter & Rutter, 1993). Nevertheless, the basic foundation of our ability to communicate effectively, our cognitive processing capability, does change as a function of time (age). Stated simply, our cognitive abilities show impressive gains in early life, followed by relative stability throughout our midlife, followed by a slow decline in late life, until a rapid decline is recorded past the age of 80 or later (Schaie & Hofer, 2001). These relative periods are reviewed separately, but remember that each later period is impacted by the individual's experiences at younger ages.

EARLY CHILDHOOD DEVELOPMENT

Haslett and Samter (1997), relying on over 50 years of research by cognitive psychologists and communication scholars, summarized the tremendous growth in cognitive abilities that occur during the first 5 years of life. No one would attempt to refute the argument that normal growth in the first years of life is highlighted by significant and meaningful gains in our ability to store, retrieve, and use information. This increased cognitive development leads to increased use of language and communicative skills. For example, semantic development, or the development of the meanings assigned to words and actions, is intimately linked to cognitive development. As young children grow, the experiences they have coupled with their innate predispositions interact to create the meanings they develop for people, situations, and things. As children acquire their first words, they also are developing concept formats and category hierarchies for understanding these words.

Cognitive development in children does not occur in a vacuum, although humans do seem to have "hard wiring" that directs some aspects of their cognitive development (Rutter & Rutter, 1993). Extensive research suggests that humans have "biological preparedness," which directs cognitive development, and that there are sensitive periods for learning certain skills (such as language acquisition, as discussed in more detail in the next chapter). However, cognitive development is not a cumulative accretion of greater complexity or ability. As children gain cognitive skills in one area, they may lose skills in other areas. For example, children under 6 months learn through visual stimulation in ways that are no longer available to them after about the age of 12 months. Most research also suggests that cognitive development is not a smooth linear process, but one that occurs in "leaps," that is, times during which children rapidly acquire new abilities.

The maturation of the brain, as an organ in a human body, is impacted not only by biological factors that stimulate physical growth but also by experiential and environmental factors. Children who live in a stimulating environment and receive adequate nutrition mature differently and continue to process information differently from children who live in a more sterile environment or who experience nutritional deprivation. Testing of very young children shows that early scores are not predictive of later scores. Researchers suggest that genetic influences are relatively weak early on, but become stronger as children age, even though intelligence is affected by environmental factors as well. Summarizing a vast body of research, Rutter and Rutter (1993) attributed about half of cognitive maturation to genetic influences and about half to the child's environment; however, they pointed out that considerable variation exists, depending on the dimension of cognitive development that is being examined.

Early environmental influences may have long-lasting effects on the individual's cognitive processing ability, but certain ages are more critical to development than are others (Rutter & Rutter, 1993). More specifically, individuals may respond differently to stressors as they experience them at different ages. For example, experiences of environmental deprivation during the toddler years have longer term consequences than those same experiences earlier in life. Studies consistently reveal that the family environment when the child is between 2 to 5 years old is the most critical in IQ development.

In spite of considerable variability in cognitive development, researchers and parents can predict the typical sequence of development. The classic formulation of cognitive development is derived from the work of Piaget. Haslett and Samter (1997) provided an excellent summary of Piaget's work as well as a comparison with the work of Vygotsky and Forrester's ecological theory that combines the views of Piaget and Vygotsky.

As Haslett and Samter (1997) pointed out, Piaget's theory of early cognitive development focuses on what appear to be universal stages. Piaget identified four major stages of development, each consisting of several substages, and the ages at which children typically move through each stage. The first stage, called sensorimotor intelligence, occurs from birth through about 24 months. During this stage, children develop by exploring their world physically, that is, their senses serve as their primary source of information. Although their senses are primary, children's cognitive development during this stage leads to an understanding of intentionality and a sense of self and that language may influence others' actions. Thus, during stage 1 of Piaget's theory, children develop a fundamental understanding of language and interaction (Haslett & Samter, 1997).

Piaget

The second stage, called preoperational thought, occurs from ages 2 to 7. During this stage, children continue to explore their physical world through concrete actions. The third stage, concrete operational thought, occurs from ages 7 to 11 and reflects children's concrete mental operations, which allows them to understand concepts such as reversability and to solve problems through mental as well as physical methods. The last developmental stage, formal operational thought, occurs from ages 11 to 18 and reflects the ability to use language on an abstract level to solve problems. Piaget argued that language does not begin to strongly influence thinking until this final stage of development. Language allows children to perform operations conceptually rather than only through physical manipulation, allowing for increasingly complex levels of abstraction and reasoning (Haslett & Samter, 1997).

Many scholars argue that the greatest problem with Piaget's work has been the rather rigid manner is which these "stages" have been applied to children's development and are used for diagnosis and intervention (Rutter & Rutter, 1993). The stage approach, although a useful framework for understanding, has been interpreted to suggest that children are biologically driven to systematically progress through the stages in a predetermined order and that they must fully complete development at one stage before "proceeding" to the next. Piaget's work concentrated on the universals of development, ignoring the considerable variability that occurs. The dynamics of change are more complex, and individuals experience considerable flux over time. Rather than being biologically driven to develop in certain ways, children are active agents in their cognitive development. They create their own patterns and try out their ideas. Ideas that receive positive reinforcement tend to be retained, whereas ideas that receive negative reinforcement are more likely to be rejected by the child. As a consequence of the active role that children play in creating meaning and understanding for themselves, they tend to move back and forth through the different stages as new information leads to a reprocessing and reevaluation of previous structures. The research also shows that children have multiple routes available for achieving these developmental milestones; therefore, the rigid universals are seen as no longer applicable when trying to create a full understanding of how cognitive processing develops in children.

Because many scholars now believe that environmental influences play an important role in cognitive development (Haslett & Samter, 1997; Rutter & Rutter, 1993), theories that modify Piaget's work are important in understanding this area of development. Both Vygotsky and Forrester focused on the connection between the environment and a child's development.

Haslett and Samter (1997) summarized Vygotsky's work, in which he suggested that both language and cognition emerge through social interaction. In Vygotsky's view, language and thought develop independently until about the age of 2 years. After that age, children begin to exhibit what Vygotsky called "verbal thought," that is, their speech reflects their underlying rationality and their thoughts become verbal, whether spoken or not. Children may begin to "talk through" problems as they work to solve them. This approach argues that cognitive development is the result of, or at least strongly influenced by, social interactions. The development of language, therefore, allows children to participate in their social environment. As children mature, their use of language becomes more flexible and their problem solving more abstract, whether interacting with others or using "inner speech."

Haslett and Samter (1997) compared three different streams of theory—the constructivist–representational, the social interactional, and the ecological views—regarding cognitive development and the role of language. The first view, the constructivist–representational view, is reflected in Piaget's work. In this view, the focus is on information processing, and language does not play an important role until the formal operations stage, in which complex, abstract thought requires language for representational meaning. One major critique of this view is that it does not create models that reflect the unpredictable nature of conversation, with its frequent shifts in topics and unexpected directions. The second view, the social interactional approach, is reflected in Vygotsky's work. In this view, language directs cognitive development through social interaction. The focus is on how conflict and confrontation serve as triggering events for cognitive development. One major critique of this view is that researchers have not been able to identify the underlying processes that lead to change. Critiques of these two views, led Forrester (1993) to develop the ecological approach.

Haslett and Samter (1997) summarized Forrester's (1993) ecological theory, which emphasized the relationship between the organism and its environment, thus reflecting a similarity to the social interactional approach. However, Forrester did not propose that language drives cognitive development. Instead, children are "driven" to understand their social surroundings in order to survive. Language and cognitive development are intertwined, so that developments in one arena influence developments in the other, but the process is mutual, not linear. Learning about the social environment occurs initially through observation and monitoring of, then followed by participation in, social interactions. These observations help children learn both the rules and dynamic flexibility required of conversation. Thus, cognitive skills are critical for understanding and participating in the social world.

Two interrelated cognitive concepts that have received considerable attention in communication are cognitive complexity and perspective taking, which are influenced by the nature of social interactions that children have with others. Although these studies are not specifically framed in a life-span perspective, they are inherently developmental in nature. Cognitive complexity deals with the number and variety of constructs that an individual has available to generate meaning(s) about individuals, relationships, and situations (Burleson, 1987; Delia & Clark, 1977; Delia, Kline, & Burleson, 1979). Individuals who are more cognitively complex have a greater number of constructs to draw on, and their constructs are more abstract than are the constructs of less cognitively complex individuals. Individuals who are more cognitively complex are better able to take into consideration the perspective of the other person. This perspective taking allows cognitively complex individuals to adapt their messages to fit the other person's needs and the situation.

In a classic study, Clark and Delia (1977) showed the developmental nature of cognitive complexity as children demonstrated increased abilities to adapt their messages to the receiver. They found that children in kindergarten and 1st grade made unelaborated requests; 2nd- through 5th-graders made personal need arguments; 6th- through 9th-graders made need arguments, but had minimal counter-arguments; whereas 10th- to 12th-graders made benefit arguments, negotiated, made elaborated need arguments, and were able to make counter arguments. Older children were better able to take the perspective of the other and to adapt their messages to the individual listener, therefore exhibiting greater sophistication in their interactive strategies.

The development of more sophisticated persuasive strategies has also been examined by O'Keefe (1988), who found that more cognitively complex individuals are more likely to use more sophisticated message design logics, that is, they generate messages that achieve the speaker's goals while attending to the needs of the listener as well. Cognitively complex individuals also demonstrate greater communicative competence when using comforting messages (Burleson, 1994), in maintaining relationships (Burleson & Samter, 1994), and in organizational settings (Sypher & Zorn, 1986). In each of these settings, cognitively complex individuals are better able to adapt their messages to the needs of the listener and, therefore, are more effective at achieving both their own and the listener's goals.

Children develop cognitive complexity through the nature of interactions they have with parents and caregivers. As a simple example, children often ask why rules exist. The parent may respond by saying, "Because I said so," which is considered to be a position-centered message. The child should comply because the person with power, the adult, says the child should comply. On the other hand, the parent might reply by providing the child with reasons for the rule, such as protecting his or her own or another's safety, considered to be a person-centered message. In person-centered messages, these more elaborated explanations help children to understand the reasons behind rules and to understand the consequences of behavior for themselves and for those around them.

By developing the ability to take others' perspectives, children also become more cognitively complex. As Haslett and Samter (1997) pointed out, greater cognitive complexity influences children's acquisition of meaning(s) for people, things, and situations. Although most studies on the development of cognitive complexity focus on children's development, none of these studies makes a convincing argument that cognitive complexity cannot be further developed in later years. As individuals have more experiences and opportunities to have their assumptions challenged, they may indeed become better able to take the perspective of the other, to become more cognitively complex, and, ultimately, to become more effective communicators.

MIDLIFE AND OLD-AGE TRANSITIONS

Most research on cognitive development has focused on the years leading up to physical maturity, typically considered to be 18 years of age. As noted previously, the environment plays an important role in cognitive development, and social interactions are an important element of humans' environment. As we continue to age, we continue to engage in social interactions that, in turn, impact our cognitive processing. As mentioned earlier, cognitive processing is not just intelligence or speed, but consists of many dimensions. Self-image, self-concept, and identity are all important elements of cognitive processes. The middle and late years consist of experiences that may affect our self-concept and identity, for example, forming long-term committed relationships, having children and raising a family, career development, job changes, and retirement all impact our sense of self. To illustrate the complex nature of these cognitive processes in the middle and later years, issues related to mental health, decision making, social interactions, and the so-called "midlife crisis" are examined briefly. Issues related to role transitions and identity are more fully explored in chap. 7.

Problems with mental health are not an inherent consequence of aging. Rutter and Rutter (1993) pointed out that physical health and psychosocial stresses have more impact than chronological age on the processes of physical and mental decline and that physical decline with age is more greatly influenced by a lack of exercise. Most individuals experience continuity in their cognitive functions, that is, if individuals function well in young adulthood, they usually function well in old age, except among those who have experienced poor physical health or drug dependency (e.g., alcohol abuse). Reviewing a number of psychiatric disorders, Rutter and Rutter (1993) found that the age at which most mental health problems peak is often in late adolescence and early adulthood. Thus, the number of individuals diagnosed with depression and psychopathology peaks in late adolescence, schizophrenia and psychoneurosis diagnoses peak in the mid-20s to mid-30s, the number of individuals with depressive psychosis remains relatively stable throughout the ages of 30 to 60 years, and senility rates begin to climb among those over age 55.

For most healthy individuals, the middle and late years are times of successful psychosocial functioning. As individuals age, they may become more competent at handling life's problems as they develop more success-ful coping styles in which they are able to plan for contingencies, learn to develop and appropriately use a social support network, and build good self-esteem by achieving objectives and receiving positive feedback from others.

Decision making provides a good example of how individuals adapt their strategies across the life span. When examining the problems of ev-eryday life, older individuals are more likely to base decisions on prior experience, whereas younger individuals spend more time collecting rele-vant data because they have fewer personal experiences on which to draw (Willis, 1996). Because of the greater potential for having more experi-ences as we age, older individuals generally have more social knowledge than do younger individuals (Blanchard-Fields & Abeles, 1996). These different styles might lead to intergenerational conflict, as each group will have a different approach for solving the same problem. For example, younger individuals experiencing their first life crisis are not likely to have the same level of coping strategies for managing these events as do older individuals. Older individuals are more likely to understand that crises arise in life, but these events can be managed and survived successfully, adopting a "this too shall pass" attitude. Younger individuals may feel that older individuals are not sufficiently concerned, whereas older individuals may feel that younger individuals are making the issue larger than it needs to be. Both generations may feel that the other is, therefore, being insen-sitive. Although older individuals do exhibit minor declines in processing speeds, they often exhibit more complex processing structures based on years and number of experiences.

An important element of cognitive processing is the development of cognitive structures that are used to help us to quickly identify others' roles, situations, and things that arise during interactions. These stereo-types are used to provide us with a "shorthand" for what to expect in interactions with others. How others treat us affects how we see our-selves. Programmatic research by Hummert (1990, 1994a, 1994b), Giles and Williams (1994), and Ryan (1991) has emphasized the importance of studying stereotyping, particularly stereotypes related to aging and the pos-itive and negative effects that stereotypes have on our communicative be-havior. Levy's (1996) work showed that exposure to negative stereotypes of aging worsens older individuals' memory performance, whereas expo-sure to positive stereotypes of aging improves their performance. Exposure to aging stereotypes, however, does not affect memory processing among young adults. Based on this research, we can assume that older individuals who are interacting with others who are treating them according to negative stereotypes of aging are likely to have their self-image and self-esteem damaged. Although we establish a categorization system that leads to stereotyping fairly early in life, these stereotypes can be altered as we are exposed to new experiences. These changes may reflect a process similar to that of cognitive complexity. As we have experiences, we fit those experiences into our current framework of thinking or alter our thinking to make sense of the new knowledge.

One psychological issue that impacts individuals and their social support network is that of the so-called midlife crisis (Rutter & Rutter, 1993). The basic concept is that during middle age, individuals not only reevaluate their lives and aspirations, but struggle to come to grips with missed opportunities or unachieved goals. The driving mechanism for this reevaluation is unclear; however, the most popular assumption is that younger individuals believe they have their lives ahead of them to accomplish their goals. As individuals enter their middle years, they begin to realize that life is finite and that they may not have forever to accomplish their dreams. These concerns may be triggered by the aging and death of one's parents or the death of friends who are near-age peers. Rutter and Rutter (1993) reviewed the research surrounding the midlife crisis and argued that, although "adult life brings with it a host of stresses, rewards, challenges, and transitions" (p. 306), a midlife crisis is not inevitable. Middle-aged individuals may well reevaluate their lives, but do not necessarily find themselves lacking in successes and abilities to cope with the vagaries of life.

Rutter and Rutter (1993) reviewed the research on the midlife crisis by summarizing whether support has been provided for the propositions presented by Levinson (1978). Levinson's first proposition is that "middle life is associated with a wide range of adaptations in life pattern" (Rutter & Rutter, 1993, p. 307). This proposition has been supported by subsequent research indicating that individuals undergo major and minor role changes that require psychological adaptation. The nature of the adaptation, however, may be minor or substantial, depending on a number of variables affecting the individual.

Levinson's second proposition states that "middle age brings with it significant changes in *internal* aspects of a person's life structure" (Rutter & Rutter, 1993, p. 307). This proposition has been partially supported by subsequent research. The research indicates that whether individuals experience external events or not, midlife often leads to reappraisal, but this reappraisal is not age-relevant or age-inherent, and the nature of the self-searching may be more ongoing as individuals adapt to their ever-changing circumstances. This reevaluation, then, is less of a crisis than a series of small adaptations as one continues to experience life and learns to cope with changes.

Levinson's third proposition states that "it is necessary to experience tumult and turmoil if one is to make the transition successfully" (Rutter & Rutter, 1993, p. 309). This proposition has not been supported by subsequent research. As stated previously, these adaptations to changing life circumstances are not inherently a crisis, and most individuals manage to cope with these changes through small adaptations. The story of the middle-aged executive "chucking it all" to go live in the mountains is an anomaly. Middle-aged individuals indeed have to contend with many changes, such as "the empty nest," becoming grandparents, looking after elderly parents, dealing with changes in definitions of their sexuality (whether because of reduced sex drives among men or menopause among women), bereavement caused by the deaths of family and friends, and retirement. However, most individuals manage to develop coping strategies, build and use effective support networks, and adapt successfully to these changes.

For most older individuals, even when they experience declines, they develop alternative strategies that allow them to continue to communicate effectively and appropriately. In spite of the generally good news that cognitive decline does not begin at age 25, or even age 55, some individuals do experience serious problems with cognitive functions in their later years, even when they have been relatively healthy earlier in their lives. Schaie and Hofer (2001) reviewed the longitudinal studies conducted in psychology and aging and found overwhelming evidence that our cognitive abilities show impressive gains in early life, followed by relative stability throughout our midlife, followed by a slow decline in late life, until a rapid decline is recorded past the age of 80. Thus, in normal aging, declines that impact day-to-day functioning usually do not occur until very late in life. Most of these declines, however, have relatively little consequence for functioning and interaction until the decline becomes quite pronounced (Schaie, 1996).

Three particular declines in cognitive processing do have consequences for older individuals in conversation and the reactions of others to those difficulties. As we age, we experience minor to severe losses in working memory and delays in cognitive processing, along with difficulty in finding words. These declines affect the discourse-processing abilities of older individuals. Working memory capacity refers to the amount of information that we can retain over a relatively short period of time. Decreases in working memory capacity lead to the production of less complex linguistic structure and comprehension failures when others use complex structures (Kemper, Greiner, Marquis, Prenovost, & Mitzner, 2001). For example, sentences with subordinate clauses require greater working memory capacity because the individual must "hold aside" the subordinate clause to evaluate its meaning in relationship to the rest of the sentence. Problems with loss of working memory also lead to greater repetition and redundancy in conversation (Kemper & Lyons, 1994). Although more simplistic sentence structure may not greatly impact the conversational flow, redundancies and repetitions are usually negatively evaluated by listeners.

Slower processing speeds increase the amount of time an individual needs to search for information (Kemper & Lyons, 1994). Even slight delays can interrupt the flow of a conversation. In the United States, the norm is for relatively "rapid-fire" exchanges, and silences are not well tolerated. When an older individual takes even slightly longer to process information, the interactional partner may "jump in" to the silence to offer suggestions or become irritated with the delays. Both partners may find these actions difficult to manage and may begin to avoid interactions in the future.

Word-finding difficulties generally are first exhibited by difficulty finding names and the use of general terms instead of specific ones (Kemper & Lyons, 1994). Forgetting the name of a neighbor or public person while in conversation with a friend or family member often results in a response of "Oh no, it's early-onset Alzheimer's," followed by nervous laughter. In reality, these difficulties are not a sign of the onset of dementia, but a normal consequence of the way in which we store and access information. Although we may not be able to remember the names of neighbors, we can remember a number of other characteristics about them, such as their occupations, number of children, and character traits. Names are relatively arbitrary, and we usually have few links in place to help us to access them. On the other hand, other characteristics have rich connections and are easier to access because we have a greater number of related items for drawing them up. As we age, however, we do begin to experience more difficulty accessing names and specific terms. Older individuals will use more vague terms for conveying information. For example, instead of saying, "Look at the beautiful cardinal in the redbud tree," a person with word-finding difficulties may say, "Look at the beautiful bird in the tree." Although the differences between these two sentences are minor, they may lead to less fruitful interactions.

These cognitive processing problems and their consequences for interaction are not inevitable, and declines must be quite severe before they significantly impact daily life. Maybe the best news, however, is that we can combat some of these problems by making healthy lifestyle choices across the life span and remaining engaged in life and activities that continue to exercise our minds (Kemper et al., 2001; Rowe & Kahn, 1998).

SUMMARY

Cognitive processing is multidimensional, with a number of important domains, but it can be simply summarized as the storage, retrieval, and use of knowledge. Cognitive processes allow us to organize and make sense of our world. Early childhood is a time of tremendous growth in cognitive processing ability. This maturation is a product of both genetic "hard-wiring" and the social environment of the child. Although the stage approach of early childhood development oversimplifies the process and implies a universality that is nonexistent, these stages do reflect a common, general pattern. As social creatures, we are influenced by the social interactions in which we participate and that we observe. Two interrelated cognitive processes that communication scholars have found particularly useful are cognitive complexity and perspective taking. Individuals who are able to put themselves in the other person's position are also able to adapt their messages for maximum effectiveness.

Following the tremendous growth that occurs in childhood, the physical aspects of cognitive processing (e.g., processing speed, working memory capacity) remain relatively stable throughout adulthood until very old age. The social aspects of cognitive processing continue to be very active as individuals adapt to life events and rework the meanings they assign to prior events. As we age, we tend to change our decision-making style, and our stereotypes for people, situations, and things may change based on new experiences. The midlife crisis is more of a myth than reality. People do reevaluate their lives, but the process is more day to day and not a crisis. Mental health problems are not a byproduct of aging, but some cognitive decline is associated with aging. Older individuals have decreased working memory capacity, have slower processing speeds, and may have trouble finding words. These declines may affect social interaction as the individual struggles to make sense of complex sentences or cannot find the word he or she wants to use. Some older individuals may suffer from severe dementia, and the percentage of older individuals in this category increases with age. However, severe cognitive processing declines are not inevitable and are not a part of normal aging.

3

Language Development

As noted in the introduction to this part, the development of language, cognition, and communication are intertwined. In this chapter, we focus on the development, maintenance, and decline in language skills across the life span. In much the same way that cognitive scientists have concentrated their research efforts at the beginning and at the end of the life span, linguists, sociolinguists, developmental psychologists, and communication scholars have placed great emphasis on the developmental gains of language in children and on the decline of language abilities in old age.

Haslett and Samter (1997) defined language as the "symbolic code that underlies verbal communication" (p. 13). Language is more than the words we use, but is used to express ourselves, to convey meaning, and to create shared understanding. Although we often think about the acquisition of language as an individual process, we learn language through social interaction. Therefore, language is the very basis of our social lives.

As with many other communication skills, the development of language skills requires the acquisition of knowledge and use, or performance, of that knowledge. Individuals may or may not know what words to choose or the proper sentence construction to use and may or may not have the ability to successfully express that knowledge. In normal development, however, most individuals apparently quite easily develop the basic skills of language use.

Although the development of language is quite rapid and apparently easy, children must develop the ability to understand the language of others and to generate their own language skills. Children must understand words, sentences, the impact of the context on the interpretation of meaning, the use of paralinguistics, etc. Haslett and Samter (1997) pointed out that children must acquire knowledge of the structure of language on at least four levels: sound, meaning, grammar, and discourse. Sound (also called phonology) consists of such elements as phonemes, pitch, stress, pausing, and timing. Therefore, children must develop an understanding of and ability to produce the appropriate noises in the language system of their culture. Meaning (also called semantics) consists of such elements as understanding the referential relationship between words and objects or abstract concepts. Therefore, children must develop an understanding of and ability to use the "right" words to express their meaning. Grammar consists of the structure of a language, including the appropriate use of suffixes, prefixes, and word combinations. Therefore, children must develop an understanding of and use the appropriate relationships among words. Finally, discourse consists of a wide range of communicative skills, often considered to be those beyond the basic use of language. Therefore, children must develop an understanding of and ability to appropriately take turns in conversation, follow the topic and threads of conversation, and know the appropriateness of topics with different relational partners in different situations. In addition, all four of these levels of language must be coordinated with each other. In this chapter, we focus on the first three elements of language, as the elements related to discourse are discussed in a number of other chapters relating to communicative competence.

EARLY CHILDHOOD

Haslett and Samter (1997) summarized the precise nature of change in our language abilities during the first few years of life. From prelinguistic development, to speech pronunciation, to our first words, to semantic development, to syntactic development, the fundamental process of language acquisition that occurs in the majority of normal humans has been well researched. One of the fundamental arguments in language development is the underlying mechanism for its acquisition. Are humans "hard-wired" for language (the "Chomsky"position), or are humans driven to learn language through social interaction (the "Skinner"position)?

Kuhl (2000) summarized the Chomsky versus Skinner arguments regarding language acquisition. The Chomsky position is that infants are hard-wired for language acquisition. Essentially, we are born with an innate knowledge of language, and the use of language by those around us triggers a particular pattern (related to a particular language). Thus, infants learn whatever language is spoken around and to them, but have the ability to learn any language that is used. The Skinner position is that infants do not have innate knowledge of language, but develop their language skills through reward contingencies. Essentially, babbling noises that generate a positive response are repeated, whereas babbling noises that generate a negative response are not repeated. Through a series of rewards, children learn the language of those with whom they interact.

Kuhl (2000) argued that both the Chomsky and Skinner positions are, to some extent, wrong. Language acquisition is the product of both innate abilities and the social environment. Infants at 6 months have the ability to discriminate between the basic units of language (the phoneme), but by the age of 12 months, they can no longer distinguish the differences between sounds that are not used in their native language (that is, by those individuals with whom they interact). Kuhl (2000) proposed that infants detect patterns in language, and their learning strategies generate "maps" of their native language. As a consequence, although all children are born with the ability to differentiate all sounds in human language, through interaction, the mental maps for speech differ for speakers of different languages.

The current consensus regarding language acquisition, then, is that humans do have some inborn capacity for language, but grammatical skills need to be learned (Kuhl, 2000; Rutter & Rutter, 1993). Individuals who grow up with limited exposure to language have slower language development than do individuals who grow up in richer linguistic environments. However, children who are removed from neglectful environments before the age of 3 years make relatively rapid progress toward "normal" levels (Rutter & Rutter, 1993). Although parental/caretaker interaction has limited impact on basic levels of language development, children who receive responsive, reciprocal interaction develop language more quickly and are more skillful in their use of language. Thus, the innate capacity for language is affected by the social environment. Luckily, children have a number of strategies or skills available to them. Therefore, if they are missing one strategy, others will "click in" (Rutter & Rutter, 1993). Fundamentally, a child with the normal genetic predispositions to acquire language who has been placed into a rich, linguistic environment will have a greater chance of developing superior language abilities.

Although the development of intelligence and language are intertwined, the pace of the development of language skills is not reflective of the child's intellectual capacity (Rutter & Rutter, 1993). More intelligent children do not develop language skills more rapidly or in a more complex fashion. However, language development is related to brain development, as both require and are stimulated by social interaction. In addition, meaning reflects individuals' experiences and a certain level of cognitive development is needed to process these experiences and assign meaning to them (Haslett & Samter, 1997). Thus, word acquisition relies on the development of category hierarchies, and concept formation is a cognitive process. With the understanding that the first 3 years are critical for language development, we briefly review the development of a number of elements of language (from listening and attending to nonverbal interaction skills to sound production of words and sentences) and the "typical" ages at which these skills are acquired by children.

When we talk about language development, we must remember that it occurs within the development of the broader range of communicative skills. Communication, or the use of discourse, requires a number of skills that do not involve the use of words. These skills, as mentioned previously, will be discussed more fully in later chapters; however, a discussion of nonverbal interaction skills is useful at this point to assist with understanding the later development of the use of verbal language (Haslett & Samter, 1997; Rutter & Rutter, 1993).

Nonverbal Interaction Skills

Before children begin to use language, they are already fairly sophisticated communicators (Haslett & Samter, 1997). They have the ability to gain the attention of others and to interact with them to achieve goals. Survival requires the assistance of others; therefore, infants are inherently driven to interact with others. Infants attend and orient to voices, often gazing at a person who speaks to them. They make eye contact with others, gaze and point at desired objects, use facial expressions, attend to the paralinguistics of others, and begin to learn to integrate nonverbal messages with verbal ones. As early as 3 or 4 months of age, infants are able to share communicative control (also called interactional synchrony) by coordinating their behaviors with the behaviors of others.

Eye gaze is important because it is used to regulate social interaction and provides feedback, especially to an infant who is developing interactional skills. Eye contact continues to be an important feature of communication throughout the life span, as it is used to manage turn taking in conversation, to express interest in the other person and to receive nonverbal feedback during the course of conversation.

Facial expressions play a key role in communication across the life span, as they are used to convey emotions. For infants, their own and their caregivers' facial expressions are crucial to the development of attachment, and children learn how to respond to situations by monitoring their parents' reactions. By 3 months, infants can distinguish between positive and negative expressions. Attempts to control facial expressions occur as early as 3 months and by 2 years, most children can plan and display a chosen facial expression (Haslett & Samter, 1997). Although the expression of emotions through facial expressions is probably universal and based in physiology, the ability to mask emotions requires a certain level of cognitive development to understand the meaning of a given expression and to regulate its production. As children age, they become more sophisticated in reading and producing facial expressions. For example, by 3 or 4 years of age, children have learned to pair facial expressions with other nonverbals and with verbal messages in order to interpret that same expression in multiple ways (e.g., understanding the difference between a smile of joy and a smile of failure). Between ages 4 and 6 years, children become more adept at discriminating the authenticity of others' emotional expressions.

Verbal Skills

The development of these nonverbal communicative skills lays the foundation for the development of more sophisticated conversational exchanges as children add language skills to their repertoire. The addition of language allows individuals to express more complex ideas, to refer to the past and future, and to explain the world in greater depth and detail (Haslett & Samter, 1997). As mentioned previously, the acquisition of language involves development in a number of areas, including phonology, semantics, and grammar. Individual children demonstrate considerable variability in the rate and sequence of acquisition of the different dimensions of language; however, the acquisition of these different elements of language is a closely interconnected process. In spite of the variability demonstrated by individual children, "typical" milestones are often noted in the research on children's acquisition of language.

At birth, infants orient to the sounds of voices. Vocal stimuli in the form of "baby-talk" (i.e., higher pitched, overexaggeration of sounds; prosodic repetition) generate a greater response in infants as they begin to develop cognitive maps of the sounds of language used by their caregivers (Haslett & Samter, 1997; Kuhl, 2000). At 3 or 4 months, infants begin to babble, making a wide range of sounds. By 7 or 8 months, babbling is used in soliloquies and social interactions in which infants are able to exert some control over the nature of the interaction. By 9 months, these babblings contain more sounds that occur in the native language, dropping the sounds that do not occur, and reproduce the cadences of speech, with rising and falling intonations evident in sentences.

During the babbling stage, infants learn which noises receive a positive response, acquiring the phonemes and morphemes of their native language. The next step in language development occurs when children begin to utter single words with meaning. The age of "baby's first word" ranges widely, but most children utter their first word between the ages of 12 and 18 months, and their vocabulary grows dramatically in the next few months (Rutter & Rutter, 1993). Typically, these first words refer to familiar people and concrete objects.

Although the use of single words is an important and exciting milestone, language experts identify the use of language as beginning with the use of two-word sentences, which typically occurs around the age of 2 years (Haslett & Samter, 1997; Rutter & Rutter, 1993). Two-word sentences convey the acquisition and integration of knowledge regarding phonology, semantics, and grammar. With the onset of two-word sentences, children are able to produce appropriate sounds for their language, to convey meaning, and to demonstrate an understanding of the structure of their language. More specifically, two-word sentences demonstrate the child's understanding of the difference between nouns and verbs and how these word forms relate to concepts and meanings.

Once children begin to produce two-word sentences, their development in all areas of language increases rapidly. They are able to construct more and more complex sentences and to express more and more abstract ideas. By the age of 5 or 6 years, normal children will exhibit mastery of all elements of language and will develop the ability to monitor their own communication (Haslett & Samter, 1997). At this point, they are able to evaluate their messages and to repair perceived mistakes while conversing with others.

Thus, the first 5 or so years of life are a time when children experience tremendous growth in their use of language. Children must learn to read and use nonverbal messages, such as eye gaze, facial expressions, and paralinguistics, and to coordinate these messages with verbal ones. They must learn the sounds and phonemes of their language. They must learn which words are connected to which objects and concepts. They must move from the use of single words, and the use of two-word sentences marks the beginning of the true use of language because this event signifies the understanding of the complex nature of language rules. Children must develop an understanding of grammar to manage interaction with others.

THE MIDDLE YEARS AND LATER LIFE

Following the rapid acquisition of language skills in early life, the middle and later years are relatively stable. Little research has been conducted on language during the middle years, but considerable attention has been given to the later years, when language skills may decline as cognitive processing declines. As mentioned in the introduction to this part, the acquisition of language and the development of cognitive processing skills are interrelated, but independent processes. In the later years, language use is impacted by cognitive processing abilities; however, different domains of language use are differentially impacted by cognitive abilities.

Research consistently finds declines in our syntactic and discourse processing abilities as we age; however, these declines are relatively subtle in normal aging. The most significant declines occur in verbal fluency, vocabulary, and verbal performance past the age of 70 (Schaie & Hofer, 2001). These declines in language performance have consequences for interaction, as others feel the need to step in and help the older individual with problems, potentially leading to greater frustration for the older participant who may become frustrated and avoid interaction altogether, thus reducing the interactive lives of older individuals.

As mentioned in the chapter on cognitive processing, declines in these abilities result in declining linguistic performance. As working capacity declines, individuals use less grammatically complex sentence structure and are less able to comprehend complex sentence structure when used by others (Kemper et al., 2001). Maintaining attention to the conversation may become more difficult. As semantic memory (a person's organization of general world knowledge, concepts, meanings, and associations) becomes impaired, the person uses less specific terms and may lose the ability to remember scripted behaviors (Kemper & Lyons, 1994). Word-finding problems may lead to uncomfortable pauses as the person searches for the right word or an appropriate substitute.

These linguistic problems generally do not have a significant effect on interaction until they become quite severe because most individuals, even those suffering from dementia, develop strategies for maintaining interaction in spite of these problems. For example, phone conversations have a typical pattern of openings and closings. Older individuals with dementia may shift their interaction styles to less specific forms, but retain the script for the interaction. Instead of asking how specific individuals are doing, questions such as "How's everyone there doing?" may be asked. These vague, open-ended questions prompt the respondent to provide information without specifically admitting that the questioner cannot remember the names of the person's children and spouse.

Most individuals with dementia continue to interact fairly successfully until the middle stages of the disease. In the middle and later stages of dementia, the individual may no longer initiate conversations or topics in conversations (Kemper & Lyons, 1994). The lack of interest in what were normal activities, such as watching television or reading the newspaper, limit the topics of conversation available and may create caregiver burden as the individual demands more direct attention and entertainment.

The problems reviewed to this point have been structural ones. Communication scholars studying language in later life emphasize the style component of language much more than the structural component. Coupland, Coupland, and Giles (1991) used communication accommodation theory to explain and describe how interactions with older adults often demand and result in adaptive language use. The adaptation can take the form of overaccommodating or underaccommodating to the perceived needs of the older interactant. In either case, the use of language has been shown to be a significant and complex factor in the overall communicative milieu of older adults.

Younger people may overaccommodate older people by speaking loudly and slowly, using oversimplified and overly polite language (Nussbaum et al., 1996). This "elderspeak" or "secondary baby-talk" treats the older person as incompetent and dependent. Underaccommodation occurs when younger people do not attempt to meet the needs of the older person by avoiding certain topics of conversation. Older people may underaccommodate younger people by disclosing painful life events that would not normally occur in conversations or "chaining" on a topic by providing more detail than is necessary and going off on unrelated tangents.

Obviously, these stylistic behaviors have an impact on the participants' assessments of the interaction and their partners in these interactions. One outcome can be that older individuals feel less competent after such an interaction, and younger individuals feel uncomfortable. Both generations may try to avoid such situations in the future, leading to less active social worlds for older individuals. As mentioned in the chapter on cognition, one of the most important activities for maintaining cognitive functioning is maintaining engagement in the world. Decreasing social interaction, then, can lead to a downward spiral as skills become less practiced.

SUMMARY

Children acquire a wide range of language skills relatively rapidly. By the age of 5 years, most children have learned the basics of language on four interrelated levels: sound, meaning, grammar, and discourse. Their ability to interact precedes their ability to communicate verbally as they use nonverbal messages. With the addition of verbal language, they can begin to share in more precise and detailed ways with those around them. The addition of verbal messages allows us to share emotions, to talk about the past and the future, and to discuss abstract concepts. After this rapid period of growth, the acquisition of language skills declines; however, vocabulary usually continues to grow throughout the life span. In our later years, problems with cognitive processing may affect our ability to access and use our knowledge of language. For older individuals, these problems with language may impact not only the nature of their interactions, but their opinions about their own competence and the opinions of others about their competence.

Language skills lay the foundation for communication. Through language, we are able to label our experiences and to share those experiences with others. We can express our emotions, attitudes, and beliefs. Language not only transmits information, but is the very basis of our social lives. The following chapters examine the communicative nature of our social lives across the life span.

III

Relational Contexts

The third part of this book examines family and friend relationships. Family and friend relationships are essential contributors to our well-being throughout the life span. The changing closeness and control dynamics of four significant relationships provide evidence that relationships are not stable entities but constantly change across time. The parent–child relationship, sibling relationships, the marital relationship, and friendships can be formed very early in life and remain vibrant until late life. Each of these relationships develops in response to individual and environmental influences over the life span. The new relationship that emerges can be fundamentally different from the previous state of the relationship and can often be more useful at serving the needs and desires of those who are actively maintaining the relationship. Relationships that become stagnate or show very little sign of life span development may no longer contribute to the dynamic relationship network each of us maintains across the life span.

A common mistake made by scholars and students who are studying or attempting to understand human relationships is to ignore the life-span developmental changes that occur within each relationship we form and attempt to maintain. Our relationships are constantly changing as a result of both individual physical and psychological development and the numerous environmental influences that we may not be able to control. No matter how desperately we hope to maintain the current state of a rewarding relationship, that relationship will not remain the same. Relational change may be painfully slow and continuous, or it may be sudden and dramatic. Each relationship develops at a pace within a larger network of relationships affected by and affecting the dynamic nature of our social world. Through our ability to competently communicate, we exert massive amounts of energy in an attempt to coordinate our relational network as we cope with the many challenges faced each and every day.

The major family and friend relationships discussed in this section contain a rhythm or a flow as they progress through the life span. At times, the parent–child relationship is dominated by the parent, combative during adolescence, and dominated by the adult child later in life. Sibling relationships are close and intense during childhood, distant and comforting during adulthood, and return to close and intense during later life. The affection spouses share with each other is interrupted by parenthood and must be regained during older adulthood. In each case, the nature of the relationship changes across time. These changes can fundamentally rearrange the closeness and power dynamic of the relationship to such an extent that a totally new relationship emerges at different points in the life span. The marital relationship at the time of the wedding is not the same relationship that transpires during the parenting of young children. The high levels of affection and balanced power that defined the marriage are replaced by affection directed toward the children and separate, gender-based roles to accomplish the multiple tasks of establishing a family.

The primary focus of this part is to provide evidence and a sound argument that relationships develop across the life span. This development is not only interesting because it happens, but is interesting because of the different functions that are served by the developing relationships as we age. Each relationship is formed to serve the social, emotional, and physical needs of the participants. Each relationship is structured to meet these needs in various ways and at various times throughout life. Early in life, our relationships serve security and socialization needs. We discover and create our self-identities through our adolescent relationships. Young and middle adulthood are dominated by relationships that accomplish parenting and career goals. In later life, our relationships help us to remain healthy and sustain active social lives.

In this part, chapter 4 examines the role of communication in families with young children through adolescence. We highlight the unique role that families play in childhood development and socialization processes, communication processes in different types of families, communication with extended family, and how family communication changes during the transition of children into adolescence. Chapter 5 looks at how communication changes in families later in life. This chapter explores changes in families as children leave home, sibling communication in later life, and the impact of common life events, such as divorce and remarriage, on family communication. In chapter 6, we explore ways in which the friend relationship is unique from other types of relationships, theories about the development and maintenance of friendships, and how friendships change throughout the life span.

4

Family Communication: Childhood Through Adolescence

The family has a profound influence on individuals throughout the course of their life span. Our perceptions of others, our attitudes, beliefs, and values, and our communication behaviors are shaped in a variety of ways through multiple interactions with parents, siblings, and extended family members. Everyday family life presents numerous opportunities for people to engage in many types of communication. For example, most people learn how to talk, how to read, how to argue, and a host of other communication skills within the family context. In addition, our families typically provide our first experiences of such diverse topics as power relationships, gender roles, small group communication, intimacy, and communication rituals.

As important as families are, however, they are just one of the many groups an individual identifies with throughout his or her life span, including peers, occupational groups, and many other important associations. The influence of family members on an individual's communication behaviors, attitudes, and beliefs may interact with influences from other important groups and, at other times, the family and other groups may send a person contradictory messages about appropriate ways of communicating or behaving in general. However, despite these outside influences, our families have an important impact on our perceptions of the world and our interactions with others as we progress through life.

Finally, family communication is dynamic in nature. Families typically progress through a number of stages throughout the life span and, in most families, we can observe changes in communication patterns over a period of time. For example, the communication patterns established when a child is young, dependent, and has little power or influence over parental decisions changes significantly as the child becomes more independent as he or she grows older. As a consequence of the child's increasing independence, more conflict arises between children and parents over the child's desire to become more autonomous, particularly during adolescence.

The focus of this chapter is on characteristics of families and family communication during early stages of the life span for the average person. Chapter 5 examines how communication patterns typically change as individuals and their family members progress through later stages of the life span.

CHANGING VIEWS OF FAMILIES
AND DEFINITIONAL ISSUES

Throughout history, family structures have been a crucial part of the developmental process for individuals, and humans have bonded together as families for a variety of reasons, including the need to nurture children, for survival purposes, for socialization, and for fulfillment of basic inclusion and interpersonal needs. The decision to raise children often had economic benefits for families. Family trades were common during the pre-industrial era, and many individuals learned important occupational skills through immediate and extended family members.

During the 20th century, our society witnessed vast changes in terms of our collective perception of what constitutes a family unit. This period saw numerous social changes that accompanied the many technological advances, increased diversity in the United States as a result of immigration, greater mobility, various social movements, including those by women and minorities, and the aging of the U.S. population during the last quarter of the century. Popular media during this time often depicted the typical American family in idealized ways (e.g., the television shows *Leave it to Beaver* or *The Brady Bunch*), ignoring the diversity of important cultural differences among immigrant families, single-parent families, blended families, and gay and lesbian families.

In the early 1990s, Vice President Dan Quayle received a great deal of criticism for his views of the decline of family values in America. Many of his critics felt that he had a limited concept of what American families were actually like during that time, and some people were offended by his conservative views that single-parent families were somehow inferior to the two-parent biological family (sometimes called a "nuclear family") in terms of the values that children would learn. In fact, during the time of this controversy, two-parent biological families were not the most common type of family (U.S. Bureau of the Census, 1991). The majority of Americans were living in blended families or step-families, where both parents are not the biological parents of children in the family because of adoption, remarriage after widowhood or divorce, single-parent families, or extended families where grandparents or other relatives (or family friends) often spend more time than the biological parent taking care of the child.

Today, our society is becoming increasingly more aware of other diverse types of families. Of the 105 million U.S. households in the year 2000, only 69% of these were family households. Only 24% of family households consisted of married couples with their own children, and there were 12 million single-parent families during this time. In addition, there were over 3 million cohabiting couples (Fields & Casper, 2000). In recent years, social scientists have begun to understand important cultural differences in families. For example, there is evidence that families exhibit important ethnic differences in terms of family structure, family rituals, and communication patterns (Baxter & Clark, 1996; McGoldrick, 1993). Gay and lesbian families are also beginning to receive more attention from researchers and the media, as well as voluntary types of families, such as communal living and cohabiting couples who choose to remain childless. Moreover, with the increase of older individuals in the United States, we are beginning to see more extended family structures that span four generations (Nussbaum et al., 2000).

As you can see from this brief discussion of how societal views of families have changed, there is no one specific type of family, and no two people experience families in the same way. However, family communication scholars have found that families often exhibit common characteristics, such as: (a) an organized network of people with a shared history; (b) legal, consensual, or biological ties; (c) sharing of a common living space over an extended time period; and (d) mutual interpersonal influence (Bochner, 1976; Galvin & Brommel, 2000).

Notice that these characteristics do not specifically mention the presence of children. However, in keeping with the book's life-span developmental perspective, this chapter focuses primarily on communication patterns in families with children and how families influence the development of children's communicative behaviors. Also, keep in mind during our discussion of family communication that there are many types of family structures and, although there are a number of similarities between different types of families in how they influence the developmental processes of children, important differences can also be observed among each type of family because of the diversity of the individuals who make up the family and the social circumstances that brought the family together.

Finally, we make the distinction between families of origin, or the family structure responsible for raising and nurturing a child, and current families, which typically change for individuals as they progress through the life span (e.g., new families formed as a result of marriage, remarriage, cohabitation, etc.). This chapter focuses mainly on the roles families of origin have in developing our communicative skills and behaviors, and how communication patterns in families of origin change from the time when an individual is born until he or she progresses through adolescence and early adulthood. Chapter 5 discusses changes in family of origin communication patterns as both individuals and their family members progress through later stages of the life span.

FUNCTIONS OF FAMILIES

Most families of origin, regardless of individual type, have a variety of functions beginning when a child is born and may continue to be influential throughout the life span of an individual. These functions include the fulfillment of basic physical and emotional needs (nurturing); socialization into family beliefs, attitudes, values, roles, and communication behaviors; fostering of a sense of cohesion and adaptability; and creation of awareness of individual and collective boundaries.

Nurturing and Providing for Basic Needs

Anyone who has spent time around a newborn child begins to realize how fragile and vulnerable an infant is. Every physical need of the child needs to be attended to by a parent or another family member during the earliest stages of human life. Children come into this world with several instincts (such as the need for nourishment when hungry), but with no abilities for physical survival. A child must learn everything through the help of others who are willing to devote time and considerable energy to help an infant emerge from a state of total dependence to become a self-sufficient individual. Parents and other family members serve a number of important roles during the nurturing phase, including caregiving and provision of basic physical needs, socioemotional development, and early cognitive development, as discussed in several other chapters in this book. Physical development is extremely important during the first 2 years of life, and families play a crucial role in providing proper nutrition for physical and neurological growth. In addition to rapid increases in height and weight, young children develop important brain and nervous system functions during the first several years of life, including basic motor skills needed to perform simple physical acts, such as walking or the ability to handle objects.

Socioemotional Development

Prior to language development, children learn how to communicate emotions, and parents learn how to respond to a child's nonverbal emotional displays (Maccoby, 1992). Most children learn to express emotions, such as interest, at birth, whereas other emotions, such as anger, sadness, and fear, typically develop over a period of months during the first year of life. More complex emotions, such as guilt, usually occur around a child's second birthday. Many researchers believe that emotional development is relational, and there is a link between a caregiver's display and regulation of emotion and the ways in which a child learns how to respond emotionally (Saarni, Mumme, & Campos, 1998).

Related to the issue of emotional development is a child's attachment style. Attachment theory (Bowlby, 1988) argues that our early experience of bonding with caregivers is an important foundation for our psychological development, and it influences how we perceive others and interact with them throughout our lives. Initial interactions with caregivers are thought to affect our sense of trust, caring, and responsiveness when interacting with others throughout childhood and into adulthood. For example, children who are fortunate enough to have been raised by parents who consistently reassure them and respond to them in loving and supportive ways tend to be more secure in their relationships with others later in life. These individuals are likely to have more positive self-perceptions and to be more affectionate and trusting of others. Children who receive inconsistent or unpredictable responses from caregivers, such as when parents have only limited time to devote to the nurturing process because of work or financial pressures, tend to develop more negative self-perceptions, and they may be less secure and trusting in relationships. In the worst cases, children who have been responded to negatively, rejected, or abused by caregivers can develop attachment styles in which they will either avoid contact with others later in life or spend their time as perfectionists who feel they must always prove themselves to others.

Gender Role Development

As we have seen in other chapters, children must learn how to acquire language and the ability to communicate with others. The family serves an important function in helping children to acquire both language and communication skills through repeated, ongoing interaction between caregivers and children. Family life provides multiple opportunities for infants to observe the behaviors of others in their environment and for the nascent stages of socialization. Chapter 7 focuses on the socialization process and the development of roles, including gender roles, in greater detail. However, because of the important implications for Life-Span Communication, we address the development of gender roles and related communicative practices here as well.

Parents and other caregivers spend countless hours interacting with children, correcting behaviors, and serving as primary socializing agents for children by helping them to learn a number of important roles and the patterns of interaction that are appropriate for those roles (Fitzpatrick & Badzinski, 1994; Sillars, 1995). The development of gender roles among children can be attributed to numerous sources, including peer groups, and family (Beal, 1994). However, our families tend to have a primary influence on our perceptions of being male or female. Gender role socialization in families is largely influenced by verbal and nonverbal communication between children and other family members, including siblings and extended family. Family members begin to interact with children very early in a variety of gender-specific ways, and they will even talk to newborn babies differently depending on whether the infant is male or female.

As a child ages, parents typically purchase different types of toys depending on the sex of the child, such as footballs for boys and Barbie dolls for girls. In addition, parents often reinforce gender stereotypes they learned in their families, peer groups, and society, through verbal communication, by repeatedly making statements to a child about how they expect a child to behave (e.g., "girls don't hit," and "be a good boy and help your father fix the kitchen sink").

There are several theories focused on specific ways that gender roles are developed. Proponents of social learning theory (Bandura, 1977) argue that children respond to the ways family members communicate gender expectations by imitating the gender roles that were conveyed to them by parents, siblings, and extended family, and by observing gender role behaviors in their family environment. In other words, children often imitate gender behaviors they learn from interacting with mothers, fathers, grandmothers, sisters, etc., and watching the activities in which these family members engage. Parents and other family members also reinforce gender roles by rewarding gender behaviors they feel are appropriate for a child to enact or punishing a child if he or she acts contrary to their gender expectations.

Two other prominent theories related to gender roles are cognitive development theory (Kohlberg, 1966) and gender schema theory (Carter & Levy, 1988). Supporters of cognitive development theory propose that children first develop an initial stable concept of their gender, and then they begin to interact with others in ways that are consistent with their conception. Over time, and with repeated interactions with others, children's initial conception of their gender is reinforced. Similarly, gender schema theory holds that children develop a variety of schemas, or cognitive structures that organize perceptual stimuli that are encountered through interaction with others and the world, including schemas that organize gender-related stimuli. Gender schema theorists argue that once a child develops initial gender schemas, these structures ultimately guide his or her gender behaviors and attention to new gender-related stimuli in ways that are consistent with the initial schemas.

Although these theories have emerged as possible explanations of gender role socialization, there is still considerable debate among scholars as to which one best explains this phenomenon. As stated earlier, families are only one of the many socializing agents when it comes to learning gender roles. In addition, gender role expectations as well as the gender role socialization process will vary among different types of families, based on variables, such as whether a child is in a single-parent or a dual-parent family, the gender combination of parents (as in gay and lesbian families), whether or not a child has same-sex or cross-sex siblings, and a host of cultural factors, including ethnic and religious backgrounds.

Cognitive Development

The family has an important role in a child's cognitive development. Although all of the ways in which parents and other caregivers influence our cognitive development is beyond the scope of this chapter, it is easy to see

that they spend a great deal of time helping children to learn to interact
with others and their environment, and instructing them in developing
basic cognitive abilities, such as attention, memory, and task analysis. Although biological differences certainly account for some degree of variability in cognitive abilities among children, a nurturing family environment
is also important. As children grow older, families are important sources
of early childhood education because families support a child's education
financially as well as helping him or her with homework assignments and
providing education experiences outside of the classroom.

Cognitive development includes helping to foster a child's sense of individuality and self-sufficiency. Family members can facilitate this process
by encouraging a child's interests and abilities, and by not stifling his or
her motivation to pursue interests by being overprotective, by enforcing
rigid family rules that limit opportunities to engage in activities, or by dis-
couraging activities that are not in the interests of parents. For example,
some parents may feel that playing a musical instrument is a waste of time,
and they may not allow a child to play in a school orchestra. Other families may gravitate toward the other extreme by having expectations that
are too high for their children when it comes to their cognitive development. They might exhaust a child by simultaneously enrolling him or her
in dance instruction, piano lessons, soccer, and a variety of other activities,
regardless of whether the child has any interest in them.

Fostering a Sense of Individuality

As children reach late adolescence and early adulthood, parents often attempt to encourage individuality by encouraging them to pursue a college
career or to seek employment, to make more decisions on their own, and
by giving them more responsibility and freedom. Of course, this is not always a smooth transition, and, as we will see later, adolescence and early
adulthood can be difficult periods for parents and children.

Supportive Functions

In addition to nurturing and individual development, families are important sources of social support for individuals throughout the life span,
which is discussed in more detail in chapter 9. For our purposes here, the
fact that support from family members has been linked to both psychological and physical well-being is important to discuss (Albrecht, Burleson,
& Goldsmith, 1994; Schwarzer & Leppin, 1991). Because families are

generally available in ways that friends are not, they are often the first people to whom we turn in times of trouble. Families typically provide instrumental, emotional, and informational support in a variety of ways. For children, families not only provide the necessities of life, such as food, clothing, and shelter, but also encourage the development of new skills and learning. Feeling loved and valued, as mentioned in the discussion on attachment theory, leads to more positive self-esteem. Adequate and appropriate support in the family during childhood lays the foundation for positive views of the self throughout the life span.

Cohesion

Cohesion refers to the perception of closeness or emotional bonding with family members and can affect an individual's sense of autonomy or independence in the family structure. Individual families typically vary in terms of this characteristic, and cohesion can be conceptualized as a continuum from disengaged families (low cohesion) to enmeshed families (high cohesion). Disengaged families tend to exhibit extreme separation among individual family members and little sense of family unity, whereas enmeshed families are characterized by strong emotional ties, loyalty, and a sense of belonging (Galvin & Brommel, 2000). Most families have cohesion patterns in between these two extremes, and some families may demonstrate continuity in their cohesion patterns throughout the life span, whereas other families may gravitate toward one extreme or the other depending on life events that may increase or decrease cohesion. For example, one of the authors of this book grew up in a relatively enmeshed family; however, after his mother died and his father remarried, he and his brother moved to different parts of the country, and he has noticed his family has become far less cohesive in recent years.

Cohesion in families is affected by the larger concept of dialectical tensions among individuals in relationships in general. Relational Dialectics Theory (Baxter & Montgomery, 1996) is concerned with a number of ongoing tensions between contradictory impulses that individuals feel in relationships, including relationships with family members. People often have inconsistent or contradictory attitudes and beliefs about relational partners, and these perceptions may create tension for a person because humans typically feel the need to manage inconsistencies between cognitions. For example, most people feel a tension between their desire for a sense of connection with parents, siblings, and extended family members and their desire for autonomy, or a sense of leading one's own life separate

from their family of origin. You may have experienced this tension if you
have been living away from your family and could not wait to be together
with them during a holiday break from college. Yet, after spending a few
days with your family, you may have wanted to "do your own thing," such
as engaging in activities you have learned to enjoy at college (e.g., drinking beer with your friends) without having your parents or siblings along
with you. The autonomy–connection dialectic is an ongoing tension that
people feel in their relationships with other family members throughout
the life span.

Dialectical tensions can be managed in a variety of ways, and most individuals use strategies, such as being connected with their family at certain times (such as holidays) while attempting to be more autonomous in
other contexts (e.g., work, school), choosing one extreme over the other
(avoiding events where you have to connect with family members), or trying to find a happy medium between the opposing tensions (see Baxter &
Montgomery, 1996).

Adaptability

Adaptability, or the ability of a family unit to respond to situational and
developmental changes by altering relationship roles, is another key function of family life. According to Galvin and Brommel (2000), "family systems constantly restructure themselves as they pass through predictable
developmental stages" (p. 33). Over time, change is the one thing a family can always count on, and the ability of family members to adapt to
these changes is important to relational satisfaction as well as to successful
psychological adjustment. Families have to make numerous adjustments
as they encounter significant life changes, such as a child entering school,
the birth of a sibling, the death of a grandparent, or when parents decide to file for divorce. Similar to cohesion, adaptability can be conceptualized on a continuum from low adaptability, where families have rigid
relationship roles and respond to change with somewhat inflexible rules
and authoritarian leadership, to high adaptability, where family members
exhibit more flexibility when facing changes and more egalitarian leadership.

Adaptability can also be conceptualized in terms of Relational Dialectics Theory with the dialectic of stability and change. Although families
enjoy a sense of stability, too much stability can make family relationships
stagnate and rigid. At the other extreme, although individuals and families enjoy the novelty associated with change, too much change can make

family members feel that they have little control over life events, which in turn may lead to higher levels of anxiety and dissatisfaction (Ross & Mirowsky, 1990).

FAMILY COMMUNICATION PATTERNS

In addition to family functions, researchers have also identified a variety of communication patterns that families as a whole exhibit as well as characteristics of interaction between parents and children, siblings, and extended family members.

Family Rituals

Family rituals are repetitive forms of communication ranging from everyday interactions and routines to more symbolic communication events, such as those that take place during family holiday celebrations. Rituals serve as a socializing function for children, and they help to shape attitudes, beliefs, and values throughout life. More mundane rituals may include times when family members watch television together, do chores, or when they catch up with each other or express affection and intimacy at certain times of the day. More symbolic rituals may involve going to church, synagogue, or other religious events together, or celebrating holidays and special occasions. Holidays often provide a context for children to interact with extended family members and to share in holiday-related interactions, such as sharing the things for which people are grateful on Thanksgiving or the annual 4th of July family water balloon fight. Obviously, the types of rituals in which family members engage are as unique and varied as families themselves. However, family rituals can have a strong influence on what children remember about their families of origin and which rituals they choose to preserve later in life.

Conformity Orientation and Conversation Orientation

Fitzpatrick and Ritchie (1994) identified four different types of families based on communication patterns resulting from two dimensions: conformity orientation and conversation orientation. These communication patterns may affect the relationships between family members throughout the life span of a family of origin, and they may also serve as socializing agents for future patterns of interaction when adult children form new families. *Conformity orientation* "refers to the degree to which families create a climate that stresses homogeneity of attitudes, values, and beliefs" (Koerner & Fitzpatrick, 1997, p. 60). Families with a high conformity orientation tend to have very similar attitudes, beliefs, and values; harmonious interaction between parents and children; and obedience to family rules. Families with a low conformity orientation are characterized by dissimilar attitudes, beliefs, and values, and interactions that reflect the uniqueness and independence of family members. *Conversation orientation* can be defined as "the degree to which families create a climate where all family members are encouraged to participate freely in interaction about a wide array of topics" (Koerner & Fitzpatrick, 1997, p. 60). In some families, people feel free to openly discuss a variety of topics, including sex, relationships, and problems individuals might be facing, whereas other families avoid these topics and only encourage a limited range of topics and discussion about them.

According to Fitzpatrick and Ritchie (1994), families with high conformity and conversation orientations are call *consensual families*, where family members feel tension between the pressure to agree and an interest in openly communicating about a variety of topics. This pattern is often seen in traditional families, and family members may be torn between wanting to encourage open communication and wishing to preserve harmonious relationships. *Pluralistic families* have low conformity orientations and high conversation orientations, and family members communicate in unconstrained ways about a variety of topics. In addition, members of this type of family tend to be more independent and value freedom of expression despite differing viewpoints. Families who have high conformity orientations and low conversation orientations are known as *protective families*. In this type of family, there tends to be less sharing between family members and more rigid obedience to family rules. Finally, *laissez-faire families* exhibit both low conformity and conversation orientations. Family members in this type of family tend to communicate infrequently and about few topics. Family members tend to be emotionally detached from each other and more influenced by peers or individuals outside of the family.

Parent–Child Communication

Although there is considerable diversity in types of parent–child communication because of factors such as cultural differences, economic conditions, life events, single- and dual-parent families, single children/

multiple children families, blended families, and nontraditional families, researchers have identified several general communication patterns in families. Parent–child communication is also influenced by patterns of interaction that parents learn in their own families of origin, individual communication styles, and unique communication patterns between couples who decide to become parents.

Many parents desire to communicate with their own children differently from how they interacted with their own parents. When a person decides to have a child for the first time, he or she must learn the role of a parent and how to communicate as a parent in a way that works for him or her. In some cases, individuals reconstruct parenting styles based on their interactions with their own parents, or they may consciously attempt to communicate in ways with their own children that are much different from what they learned in their family of origin.

Some parents engage in an authoritarian parenting style, or a restrictive and demanding communication style that exhibits little verbal interaction between parent and child (Baumrind, 1991). Authoritarian parents decide what is important for children and expect children to adhere to strict rules without input or debate. A parent who says, "You will not play with your friends today ... end of discussion," is communicating in an authoritarian manner. Many times, children of authoritative parents know that they will face strict forms of punishment if they decide to disobey a parent's rules. Although this style has certain advantages for parents in that they can assert their rules and perhaps gain short-term compliance, research has found that children of parents with strict authoritarian styles often fail to initiate activity with others, have poor self-esteem, and low communication competence compared with children whose parents have nonauthoritarian styles.

Other parents have a permissive parenting style, which often takes two forms: neglectful and indulgent (Maccoby & Martin, 1983). Neglectful parents tend to be uninvolved in their child's life, and they are unclear when communicating about their concerns for the child, if they convey them at all. Parents who privilege other roles over parenting (such as work) may find the neglectful parenting style feasible, especially if they remain unaware of problems a child is encountering. Parents who take an "if I don't know what they are doing, it won't hurt me" attitude toward their children are demonstrating the neglectful style. However, this approach may also communicate to children a lack of concern by parents, and it often provides children little direction about important choices in their lives.

Indulgent parenting is a second form of the permissive style. Unlike the neglectful parent, the indulgent parent is very involved with his or her child. Yet, the indulgent parent places few demands or asserts little control over the child's behavior. Over time, this style may influence a child in a negative way in that he or she will develop little sense of self-control. In some ways, a nonrestrictive environment can foster a sense of creativity and freedom for a child, but it can also lead to the development of a child who is overindulgent, spoiled, and who behaves inappropriately around others later in life when he or she does not get his or her way.

Authoritative parenting is more responsive and nurturing than authoritarian parenting, and children are encouraged to make more independent decisions. However, unlike the permissive parenting style, authoritative parents make their wishes and expectations clear to children. Authoritative parents often let children make mistakes, but they will also spend time with children in helping them to understand the implications of certain choices. Instead of imposing harsh punishments when a child goes against his or her parents wishes, authoritative parents may simply express their disappointment to the child or discuss ways the child could act differently when he or she faces similar choices. Children of authoritative parents often have higher self-esteem and better communication skills than those of authoritarian or permissive parents.

Sibling Communication

Siblings are typically the most enduring family relationships we have throughout our life span, and they tend to be more egalitarian than parent–child relationships (Cicirelli, 1980; Stocker, Dunn, & Plomin, 1989). Most families have more than one child, either by birth or adoption, and roughly 80% of U.S. children have one or more siblings (Nussbaum et al., 2000). Siblings have an important impact on a child's development in a variety of ways. Cicirelli (1994) contends that siblings may be a stronger socializing influence on a child than parents and that siblings who are close to a child's age may exhibit more understanding about a child's problems and communicate more effectively than his or her parent(s). This understanding may especially be the case when problems center around issues such as peers, when siblings may have more experience than parents with current trends, or for issues concerning dating and sex about which adolescents may be more comfortable talking with siblings than parents.

Most people will acknowledge that rivalry and conflict also exist in sibling relationships. Family life presents many opportunities for conflict between siblings, but although sibling rivalries often occur in families of origin, little empirical evidence supports the idea that these rivalries continue throughout the life span, although more research is needed in this area (Nussbaum, Thompson, & Robinson, 1989).

One area of sibling relationships that has been studied extensively is birth order in families. Children who are born first may have different experiences from children who are born later because they do not have older siblings for interaction and because parents often exhibit different behaviors toward a first-born child. For example, parents may be overly cautious with a first-born child when it comes to letting him or her play with certain toys, interact with peers, or engage in other activities because they are not sure how these things will affect the child. However, when a younger sibling is born, parents may relax more about letting the second-born child participate in these events because they have reduced their uncertainty about them. This different treatment often leads to jealousy between siblings, especially if the younger sibling is allowed to do things that the first-born child was not allowed to do when he or she was at a similar age.

Birth order affects other aspects of family communication. For example, because newborn children require more attention than older children, first-born children may resent a younger sibling if parents begin to spend less time with him or her. Parents have also been found to have higher expectations of achievement and responsibility for first-born children than later-born children. Parents may be more nurturing when raising a first-born child, but they are often more protective of younger siblings. First-born children are often expected to take on more responsible roles when interacting with younger siblings. In single-parent families, where a parent has to spend a great deal of time at work for financial reasons, older siblings often take on a parental role, although this is also a common behavior in dual-parent families when older siblings can effectively handle the responsibility of caring for a child. For example, the wife of one of the authors of this book was 12 when her younger sister was born, and both she and her parents (both of whom worked) claim that she raised her sister more than her parents.

A number of stereotypes of the effects of birth order exist in our society, such as the youngest sibling being "spoiled," or middle siblings being "troubled" children or mediators. Although some youngest siblings may receive more attention in families and some middle children do experience problems, life-span researchers have found that <u>birth order is not a good</u> <u>predictor of individual behaviors later in life</u>. In addition, given the considerable variability among different types of families and the influence of relationships outside of the family on individuals, it is difficult to make generalizations about the impact of birth order on the developmental process.

Communication with Grandparents

The increase in life expectancy has led to greater opportunities for individuals to have long-lasting relationships with grandparents. Although each family situation is unique, grandparents often play an important role in families of origin in terms of connecting children with family history, perpetuating family rituals, and the socialization process. In some families, such as in single-parent families and in certain ethnic groups, grandparents take on more direct responsibilities for child rearing and parenting functions (Kivnick & Sinclair, 1996). In other families, grandparents may be distant figures with whom a child has only limited interaction via telephone, the Internet, or on special occasions, such as holidays. Moreover, considerable variability exists in terms of the age a person becomes a grandparent, because some individuals become grandparents in their early 30s whereas others do not begin this role until they are in their 70s or 80s. Despite the impact grandparents have on our lives as we progress through the life span, there are relatively few studies on grandparent–grandchild communication, but researchers have found several patterns of communication across the life span.

Because of gender role socialization in our society, women tend to shoulder the responsibility for maintaining ties with grandparents and other extended family members and, in most families, grandchildren tend to have closer ties with their maternal grandparents (Hagestad, 1985). In addition, grandchildren tend to have closer relationships with grandmothers than with grandfathers, regardless of the gender of the grandchild. Some evidence suggests that grandmothers may talk to grandchildren more than grandfathers, especially about topics such as family history (Nussbaum & Bettinni, 1994). Grandparents often experience a dialectical tension between desiring to be actively involved in their grandchildren's lives while simultaneously not wanting to interfere with their adult children's parenting or in their grandchildren's lives (McKay & Caverly, 1995).

A number of communication styles that grandparents have with their grandchildren have been identified, ranging from very involved and frequent communication to sporadic communication or interaction only in specific contexts. In some cases, grandparents may serve as surrogate parents or take on the typical role of the parent (usually grandmothers). In other situations, grandparents may serve as keepers of family wisdom and history, especially during holidays or other ritual events (Nussbaum et al., 1989; Troll, 1983). Some grandparents seek a more hedonistic relationship with their grandchildren, preferring to engage in leisure activities with them, such as taking them to the zoo or playing games, while leaving the less pleasant tasks of childrearing (such as changing diapers) to the parents. Finally, some grandparents remain distant figures (especially those who are separated by long distances), interacting with the child via telephone on an infrequent basis.

In terms of developmental changes in the grandparent–grandchild relationship, younger grandparents tend to be closer to grandchildren than older grandparents, and younger grandchildren have been found in some studies to have a closer relationship with grandparents than older children, whereas other studies have found just the opposite. In addition, younger children may perceive the grandparent role differently than older children (McKay & Caverly, 1995). As a child ages and begins to understand the relationship between his or her parents and grandparents better, and as his or her understanding of the meaning of aging develops, this often lays the foundation for perceptions of older adults in general.

Some evidence suggests that grandparents may serve an important role in terms of providing a sense of stability and social support during times of family crises. If a parent becomes terminally ill, if parents divorce, or if a teenage child gets in trouble with the police, grandparents often become more involved with their adult children and grandchildren. During these stressful periods, grandparents may provide a sense of stability by offering advice, and instrumental support or by being there for family members. However, grandparents do not always want to get involved in family crises because they do not want to be perceived as "butting in" or because they desire to maintain a sense of peace of mind and stability (especially after retirement). Grandparents in families with lower socioeconomic status and those with adult children who are single parents may play more active roles in the family and may not have the opportunity to distance themselves and enjoy their "golden years." In fact, an increasing number of seniors are finding themselves taking on primary child caregiving responsibilities.

Studies of grandparent–grandchild relationships have concluded that both grandparents and grandchildren perceive the relationship positively

(Folwell & Grant, 1999; Harwood & Lin, 2000). However, grandparents often feel frustrated over emotional and communicative distance between themselves and their grandchildren. Sometimes these feelings of distance are associated with physical distance when grandparents and grandchildren are separated geographically, whereas at other times, psychological distance can occur between grandparents and grandchildren because of perceptions based on the social identity of each age group (Harwood, Giles, & Ryan, 1995). For example, a grandfather may feel that he is psychologically distant from his grandson because of their different tastes in music or ideas about marriage. Similarly, the grandson may feel that his grandfather cannot understand the pressures he faces at school because he believes life was much different when his grandfather attended school. Harwood and Lin (2000) found that grandparents rarely blame their grandchildren for the distance they sometimes feel between them, and they often desire more one-on-one communication with grandchildren, although this is often difficult because most grandparent–grandchild communication takes place in the presence of parents and other family members.

Communication with Other Extended Family

Obviously, families include other important members besides parents, siblings, and grandparents. Uncles and aunts, nieces and nephews, great-grandparents, and family friends may also play important roles in terms of caregiving, social support, and the socialization of a child. The interactions between children and extended family members may take on characteristics of the parent–child relationship in families where parents, siblings, and grandparents are not available. This dynamic may be the case in many single-parent families, where a parent may require assistance from numerous people to manage the overwhelming task of working full time and raising a child. Other extended family members may enter a child's life infrequently at family gatherings, such as weddings and funerals. Extended family members may exhibit communication patterns similar to the grandparent–grandchild relationships, or they may also be unique, depending on the characteristics of the family or the age of the extended family member in relationship to the child's age. Only a small amount of research exists that examines communication between children and extended family other than grandparents, despite the fact that these relationships likely play an important role in the child's development process.

ROLE CHANGES IN FAMILIES THROUGH
ADOLESCENCE AND EARLY ADULTHOOD

Adolescence is an important transitional period between childhood and early adulthood, and is associated with numerous role changes among the adolescent child, parents, and other family members. Adolescence is also associated with important physical changes for the child as he or she reaches puberty. During this time, male adolescents experience a release of testosterone hormones from their endocrine glands, whereas female adolescents release a similar hormone called estradiol. These hormones trigger rapid muscle and skeleton growth as well as development of sexual organs. Moreover, adolescents experience cognitive development, such as the ability to engage in formal operational thought and changes in social cognition, particularly in terms of understanding their own personality and the personalities of others. Parents and other family members may be important sources of support in some families during this time, as a child may begin to question physical changes he or she observes in his or her body. Other families may shy away from discussing reproductive organs and sexual matters with adolescent children, especially if sex is a taboo subject in the family in general.

In addition, adolescents experience a number of social changes as their bodies mature. Some individuals may develop faster than others, and this can lead to negative feelings if a person feels that he or she is not maturing as rapidly as his or her peers. Again, it may be important for parents and other family members to be supportive of the adolescent child during this time. Junior high school and high school provide numerous opportunities to adjust to adolescence and to learn important new social skills. Peers typically become more important during this time, and parents may struggle with maintaining influence on their children's behavior. A teenager may learn quite a bit about some topics (e.g., sex, dating, drug use) from interactions with peers, but may avoid discussing these topics with their parents. Relational Dialectics Theory may be helpful in understanding the shift from communicating primarily with parents and siblings to communicating with peers. Pearson (1993) suggests that the dialectical tension between judgment and acceptance may increase communication with peers at times when acceptance is desired from peers. In addition, although teenagers also desire acceptance by parents, they may fear that communicating about some topics or issues will lead to negative judgments of behavior, particularly if the topics center around sexual matters or drug and alcohol use. Peers also influence an adolescent's desire for autonomy and independence from parents, especially when behaviors are expected or rewarded by peers, such as staying out late, dating, or drinking alcohol. Although teenagers also want a sense of connection with their family, they may feel the desire for independence if they perceive greater social rewards are available by following their peers or if parents are too restrictive when allowing them to interact with friends.

The simultaneous desire for independence from parents and acceptance by peers may lead to conflict between teenagers and parents. Although adolescents are fully capable of making many of their own decisions, they often lack the perspective that comes with life experience that is typically seen as individuals reach their late 20s and early 30s. What may be seen as fully appropriate behavior from a teenager's perspective will often be met with great caution by parents, because they may understand the larger implications of behaviors that have potential negative repercussions (e.g., having sex, driving too fast, etc.). Although parents may desire to give teenagers independence and the ability to make their own decisions, it would be irresponsible on the part of the parents to let their child engage in behaviors that may endanger his or her life or negatively impact the future.

Given the recent prevalence of school shootings, date rapes, and alcohol-related accidents, it is understandable how a parent may feel the need to be cautious when giving an adolescent permission to participate in certain events with peers or privileges such as use of the family car. Parents vary in their desire to have open or closed boundaries between children and outside influences such as peers, and parents who attempt to maintain closed boundaries may find themselves in conflict with a child who desires to be like his or her peers. However, positive and open interaction between parents and teenagers may help to reduce parental fears and help parents convey concerns and expectations to teenage children.

Yet, some conflicts between parents and adolescent children may be inevitable. Recent research suggests that the family environment provides an important training ground for the way adolescents learn to manage future conflicts (Dumlao & Botta, 2000). Unresolved conflicts between parents and children in families of origin often continue throughout the life span, and they can affect parent–child communication throughout the duration of the relationship. The role of parent–child conflict in the child's development is discussed more thoroughly in chapter 8.

As adolescents become young adults, their desire for independence grows, and they often achieve financial independence from their parents. However, some individuals may prolong their financial dependence on parents well into their 20s (or later) because of a lack of occupational opportunities, education, or the desire to remain close to their family. Although these individuals may become mature adults, they may simply not have the means to make it on their own without help from their parents. Other individuals may experience a prolonged stage of adolescence, especially if they continue to live under the rules of parents or if they do not take responsibility for their lives (e.g., still allowing parents to do all of the cooking, cleaning, etc.). However, most families continue to experience important changes as they progress into later stages of the life span. These changes are the focus of the next chapter.

SUMMARY

Our family members provide us with the foundations for communication with others, and they are the first relationships we experience. Physically and emotionally, our families aid in our development by nurturing and supporting us. Psychologically and socially, our interactions with family members help us to form perceptions of others, the world around us, and ourselves. We learn many roles through our families, including gender roles and our sense of self. Families often exhibit different types of communication patterns based on whether a family is cohesive, how they adapt to life events, and parental communication styles. Our family roles and communication patterns change as we develop individually and progress through different stages of the life span. The concept of family is changing in our culture, and most families now tend to be nontraditional. More research is needed to examine how family communication changes over time in blended families, single-parent families, and families representing a wide variety of ethnic and racial groups.

5

Family Communication
in Later Life

Families experience numerous changes as each member goes through developmental changes throughout his or her life, and the cumulative effect of these changes keeps family units in a constant state of transition. In other words, both parents and children continue to develop as they progress through the life span, and each of these changes among individuals affects larger family communication patterns. These shifts in communication, along with constantly changing life events, can affect families in a variety of ways (Nussbaum et al., 2000). Some families become disengaged or suffer problems as a result of change, whereas others are more successful at adapting to new circumstances. Negative forms of conflict between members can escalate in some families and damage relationships as each person encounters change and responds to it in individual ways, whereas other families may find that conflict and other forms of communication about the changes they are experiencing help them cope more effectively.

Chapter 4 explored the impact of the family on child development and patterns of communication associated with families earlier in the life span. Although many of these forms of communication certainly continue as family members age, new issues emerge at later points in the life span that affect communication in new ways. This chapter explores a number of these communicative changes, including changing roles in the family; interaction between older parents and adult children; the sibling relationship later in life; the triadic relationship between new grandparents, adult children, and grandchildren; and the effects of cultural conceptions of aging on intergenerational communication.

ROLE CHANGES IN THE FAMILY

Individuals find themselves playing multiple roles in the family throughout their lives. Much like an actor in a play, we learn certain roles as family members and how we are expected to behave when interacting with parents, siblings, and extended family. The roles that we play reflect norms and values that we learn through daily interaction, and they help to define our relationship with other family members. Our family roles often change throughout the life course as we encounter various life events or stages, and we must learn new roles as well as learn to adapt to the changing roles of others.

For example, in our earlier years we play the role of children who are dependent on our parents, and we learn to live by certain rules that are imposed on us by them. As we get older, we may become parents ourselves, while simultaneously playing the role of an adult child when we interact with our parents. People often experience role reversals later in life when they find themselves taking care of aging parents, and our parents may become dependent on us to take care of them. Of course, roles and role changes may differ from family to family. Other roles, such as the role of a sibling, uncle, or grandparent may be even less clearly defined than the parent or child role depending on the type of family or life situation.

Changing Power Roles

One important aspect of family roles is the way in which they help to define power within the relationships among family members. Power refers to a person's ability to influence another person's thoughts or behaviors, and the resistance to these attempts by the other person (Berger, 1985). Family members can exert power in a number of ways, such as by controlling resources and attempts to gain compliance (Noller & Fitzpatrick, 1993). Parents control a number of resources, such as money, affection, and material possessions, and they may try to influence a child's behavior by providing access to these resources as a reward or by withholding them as a punishment.

The power that an individual family member possesses typically changes throughout his or her life span. As we grow older, we acquire more power as we learn more about life and acquire resources of our own. For example, a teenage child may decide to take on a part-time job after school, and he or she gains financial resources by earning his or her own money. As a result, he or she is somewhat less dependent on parental sources of money and may have the power to buy a car or another desirable item. Resources theory (McDonald, 1980) has been used to explain the relationship between controlling more resources and individual power. Essentially, the more resources a person controls in a relationship, the more power he or she has. As an adolescent child controls more resources (e.g., finances, decision making, etc.), he or she gains more power.

Conflict between parents and adolescent children often develops as a result of changing power roles. As teenagers begin to understand more about life, they may begin to question a parent's authority and attempt to exert their own power in situations. For example, teenagers can decide to purchase certain things with their own money against a parent's wishes, or they may decide to challenge parental rules perceived as unfair or inappropriate. As children become young adults, they often become less financially and emotionally dependent on their parents, especially when they are old enough to support themselves and rely on peers for emotional support.

Later in life, aging parents may become dependent on adult children for assistance, particularly when they experience health problems. Adult children are often involved in decision making for their parents, and they may find themselves helping their parents deal with financial matters so that they can move into a retirement community, or they become primary caregivers for a parent if they decide the parent should live with them. In these cases, older parents often find themselves with less power than their adult children. Negative stereotypes of older people, which are often related to misconceptions about aging, can influence negative types of communication related to power and control issues between adult children and their parents, such as patronizing behavior (e.g., treating an older parent as if he or she was a child).

Differences in power are often seen in other family relationships as well. Older siblings, because of their age and greater life experience, may assume more power than younger siblings. Some older siblings play a surrogate parent role when their younger sibling is a child to help a parent who may have limited time for some parental responsibilities because of work schedules or other factors. However, later in life, the older sibling will likely no longer play this role, and he or she may have to redefine his or her relationship with the younger sibling. In addition, grandparents and parents can experience power conflicts over the best way to discipline a child and a host of parenting issues that might be perceived differently by both parties. Parents might not appreciate advice that their own parents give them about child rearing, and this struggle may be seen as a conflict over power in their relationship.

LIFE EVENTS AND FAMILY CHANGE

As families progress through the life span, they encounter multiple life events that can affect the structure of the family and communication between them. These events may range from expected happenings to substantial or traumatic crises that can lead to family upheaval, and they typically lead to a reevaluation of self and relationships with others. Although not an exhaustive list, we examine a number of common life events that often occur in families and change the nature of relationships between family members.

Launching Children and Family Reorganization

The departure of adult children from the household is a common life event in most families, and although the length of this transitional period may vary from family to family, it generally affects interaction among family members in a variety of ways. Despite the fact that a growing number of young adults are living with one or both of their parents, most children begin to desire more independence from their parents during adolescence, and these feelings typically increase as a child reaches his or her late teens and early 20s. This desire, along with societal norms that encourage young adults to take responsibility for their own lives, influences young adult children to move away from parents and to start living on their own. Obviously, adult children vary in terms of their maturity level, financial means, and opportunities for beginning a life independent of their parents. In addition, such variables as parents' tolerance and expectations for financially providing for adult children, their readiness to grant a child greater freedom, the presence of other siblings living at home, their emotional attachment to a child, and their financial situation, may hasten or delay the child launching stage.

In many families, adult children leave home to pursue a college education or career, whereas in other families children may live at home while attending college or being employed locally. In some cases, adult children may leave home temporarily with the expectation that they can move back during breaks at school or if they are having trouble financially. Some families experience a "revolving door" situation when adult children move away from home and return several times over a period of years, whereas in other families, adult children may live with parents into later stages of the life span, especially if they are caregivers for aging parents.

Developmental Changes for Adult Children and Parents. Carter and McGoldrick (1989) contend that the launching phase is associated with several developmental changes for both adult children and their parents. Launching provides adult children with an opportunity to differentiate themselves from their family of origin by allowing them to make choices on their own, foster a greater sense of individuality, develop a sense of financial independence and responsibility, and develop their own unique network of friends and other relationships outside of the family. When children who leave home form families of their own through marriage or cohabitation, they learn to commit themselves to a new family system, realign relationships with extended family members, and develop unique patterns of family communication for their immediate family while integrating patterns from their family of origin. When adult children form new families, this allows them to carry on traditions learned from their family of origin, while they also learn new traditions and communication patterns from their partner.

Parents also experience a number of developmental changes during this time, including a psychological adjustment from parenting responsibilities back to the marital dyad. For some parents, who have been actively engaged in the child-rearing role for many years, the absence of children can cause considerable psychological trauma (Notman, 1982). In addition, they begin to develop a new relationship with adult children in that they perceive them as independent adults with their own goals, interests, and problems. Until relatively recently, parents were involved with raising children until old age, but with our increased life span, most parents now experience about a 20-year span between launching children and retirement. Middle-age couples now have to learn to adjust to this period of their lives as individuals and as relational partners in ways that previous generations did not have to manage. Midlife offers a number of opportunities for personal and relational growth for aging couples.

Communicative Changes. As families cope with the changes associated with the launching of a child and attempt to reorganize, they usually develop new patterns of communication and relating to one another (Pearson, 1993). The absence of adult children from the family home reduces interaction among parents, adult children, and siblings living at home because of the lack of opportunities for mundane and informal types of daily communication associated with people who occupy a common physical space. Although children may still frequently communicate with their parents (even on a daily basis), the interaction tends to follow certain patterns (e.g., phone calls at a certain time, e-mail, etc.), and it usually *interaction* becomes more formal than when the family lived together.

Sibling communication may also become less frequent and more ritualized; however, the new experiences that an older sibling has while away at college or living on his or her own may be of interest to a younger sibling, and this may stimulate new topics of conversation when the two interact. The departure of an adult child from the household can affect the relationship between remaining children and parents, because parents may be able to devote more time to their relationship with them.

Conflict may occur between adult children who leave home and their parents, especially when the adult child is exposed to new ideas or engages in a life style that is incongruent with parental values, rules, or expectations. Although they may no longer occupy a common living space, parents are often surprised or disappointed when they discover their child has frequent parties, sexual partners spending the night, or does not maintain a neat household since leaving home. This conflict can escalate if the adult children move back home or stay with parents temporarily (e.g., summer break from college), but also wish to live their lives with the freedom they have enjoyed while living on their own. Undoubtedly, you have heard your parents or someone else's parents say, "While you are living in my house, you will live by our rules," which often expresses a parent's dissatisfaction with an adult child's desire to engage in behaviors that the parent views as inappropriate. Moreover, adult children often resent being treated like children, even when they abide by their parents' rules. Some parents are condescending when communicating with adult children and tend to treat them as if they were incapable of making appropriate decisions, despite the fact that the adult child lives on his or her own. In other families, parents may be more tolerant of an adult child's lifestyle, and they may be more accepting of his or her choices and behaviors. Parents and adult children often communicate about these changing aspects of their relationships, and they may negotiate new rules or simply attempt to understand each other from a new standpoint.

In addition, marital communication in the family may also go through a number of changes during the launching phase. During the child-raising years, parents devote much of their time to the children, and these demands may limit the amount of time parents can spend with each other or psychologically focus on the marital dyad, affecting many aspects of communication, such as topics of conversation, levels of intimacy, and perceptions about each other and the marital relationship itself. The departure of children from the household provides an opportunity for parents to renegotiate marital roles and to engage in activities and interaction that may have been more difficult while raising children. Research on marital communication after the child-launching phase gives us a mixed picture of how couples adapt to this change. Some studies have found that couples adapt quite successfully to the departure of children within a relatively short period, whereas other marriages may suffer from increased conflict and eventually divorce.

Many couples do, however, find the period after launching children to be extremely satisfying because they are able to devote more time to their relationship, and they may experience an increase in sexual activity and marital satisfaction. Without the responsibilities of raising children, some couples travel more, renew old hobbies that had taken a backseat to children, or they discover new interests that they now have time to pursue. Parents may still communicate frequently with adult children during this time, yet they also have the ability to be a part of their children's lives while simultaneously living lives that are independent from them. However, other marriages suffer during this phase, because of factors such as financial costs associated with sending children to college or helping them live on their own, the inability to reconcile differences or problems that were avoided during the child-rearing years, and individual changes in desires and goals that may have been ignored or downplayed while children were home.

Taking Care of Elderly Parents

Another recent issue couples in their middle years are facing is caring for aging parents, and a growing number of people are finding themselves simultaneously supporting both their adult children and their parents, a phenomenon known as the "sandwich generation" (Richards, Bengston, & Miller, 1989; Williams & Nussbaum, 2001). As the length of the human life span increases, our parents are living longer, and although the majority of older people are healthy, many seniors face illnesses or conditions that may limit their mobility or make them incapable of living on their own. Most dependent older adults in the United States who require long-term assistance currently receive care from family members (Bethea, 2002), and the number of couples in their middle years who will have to care for their parents is expected to continue to increase (Moody, 1994). Relatively few people in our society have the financial means to afford a professional caregiver for their parents, so many couples take on the responsibility themselves. As caregivers, marital partners may have to spend an enormous amount of time meeting the physical needs of a parent, and most people do not have the experience, skills, or training that are necessary to handle the immense responsibility of caregiving.

Communication between marital partners may exhibit a number of changes when they take on caregiver roles. Although the research on marital satisfaction while caring for an elderly parent is somewhat mixed, caring for an aging parent appears to change the nature of relationships in the family (Bethea, 2002; Williams & Nussbaum, 2001). Marital satisfaction can be damaged by the financial cost of providing for children and parents, as well as the emotional costs associated with the caregiving relationship. Married couples caring for a parent who report lower marital satisfaction find that the presence of a parent in the home reduces the amount of overall communication time in the marital dyad and the amount of private time between couples, but increases certain types of communication between the couple, such as decision making. These changes in dyadic communication appear to affect even long-term marriages, because even these couples experience declines in marital satisfaction when the partners are caring for an aging parent (Bethea, 2002).

Marital partners often struggle with the difficulty of simultaneously providing support to an older parent and a spouse. The marital relationship and the parent–child relationship are typically two of the most important relationships that people experience in life (Nussbaum et al., 2000), and it can be extremely stressful for a person to manage the tension between wanting to please both parties and having limited time to do so. The introduction of a third party into any dyadic relationship significantly alters the communication, but the relational history that a person has with a parent and his or her spouse makes the interaction in the triad even more complex. Conflict between adult children and their elderly parents as well as tension that may have existed between a spouse and his or her mother or father-in-law, can escalate once the parent becomes dependent.

Although there is little available research on the impact a dependent older parent's presence in the household has on other family members, such as the marital couple's children who are still living at home, it seems likely that this life event would have an impact on all family relationships. Just as couples have limited time to devote to their relationship when they are caregivers, they likely spend reduced amounts of time with their own children. In addition, parents caught in the middle may be torn among providing emotional support to each other, the elderly parent, and their children. Children living at home may resent having to participate in caregiving tasks, and this could damage the relationships between children and other members of the family. On the other hand, children may find having a grandparent in the household a positive event and fondly remember their interactions many years later. Certainly, more longitudinal studies of how caring for an elderly parent changes the nature of family communication are needed.

Divorce or Separation

Divorce and separation are common life events that can significantly change the nature of family communication and relationships. Although not all family types experience divorce, such as a single parent who never marries the biological father or mother of his or her child, or a cohabitating couple with children who never legally marry, divorce has become more prevalent in our society during the last several decades.

Recent estimates of divorce rates in the United States have found that somewhere between 43% to 50% of marriages end in divorce, and although divorce rates had slowed in recent years, they are beginning to increase again (Bramlett & Mosher, 2002). Couples appear to be most susceptible to divorce in the early years of marriage. After 5 years, approximately 10% of marriages end in divorce, whereas another 10% (or 20%, cumulatively) are divorced by about the 10th year after marriage. However, it appears that the probability of divorce tends to slow after a couple has been married for more than 10 years. Variables, such as the age of the couple when they marry or cohabitate, whether they have been raised throughout childhood in an intact two-parent family, the importance of their religious beliefs, and whether they come from families or a community with a relatively high median income, are related to divorce and separation. Another reason for the increased divorce rate is that there is less of a social stigma for divorce than in previous times.

A recent study found that couples who cohabitate tend to have less stable unions than marriages. The probability of a first marriage ending in separation or divorce within 5 years is 20%, but the probability of a premarital cohabitation breaking up within 5 years is 49% (Bramlett & Mosher, 2002). In addition, separation is a second option for a growing number of individuals, particularly cohabitating couples who wish to discontinue living together or married couples who cannot afford a legal divorce because of financial reasons. The decision to pursue a divorce among separated couples appears to be affected by ethnic groups as well. According to Bramlett and Mosher (2002), separated White women are much more likely (91%) to divorce after 3 years, compared with separated Hispanic women (77%) and separated African American women (67%).

When a couple decides to divorce or separate, this event often leads to increased financial pressures for families. In families where both parents work, couples often rely on the financial benefit of having a dual income, and many parents find it difficult to support children on a single income following divorce. Most of the research on divorce has found that women tend to fair worse financially and emotionally than men after divorce (Troll, 1982). This fact is largely the result of the ongoing problem of unequal salaries for women in our society, and many divorced women find it difficult to financially provide for children despite alimony and child support payments from the father. Exacerbating the problem is the relatively large number of men in our country who fail to make child support payments. Some men may fail to make the payments because of irresponsibility, whereas others may find it difficult to make the payments on their sole income.

Financial strain on divorced couples can lead to increased conflict between them as well as strained relationships with children. Conflict between couples over the financial responsibility for children may continue for many years following a divorce or separation. This conflict can lead to one of the parents spending less time with the children or difficult communication when divorced parents and children are able to see each other because of tensions between the parents. Custody over children is a common issue during the divorce process, and women are more likely to win custody of children. The parent who does not win custody of children may only be able to interact with them during certain times, and these interactions may become more formal, whereas the parent who gains custody of children has more opportunities for everyday mundane communication with children.

Divorced individuals are also likely to experience emotional difficulties as well. Women are more likely than men to experience emotional distress following a divorce than men (Noller & Fitzpatrick, 1993). While married, couples have an overlapping social network of friends and family members, but after a divorce both men and women are likely to experience a greater degree of social isolation as members of their former combined social network side with one partner or the other. And although it is true that the stigma associated with divorce has lessened in recent decades, many friends who enjoyed engaging in social activities with couples prior to divorce often feel uncomfortable maintaining relationships with each partner individually following a divorce.

Divorced couples vary considerably in terms of their communication patterns following the divorce process (Ahrons & Rodgers, 1987; Noller & Fitzpatrick, 1993). Some couples maintain relationships that are cordial and cooperative for the sake of their children, and they are willing to put aside differences that negatively affected their own relationship when communicating about issues regarding the well-being of a child. Other divorced couples experience more limited and negative interaction, and their negative feeling towards each other may interfere with their co-parenting. Finally, some couples gravitate toward the extremes in terms of relationship styles. A limited number of couples are able to maintain a friendship after divorcing, whereas others may have a fierce hatred for one another and may severely limit or cut off all ties between themselves and their children.

Relationships with extended family are also affected by divorce and separation, so that children may have limited access to grandparents, aunts and uncles, and other relatives when their parents divorce or separate. Because extended family members are often important sources of instrumental, emotional, and informational social support, children in these families may find themselves in a position where they have less access to these types of family support or the opportunity to maintain relationships with these individuals.

Although divorce and separation certainly negatively affect families, they can produce positive outcomes, particularly when they are a positive alternative for couples who are unhappy with each other or when children benefit from their parents' divorce or separation because one of the parents is abusive or neglectful.

Some researchers contend that divorce may affect children developmentally and have found that factors such as the age and maturity of a child at the time of the divorce, the relationship between the custodial parent and the ex-spouse, and the availability of other support systems (e.g., other relatives, friends) influence the child's ability to successfully adapt to the divorce over time (Hetherington, 1989; Hetherington & Stanley-Hagan, 1995). Although findings vary from study to study, children from divorced families have anger over their parents' divorce many years after the fact, and some children experience lower self-esteem, behavioral problems with peers and at school, and increased conflict with other family relationships.

Remarriage

Although couples are marrying less frequently, remarriage is still a common occurrence in our society (Ganong & Coleman, 1994). Bramlett and Mosher (2002) found that the probability of remarriage among divorced women was 54% within 5 years. At one time, divorce had a particularly negative social stigma for women; however, divorced women are about 15% less likely to remarry today than in the 1950s.

Remarriage often creates stepfamilies or blended families, which are a common family structure (Ganong & Coleman, 1994). In 1998, approximately one third of American families were blended families (Glick, 1990), and this number has continued to increase. Communication in blended families can become very complex as a result of uncertainty over relational boundaries, the manner in which family members manage their individual and collective identities, and expectations for appropriate behaviors and interaction between members. For example, after a remarriage, a new stepmother may notice that her stepson appears to be depressed about something, but she may be uncertain about when and how she should approach the subject with him. Step-siblings may also experience uncertainty about entering each other's rooms, talking about certain topics, or how to deal with a conflict.

According to Galvin and Brommel (2000), family members typically establish internal boundaries to protect self-identities. However, when these boundaries become too rigid, family members may begin to feel disengaged from one another, and the family may lack a sense of collective identity (i.e., how the family as a whole sees itself). In terms of blended families, members may struggle to develop a new collective family identity, and they have to integrate individual identities and collective identities learned from previous family structures into the new family. This renegotiation can lead to conflict between blended family members, especially over traditions and rituals that may have been common in a previous family structure. For example, two siblings who were socialized together in a previous family may want to open Christmas presents first thing on Christmas morning, whereas their step-father and step-sibling may feel that it is appropriate to go to church.

Remarried couples with children face a number of other challenges when starting a new family. Children often do not approve of a step-parent and may feel that their biological parent is being forgotten in cases of widowhood (Nussbaum et al., 1989), or they may feel cut off from a biological parent after the divorce and remarriage process. Step-parents may struggle to gain a step-child's affection, respect, or attention. Children in step-families often exhibit behavioral problems and tend to have more positive relationships with their biological parent, but it appears that younger children are likely to form an attachment to a step-parent over time. Adolescent children, however, tend to experience more difficulty with accepting a step-parent (Henderson, Hetherington, Mekos, & Reiss, 1996), and this struggle may lead to emotional and behavioral problems during a period of time when the adolescent child is also coming to terms with his or her own identity and need for autonomy.

One source of conflict is that step-parents and step-children may have different perceptions of the role of the step-parent. Fine, Coleman, and Ganong (1998) found that step-parents perceived that they should take a more active role in parenting in a step-family, whereas step-children felt that they should assume a less active role of "friend." However, it appears that blended families can overcome many of the difficulties they face, and members may eventually adjust to the new family structure over time. Baxter, Braithwaite, and Nicholson (1999) examined turning points, or events that alter relationships in important ways, in the development of blended families, and they found that changes in household composition, [2]conflict, the [3]celebration of holidays and special events, [4]quality time among family members, and [5]family crises were the five most common turning points and that these events may put a step-family on different trajectories toward unification or problems, depending on whether family members perceived turning point events positively or negatively.

SIBLING COMMUNICATION IN LATER LIFE

Sibling relationships are probably the best example of a life-span developmental relationship because they typically last longer than marriages, parent–child relationships, friendships, and most other relationships we encounter in life (Cicirelli, 1989; Nussbaum et al., 1989). They are uniquely different from other types of family relationships because of their duration, adaptation to life events, and shared experiences (Folwell, Chung, Nussbaum, Bethea, & Grant, 1997). About 90% of older adults have at least one living sibling (Lee, Mancini, & Maxwell, 1990), and this number is likely to grow in the next several decades, as the projected number of people who will be above the age of 65 come from a cohort in which multiple-child families were the norm. Despite the large number of sibling relationships, there are relatively few studies of sibling communication, especially between adult siblings (Noller & Fitzpatrick, 1993). However, the research that does exist indicates that, although the amount and quality of communication between siblings tends to fluctuate depending on the stage of life or life events, siblings have the opportunity to provide each other with distinct resources throughout life, and the relationship may have important implications for a person's sense of well-being later in life.

In general, people tend to have a great deal of interaction with siblings while living together with them in their family of origin; however, the frequency of interaction usually decreases in the middle years of life because of factors such as starting one's own family, careers, and responsibilities (Atchley, 1977). Other variables, such as the gender composition of the sibling dyad, relate to emotional closeness. Dyads with a least one female (i.e., brother–sister or sister–sister) tend to be closer than dyads in which both siblings are male (Cicirelli, 1989). These differences may be the result of the fact that females are socialized to take a more proactive role in maintaining family relationships in our society. In addition, siblings who live further apart tend to have less interaction with each other. However, most siblings feel some degree of familial obligation for maintaining their relationship at some level, and although not all siblings communicate on a regular basis, most have the expectation that the relationship will continue throughout the life span (Noller & Fitzpatrick, 1993).

Siblings often become closer later in life because of life events, such as the death of a parent or extended family member, having to care for elderly parents, divorce, widowhood, and the desire to reconnect with one another later in life or reminisce about childhood experiences (Ross & Milgram, 1982). These events often provide opportunities to re-connect with siblings, and they may lead to increased contact between them. The death of parents and other extended family members in particular may create a desire among siblings to interact more frequently in an attempt to have some connection with one's family of origin.

Siblings may be well positioned to provide companionship and so-cial support throughout the life span. Siblings who have experienced life events such as having a family, divorce, or a career change can provide each other with helpful information, emotional support, and instrumental support. For example, an older sibling who has children can help a younger sibling who is just starting a family by giving him or her advice on child rearing as well as instrumental support in the form of hand-me-downs (e.g., used clothing, toys). Riggio (2000) found that common experiences with life events in the family can also increase solidarity between siblings, and although it is also true that siblings experience conflict, problems associ-ated with their family of origin (e.g., sibling rivalry) do not appear to cause major problems for siblings over time.

Folwell et al. (1997) examined interpersonal closeness in older sibling relationships and found that older individuals were able to clearly differ-entiate between close and distant siblings in their families. Perceptions of closeness between siblings tended to increase when they both participated in family events, such as dealing with the death or illness of a parent; when there were similarities in terms of interests, opinions, and beliefs between them; and when they were closer in chronological age. Siblings felt more distance between one another when they had less contact; perceived that there were few commonalities between them in terms of interests, etc.; and when they felt there were major differences in personalities. The sibling relationship may be similar to other types of relationships that we enjoy in terms of our desire to interact with similar others, and even the com-monality of being born into the same family may be offset by individual differences.

OLDER PARENT AND ADULT CHILD COMMUNICATION

Relationships between adult children and their parents are highly variable and may differ by family type, the life events these individuals experience, and their relational history together. Some communication patterns be-tween adult children and parents are established at earlier points in the life span, but the interaction is likely to be affected by developmental changes. Although the majority of adult children and their parents live apart, the relationship persists, and it appears to be important for most people (Cicirelli, 1983). And although each family situation is different, there is usually frequent contact between adult children and their parents.

Gender appears to be an important variable in terms of the frequency of contact. Adult daughters are more likely than adult sons to communicate frequently with parents, and they are also more likely to become care-givers if a parent becomes ill. Older men tend to have less conflict with their daughters than with sons, but they are also likely to be highly in-volved with their sons. Although the mother–daughter relationship tends to be the strongest parent–child relationship throughout the life span, the mother–daughter relationship is also prone to conflict, and it may be more complex than other types of family relationships (Troll, 1987).

Scholars debate the reasons the adult child/older parent relationship endures. Some researchers suggest that positive feelings of attachment drive relational partners to maintain the parent–child relationship. Life-span attachment theory, which is an extension of Bowlby's (1979) attach-ment theory of mother–child relationships during the child-rearing years, holds that attachment bonds formed between parents and children during childhood continue to follow us throughout life, and this helps account for the sense of closeness and obligation to our parents as we become older (Atkinson, 1989; Cicirelli, 1983). Other researchers have pointed to strong social norms that reinforce our sense of parental and filial obli-gation, thus fostering a sense of responsibility to maintain the relationship (Mancini & Bliesner, 1989; Umberson, 1993). Yet, depending on the fam-ily situation, there may be a great deal of variability in terms of frequency of contact between adult children and their parents, reciprocity in terms of providing support, and the valence of feelings (i.e., positive or nega-tive) adult children and their parents have toward one another. Henwood (1995) argues that researchers investigating this relationship should de-vote more effort to examining how communicative processes may help the relationship to endure.

Functions of the Adult Child/Older Parent Relationship

Two important functions of the adult child/older parent relationship are mutual affect and mutual aid (Galvin & Brommel, 2000; Nussbaum et al., 2000). People have a basic need for affection and interpersonal close-ness, and adult children and their parents help each other to fulfill these needs. Atkinson (1989) contended that mutual affection motivates con-tinued involvement between children and parents at later points in the life span. Researchers have found that older people who perceive more posi-tive affect from their children tend to have a greater sense of psychological well-being (Barnett, Kibria, Baruch, & Pleck, 1991; Kivett & Atkinson, 1984). In addition, studies find that childless older couples tend to be less satisfied with family life (Singh & Williams, 1982), and may have a lower sense of well-being.

A second function of the adult child/older parent relationship is mutual aid. As was discussed in chapter 4, social support between family members is an important function of the family at earlier points in the life span, and it typically continues as family members age (Dean, Kolody, Wood, & Ensel, 1989). Although we have seen that more and more adult children are finding themselves in the role of caregiver when older parents experience health problems, most parents continue to provide emotional and tangible assistance to their adult children later in life as well. This support may take the form of caring for grandchildren, helping out adult children during times of crisis, providing financial assistance, and offering advice based on life experience when adult children are faced with difficult decisions.

Conflict Between Adult Children and Parents

Both older parents and adult children become aware of shifting power roles in their relationship at later points in the life span, and they often have a difficult time adjusting to these shifts and managing conflicting desires between wanting to allow each other's independence and the desire to protect the other from harm (Morgan & Hummert, 2000). Conflict often occurs over these issues of independence and control. Parents typically wish to be involved in the lives of adult children and protective of them, but they also do not want to interfere. Moreover, adult children often struggle with the desire to protect parents from harm while simultaneously allowing them to be independent adults. Advice from older parents is often perceived as interference by adult children, and it may not be welcome if it is perceived as encroaching on one's ability to live his or her life as an independent adult.

For example, a middle-aged adult child may find it irritating to receive marital or child-rearing advice from his or her parents. Similarly, aging parents may resent an adult child's attempt to protect them "for his or her own good," by suggesting that they should no longer drive or move into an assisted-living community. Unfortunately, many adult children have negative stereotypes or inaccurate beliefs about an older parent's ability to effectively manage his or her own life after a certain age, despite the fact that he or she may be fully capable of making independent decisions. When conflict over independence and control arises, managing these tensions is never an easy task, but effective communication about one's concerns while simultaneously addressing the other person's feelings may help to minimize conflict or at least promote constructive conflict.

GRANDPARENTHOOD

The majority of older adults over the age of 65 currently have at least one living grandchild, and it is likely that this trend will remain relatively constant in the future. As we discussed in chapter 4, individuals may become grandparents at different points in the life span (depending on their age when they had children and their children's age when they become parents), and the grandparent role is not necessarily associated with old age. However, it is likely that people who have children will eventually have grandchildren, and becoming a grandparent usually leads to a number of developmental changes in individuals as they learn this new role.

Meaning of the Grandparent Role

For most individuals, becoming a grandparent is an exciting time, and the majority of grandparents report being happy with the grandparent role and their relationships with grandchildren. However, the meaning of the grandparent role may differ for individuals because of differences in self-perceptions, type of family, culture, age, and the nature of the relationship with their adult children and grandchildren. Several studies have examined the meanings people attach to the grandparent role. Some individuals perceive the grandparent role as a source of stability in the family in terms of preserving family values and rituals and maintaining the family system (Bengtson & Robertson, 1985; Troll, 1983). Grandparents will often tell stories about family members when interacting with grandchildren that give insights into family values and norms of behavior, and they typically play a vital role in reinforcing family rituals, especially during special events and holidays.

For others, the grandparent role presents a new opportunity to develop a satisfying relationship with a family member, especially if they were not satisfied with previous family relationships, such as with their adult children (Sanders & Trygstad, 1993). Becoming a grandparent also appears to provide self-fulfillment because it allows individuals to relive the experiences they had when raising their own children (Walsh, 1988), and the opportunity for a new source of companionship. Some grandparents enjoy the rewards associated with interacting with their grandchildren without many of the constraints and responsibilities of the parent–child relationship (e.g., having to discipline children). And although many grandparents play a role that is similar to parents in terms of being actively involved in caring for their grandchildren, others enjoy the ability to take on child-rearing responsibilities when they desire to do so and with the flexibility that comes with not being a primary caregiver.

Neugarten and Weinstein (1964) and Kivnick (1983) found that people perceived being a grandparent as a source of continuity between the past, present, and future of their family life. The role gives individuals opportunities to discuss past life events and family history with their grandchildren, and this interaction helps to extend the life of the grandparent through the memory of the grandchild. The experience of having grandchildren may help older grandparents to gain a broader perspective of life and their experiences.

The birth of a grandchild also changes patterns of communication between grandparents and their adult children. Researchers have found that the perception of closeness a grandchild feels towards his or her grandparents depends in part on the closeness of the relationship between his or her parents and grandparents. As we have seen, grandparents may take a more active role in single-parent families, families from certain cultural groups, and families who may require more financial or instrumental assistance. Divorce and remarriage also change the nature of the relationship between grandparents and grandchildren, and many people find themselves in the role of step-grandparent. More research needs to address grandparent roles and the relationship between grandparents, parents, and grandchildren in blended families. When parents divorce, researchers have found that some grandparents lose contact with grandchildren and must use the legal system to gain visitation rights (Noller & Fitzpatrick, 1993), whereas others have increased contact when the custodial parent and the grandchildren move in with them. Unfortunately, there is only a relatively small amount of research available on the effects of divorce on the grandparent–grandchild relationship.

PERCEPTIONS OF AGING AND INTERGENERATIONAL COMMUNICATION IN THE FAMILY

Our families are one of the few sources of intergenerational communication in our society, and our interactions with older family members are an important influence on our perceptions of older people (Ng, Liu,

Weatherall, & Loong, 1997). These perceptions are related to the ways in which we learn how to interact with older individuals throughout life as well as our attitudes about older people and the concept of aging itself. Our youth-oriented society tends to promote negative images of growing old, and our families may be one of the few places where we can develop a different perception of aging. However, family life may also reinforce certain stereotypes about aging, depending on our relationships and experiences with older family members. Feeling close to a grandparent has been linked to the development of more positive stereotypes of aging, whereas feeling distant from a grandparent reinforces negative stereotypes (Pecchioni & Croghan, 2002).

SUMMARY

Life events and developmental changes among children and parents alter communication patterns in families over time. These changes in communication are typically associated with role changes that family members must learn, and in some cases, changing roles can lead to conflict between family members. Some life events, such as a parent who needs to be cared for by an adult child, can lead to major changes in family communication. However, most families appear to cope well with role changes over time and adapt to common life events, such as launching children or becoming a grandparent, quite well. Siblings, the longest family relationship, tend to communicate less frequently as they grow older, but often reconnect later in life. The grandparent–grandchild relationship is a very common relationship as adult children have children of their own. Most grandparent–grandchild relationships tend to be positive, and they are an important family relationship in terms of carrying on family traditions and helping children to form perceptions of older individuals. Changes in families over time would benefit from additional communication research, especially changes in nontraditional families over time.

6

Friendship Throughout the Life Span

Friendships are among the most significant and unique types of relationships we experience in life. Although our immediate family members typically care for us physically and emotionally during infancy and early childhood, we eventually learn to socialize with other children, develop a concept of friendship, and form a variety of friendships, ranging from superficial ties to more enduring bonds. The nature of our friendships often changes throughout the life course, although we may exhibit some continuity in terms of what we look for in a friend. For some individuals, friendships formed at an earlier stage of life may last well into older adulthood, whereas other individuals may have short-term friendships that are maintained only during certain periods of their lives. Although the concept of friendship may differ for each person because of his or her experiences, most friendships exhibit common characteristics, and friends are important sources of support and companionship. In fact, a growing body of research indicates that friends are important to our psychological and physical well-being, and they may serve an important role in helping us adjust to problems and changes experience in life and elevate mood or outlook toward changing life ~vents.

This chapter begins by exploring the unique nature of the relationship between friends. In addition, we examine the role of communication in developing and maintaining friendships. Finally, we discuss developmental changes in friendship across the life span, focusing on important similarities and differences at different stages.

CHARACTERISTICS OF FRIENDSHIP

The discipline of communication has not concentrated much research effort on the understanding or explanation of the formation and maintenance of friendship throughout the life span. With the exception of the excellent scholarship of Rawlins (1995), we must look primarily to social scientists in the disciplines of sociology, anthropology, and social psychology for an understanding of friendship. Allan (1979) distinguished a friend relationship from a family relationship based on the fact that "friendship is a personal relationship in that it is seen as involving individuals as individuals and not as members of groups or collectives" (p. 38). We can pick our friends, but we cannot pick most of our family members. Thus, friendships are inherently different from family relationships.

Certain unique characteristics of the friendship relationship distinguish it from other types of relationships we encounter throughout our lives. Yet, at the same time, it is also important to keep in mind that people's perceptions of what constitutes a friendship and the meaning of these relationships varies widely. Friendships lack the formality of certain family relationships dominated by ceremony or rules, and friendship is based on both individuals freely choosing to form the friendship. Friendship is based more on similar likes and dislikes and is not genetically bound; it is a nonexploitive relationship, and friends do not take advantage of each other for personal gain. An important characteristic of friendship is the balanced or symmetrical nature of the relationship. Status distinctions or life-long power differentials are nonexistent in the friendship relationship.

Researchers have focused on other characteristics of friendship, such as intimacy and friendship styles. Rawlins (1992, 1995) contended that friendships differ from other types of relationships because they are typically voluntary, egalitarian, roles privately negotiated between individuals, and they require mutual involvement from partners.

Voluntary Relationship

Friendships are voluntary because we decide which individuals we choose to be our friends, and they, in return, must voluntarily choose us as friends. Other types of relationships, such as family members, teacher–student relationships, and the people with whom we work are not usually completely voluntary. We are born into families, we take classes from certain teachers because the classes are required, and we interact with many people at work because it is part of our job description. This does not mean that family members, teachers, and individuals at work cannot become our friends; however, each partner in these situations must consent to become the other's friend.

Egalitarian Nature

Friendships are usually egalitarian, which means partners stress power and status equality in the relationship. We tend to be attracted to people who treat us as equals and who have similar status backgrounds. In addition, friends often stress equality in terms of the effort that each partner puts into the relationship and the benefits each person receives. Although individuals who differ in terms of social status or power (e.g., teachers and students, bosses and employees, etc.) often do become friends, these people usually stress equality in the relationship whenever possible. In many cases, friends of different power or social status may maintain a more egalitarian relationship in private, while communicating in expected ways associated with power or status roles in public settings (e.g., playing the role of the student only during class).

Privately Negotiated

Friends tend to privately negotiate different aspects of their relationship, and their negotiations may occur formally or informally. Partners need to communicate expectations, desires, and needs to each other for friendships to function effectively. For example, problems can occur in friendships when partners differ in their expectations about such things as the amount of time they should spend together, the types of activities they should engage in together, and a host of other behaviors associated with their conception of friendship. In addition, their communication typically takes the form of a unique code (verbal and nonverbal messages that are understood by each partner within the context of the relationship) that is developed between partners through the course of the friendship. As time goes by in the relationship, friends draw on their relational history and their perceptions of the relationship based on previous interactions as a means for understanding one another.

Mutual Involvement

Friendship is not a one-way street. Both partners must exert effort for the relationship to work. Each person must invest time, emotion, and energy into the friendship, and most friends usually are willing to do so because of the rewards that friendship can offer (e.g., companionship, loyalty, and shared activity). Friends typically enjoy spending time together and communicating about mutual interests. Yet, it is possible for problems to occur among friends when one person becomes less involved in the relationship than the other.

INTIMACY AND FRIENDSHIP

Friendships also vary in terms of their level of intimacy (Nussbaum, 1994). You may have a relationship with someone who you consider to be your "best friend," and this is usually a person with whom you feel you can reveal very intimate information about yourself. Most people feel comfortable communicating intimate thoughts, such as fears, frustrations, and desires with only a select number of individuals because of the interpersonal risk involved in disclosing such information. You may consider other individuals in your social network to be "friends," but you do not feel comfortable revealing intimate things to them. Some friends who are less intimate than best friends, may serve more of a companionship function. These may be people with whom we like to engage in certain activities, such as going to movies, playing softball, or shopping, but we do not necessarily feel that we have an intimate bond with them. Companions can certainly become more intimate friends, but we often feel comfortable keeping some relationships at a relatively low level of intimacy.

The least intimate types of friendship may be with people we consider to be "weak ties." The term *weak ties* refers to the relationships we engage in that differ in terms of intimacy and frequency of interaction from close relationships. These are typically individuals with whom we communicate on a daily basis, but we are not necessarily close to them

(Granovetter, 1973; 1982). In some cases, we may consider these people to be friends, although we would probably use this term loosely. For example, many people may consider their hairdresser or an associate at work to be a friend, even though they only communicate with them in very specific contexts. However, weak ties can serve an important function because they are often more removed from closer ties, such as family members and best friends. A person can sometimes reveal quite intimate information about themselves with less interpersonal risk than if he or she were to reveal the same information to a closer friend (Adelman, Parks, & Albrecht, 1987a). For example, a person who is considered to be a weak tie may be able to listen to your problem and offer you advice without your closer friends ever knowing about it. In addition, people who are interpersonally closer to us sometimes have a tendency to judge us more critically than do people who are less close to us, especially when we reveal information that involves greater interpersonal risk, because we fear that such information may challenge their good opinion of us. We may not want our closest friends to know about bad decisions we have made, behaviors or situations about which we are embarrassed, or information about people or situations about which they are likely to have strong feelings.

Finally, Nussbaum (1994) asserted that "friendship can be a lifelong relationship as well as a relationship that forms at any given point in the life span" (p. 211). Some friendships may be formed in childhood and last throughout the life span of both partners, whereas other friendships may be associated with defined periods of time in a person's life. For example, some friendships are developed during times when an individual is working in his or her career, and partners may grow apart after retirement or a job change. Other people may form relatively short relationships with friends during periods of crisis or adjustment, such as after a divorce. One variable that may help to explain the length of friend relationships is the type of friendship style a person has.

FRIENDSHIP STYLES

Matthews (1986) identified three primary friendship styles, or broad patterns of interaction between friends over time. Individuals with an *independent* style tend to change friends as their life circumstances change, forming and maintaining friendships as they encounter new situations. Physical proximity may be an important factor in terms of forming new friendships and dissolving older ties for individuals with this friendship style, although other life events can account for these changes. For example, a person with an independent friendship style might develop relatively close friendships during high school or college, but he or she will tend to lose contact with these individuals after moving to a new state for a new job, after marriage, or as interests and needs change. One potentially negative aspect of the independent style is that, although independents typically develop new friends as they enter into new situations, the quality of friendships may vary because of the available pool of individuals. However, independents usually experience less emotional distress than people with other friendship styles if current friends move away or other life changes keep people apart. Although independents may stay in contact with friends from an earlier point in their life span on a relatively infrequent basis (e.g., holidays, weddings, etc.), these relationships are usually characterized by less intimacy and depth than relationships between people with other friendship styles.

Individuals with a *discerning* friendship style exhibit lasting deep attachments to specific friends over the life course despite any personal changes each partner experiences. Unlike independents, people with discerning styles maintain friendships formed at earlier stages of life for long periods of time, even if partners are separated by geographical distance or if they go through significant life changes. Discerning friends often feel that "old friends are the best friends," and may feel less affiliation for new friends or resist developing new friendships. In addition, the loss of a friend is the most emotionally devastating for people with this style.

Finally, the *acquisitive* friendship style is somewhat of a combination of the other two styles, with individuals being open to developing new friendships while simultaneously wishing to preserve bonds with older friends. For people with this friendship style, changing life circumstances may bring about opportunities to meet new people and develop new friendships centered on changing interests and needs. However, these individuals strongly value and attempt to maintain friendships formed at earlier points in the life span.

In terms of life stage and friendship style, Patterson and Wright (2001), in a study comparing young, middle-aged, and older participants, found that younger and middle-aged individuals were more likely to report having an independent friendship style, middle-aged and older respondents were more likely to mention having a discerning friendship style, and younger people were more likely to indicate an acquisitive friendship style than the other age groups.

THEORIES OF FRIENDSHIP DEVELOPMENT
AND MAINTENANCE

Rawlins (1981) proposed that friendships typically progress through six stages: (a) limited initial interaction based on role expectations, where potential friends interact in ways similar to other types of relationships, adhering to social politeness norms and everyday public role expectations; (b) friendly relations, or communication behaviors that exhibit characteristics associated with being friendly, such as positive talk, humor, and nonverbal affect displays, that go beyond what would be expected between people with little affection toward each other; (c) moves toward friendship, where partners voluntarily begin to take steps toward future interaction, such as making plans to meet or engage in activities together; (d) nascent friendship, or when partners begin to see themselves as friends, and they start to develop role expectations for their relationship; (e) stabilized friendship, in which partners communicate on a routine basis and have established expectations of trust and commitment to one another; and (f) waning friendship, where efforts to maintain the relationship decrease, communication becomes less frequent, and partners begin to "drift apart." In some cases, the relationship may be terminated, whereas other partners may decide to reconcile.

Relational Dialectics

Rawlins (1995) identified a number of dialectics that occur in friendships. Relational dialectics theory maintains that relationships are characterized by ongoing tensions between contradictory impulses (Baxter & Montgomery, 1996). Friendships are achieved throughout the life span through ongoing communication that must be used to manage the tension between the two ends of the dialectic poles. Dialectics, such as expressiveness versus protectiveness; dependence versus independence; novelty versus predictability; and judgment versus acceptance, create the interesting dynamic in which friend relationships are formed and maintained. The dialectic of expressiveness versus protectiveness deals with the idea that we desire the opportunity to express our feelings, concerns, fears, and other facets of self in our interactions with friends. At the same time, there are some aspects of our self that we do not want to reveal to others, even if they are close friends. For example, although you may like the opportunity to vent your frustrations to your friend over drinks, you may never feel comfortable talking about some aspects of yourself, such as insecurities or sexual problems. The dialectic of dependence and independence is concerned with the tension between our desire to be connected with our friends and depend on them for certain things, such as companionship or material assistance, and being independent of them. For example, when we spend too much time with friends, we can feel stifled by them, and we may begin to crave time away from them so that we can have some "alone time." Similarly, the dialectic of novelty versus predictability refers to the conflict between our need for stability in friendships and the novelty of change. We like to be able to count on our friends, but if things are too predictable, then the relationship can become stagnant and boring. The dialectic of judgment versus acceptance deals with the idea that we like the fact that our friends accept us despite some of our faults, but there are times when we also crave a more objective viewpoint about ourselves that friends may not provide us in an effort to spare our feelings.

Dialectical tensions are never resolved in friendships, but friends can manage these tensions through a variety of strategies (Baxter, 1988). One such strategy is cyclic alternation, or choosing one extreme over another at different points in time. For example, you may choose to spend weekends with a friend and keep your weekdays for yourself in an effort to manage the dependence/independence tension. Another strategy for managing dialectical tensions is selection, or making a choice between opposites. For example, some friends might agree to be accepting of each other at all times. The strategies that friends choose to manage dialectical tensions vary between different types of friendship relationships, and they are typically negotiated between friends.

Social Exchange Theory

Social exchange theory examines how relational partners negotiate costs and rewards (Roloff, 1981; Thibaut & Kelly, 1959). Using an economic metaphor, this theory contends that certain aspects of relationships, such as the amount of time we spend with friends, the effort we put into the relationship, and actual financial cost of participating in activities with friends, such as purchasing gifts for them and loaning them items, can all be perceived as relational costs. Relational rewards, on the other hand, can range from receiving tangible items, such as when a friend buys you dinner or allows you to use his or her car, to more psychological rewards, such as when a friend cheers you up when you are feeling down or if he or she gives you helpful advice when you need information about how to deal with a problem. According to this theory, individuals make judgments about whether they are experiencing more costs than rewards in a relationship or the other way around. The theory holds that problems can arise in a relationship when partners feel that the cost to reward ratio is out of balance, and it predicts that the relationship is not likely to continue. Conversely, when rewards exceed costs in a relationship, it is more likely to continue developing.

Reciprocity is an important aspect of social exchange theory. We tend to feel troubled in a relationship when we feel that we are underbenefitted, that is, when we perceive that we are incurring too many costs in a relationship while simultaneously receiving too few rewards. For example, if you devoted many hours of time to friends by taking the initiative to call them or listen to their problems, but they never seem to have time to call you or listen to your problems, or if you have given a friend money when he or she needed it, but you were never offered any financial assistance by your friend when you needed help, you would probably feel underbenefitted, or that the relationship was inequitable.

A similar problem can occur when a person in a relationship feels overbenefitted. In this case, you may have received a number of favors from friends without having the opportunity to reciprocate. Most people feel uncomfortable in situations when they perceive they are overbenefitted in a relationship, particularly when they feel unable to reciprocate rewards they have received. For example, you might find yourself in a position where you become good friends with your boss. Your boss can protect you from problematic coworkers because of his or her supervisory position, and he or she may even advocate a salary raise for you. However, because you are not in the same position as your boss, it is unlikely that you can reciprocate with similar types of rewards. This imbalance may cause you to feel uncomfortable, unless you can find a way to give other types of rewards (e.g., being supportive during staff meetings, taking on extra assignments, etc.).

Most friends strive for *equity* in their relationships. As mentioned earlier, friendships are typically privately negotiated, and partners may form unique expectations for the relationship or communicate about the best course of action to balance the ratio of costs and rewards. For example, in the situation mentioned previously, your boss might expect you to support him or her during staff meetings when conflict arises in return for the favors he or she has bestowed on you and may feel betrayed if you do not provide that support. Some friends communicate directly about equity in their relationship, whereas others may develop tacit understandings about the distribution of costs and rewards, and they may only talk about inequities when a problem arises.

You may know someone who continues to stay in a relationship with a friend despite the fact that the costs for this person clearly outweigh the rewards. Another aspect of social exchange theory that may help to explain this is the notion of comparison levels and the comparison level of alternatives. The *comparison level* can be conceived of as a standard people have developed regarding relationships based on their cumulative experience with other similar types of relationships throughout their lives. For example, it is possible for someone to have a history of bad friendships since he or she was a child. In the current friendship, he or she might be experiencing verbal abuse, but by comparison, the relationship might be perceived positively, especially if he or she experienced more negative behaviors in past friendships (e.g., being ignored or teased). As an outsider to the relationship, you might predict that it is likely to fail, but you are most likely evaluating the relationship from a different comparison level.

The *comparison level of alternatives* deals with judgments people make about their relational partner vis-à-vis the potential alternatives they perceive to that relationship. In other words, a substantial pool of individuals is available with whom we could potentially develop a friendship. However, we might perceive that our current friend possesses qualities that other potential candidates for friendship do not have, or we may prefer our current friend to being alone, despite flaws we perceive he or she may have.

Maintenance Strategies in Friend Relationships

Relational maintenance is necessary to keep friendships in a stable and satisfactory condition, and proactive maintenance may help relational partners circumvent problems that may lead to relational dissolution. Interpersonal scholars have identified a number of relational maintenance behaviors that range from mundane everyday routines (such as sharing tasks or engaging in joint activities) to more strategic behaviors (such as intentionally calling a friend to convey support for some crisis he or she is facing) in everyday communication (Canary & Stafford, 1994; Canary, Stafford, Hause, & Wallace, 1993; Duck, 1994; Dindia & Canary, 1993). These strategies also include conveying openness or willingness to communicate with a partner, being positive during interaction, assuring and supporting each other, communicating affection, spending time with important members of a partner's social network, sending mediated messages, and avoiding potentially negative topics or unfriendly behaviors.

FRIENDSHIP AND SOCIAL SUPPORT

Social support is an important element of friendship throughout the life span, and it has been found to have important implications for our psychological and physical well-being (Krause, 1990; Nussbaum, 1994; Rook, 1995). Chapter 9 covers social support in greater detail, but in this section, we examine both positive and negative aspects of social support in friendships.

Nussbaum (1994) contended that the friend relationship is well suited for giving and receiving social support because it is less likely to have as stringent role obligations as family relationships based on the fact that we choose our friends, so we are more likely to help friends because we want to rather than because we have to. The voluntary nature of such social support increases the likelihood that the support offered in friend relationships will be appraised positively. Support researchers find that when supportive behaviors are perceived as positive and satisfying, they are more likely to have beneficial effects on a person's psychological and physical well-being (Albrecht et al., 1994; Barbee, 1990).

Social support is thought to have a positive effect on an individual's psychological and physical well-being by providing a buffer against stressful situations. Your friends can help reduce the stress you are experiencing after breaking up with your significant other by listening to you, giving you advice about how to deal with your emotions, or providing you with an escape from thinking about the situation (e.g., by taking you to a night club or movie). Friends can also help you minimize a stressful situation or avoid it all together by providing information or tangible support.

CHANGES IN FRIENDSHIP OVER THE LIFE SPAN

Willmot and Sillars (1989) were among the first communication researchers to examine the issue of life-long changes in interpersonal relationships, finding that relationships are likely to change over time because people undergo cognitive changes as they develop and therefore form new relational schemata as they mature. Schema theory (Cohen, 1981) suggests that human beings develop mental structures called schemata (schemata is plural for schema) that organize information gathered through our experiences and perceptions of the world. We rely on schemata to make sense of the world and our relationships with others.

Essentially, these mental structures give us the ability to store information about our experiences with others so that we have a frame of reference for future interactions. Starting with our earliest experiences with friends, we develop friendship schemata that influence our perceptions of friendships as we develop through the life course. Schemata are thought to continue to change throughout our lives as new issues, experiences, and roles arise. According to Patterson (1995), few relationships are as subject to relational change as friendships, and they may be subject to modification depending on the events and issues of more central relationships such as family.

Although the ways in which friendships change across the life span has received some attention by communication researchers, there are still many things we do not know on a macro level about changes in friendship over the life span or how relational partners in a friendship change as each person lives through new experiences and encounters changing life events. However, some researchers have begun to explore the broad patterns of friendship over the life course.

Developmental Changes and Conceptions of Friendship

Conceptions of friendship in later life exhibit many of the same characteristics as other points in the life span; however, some important differences develop in how older individuals conceive of friendship. In addition, the functions of friendship may change for an individual as he or she ages, and there is some evidence that friends may play an important role in influencing an older individual's mental and physical well-being.

Patterson, Bettini, and Nussbaum (1993) reasoned that the developmental changes found in the friend relationship throughout the life span might be as dramatic as those changes found in family relationships. These developmental changes can be quite significant, given the research findings suggesting that friendship is as important as or may even be a more important predictor of successful adaptation to life than our family relationships (Nussbaum et al., 2000). Unlike the parent–child relationship, most marriages, and the sibling relationship, we are free to maintain numerous context-based levels of friend relationships as we progress through the life span. By this we mean that friendships are formed with our neighbors and school mates in childhood and adolescence, that we meet and form close friendships with a new set of individuals in college and in our workplace, that we move numerous times and form friendships as we build our careers or form friendships surrounding the activities of our children, and then may move into retirement communities and form friendships during later life with our new neighbors. Friendships can last a lifetime or can be formed and maintained based on events that occur at different points in our life span.

Communication and aging scholars have identified several ways in which perceptions of friendship possibly change throughout the life span. Patterson, Bettini, and Nussbaum (1993) examined how elderly individuals define friendship by conducting in-depth interviews with members of a retirement center. These researchers categorized responses from interviews with retirees into nine different dimensions of the meaning of friendship for older people. The majority of the responses from the interviews were classified into the devotion category; therefore, the researchers concluded that devotion is a key dimension of friendship for older adults. In addition, for older individuals, friend relationships appear to be characterized by a special uniqueness, intimacy, and depth, with the understanding between partners that "friends stick together no matter what they know about each other or what happens." Moreover, older adults appear to value reciprocity in friendships, with the notion that there should be equity between partners in terms of relational costs and rewards.

Patterson et al. (1993) also developed a definition of friendship scale and compared responses to a questionnaire between older and younger participants. The younger sample had similar perceptions of the devotion and reciprocity dimensions of friendship as the older sample, but they differed in terms of the relational stratification dimension. For example, older individuals appeared to be more discriminating and hierarchical about whom they considered best friends, as opposed to less intimate friends and acquaintances. The authors argued that perhaps older persons take a more discriminating view of friendship and hence have a greater concern for relational stratification because of their life experience and the number of relationships they have had with others. An older person's greater experience with friendship over the life span might allow him or her to be more retrospective in making choices about friends when making decisions about whether to initiate, intensify, or dissolve a relationship.

In other research comparing older people with younger people in terms of friendship, Patterson and Bettini (1993) found a positive correlation between friendship strength scores and age, suggesting that, as we grow older, our friendships become stronger. They also found friendship strength and devotion are inversely related to levels of depression regardless of the age of the participants. Although more research is clearly needed in this area, it appears that strong friend relationships are important to older individuals, and they may exert a positive influence on mental health and well-being.

Patterson (1995) examined relational network and communication patterns between younger adults and older adults. He found that older people have more communication with family members than younger people, whereas younger people had substantially greater communication with friendship networks than older people. He contends that people may have a comfortable level of social interaction at which they operate, and when some life event produces a shift in the contact mix, individuals reduce one dimension (family) to deal with the increased demand from the other (friends). Similarly, when movement occurs toward increased family communication, we may see a decrease in friendship solidarity. In general, he found that people tended to perceive communication with nonfamily members less positively as they age and that people who communicate frequently tend to communicate less with friends and vice versa. However, the author suggests that there may be a dialectical relationship between the need for a strong friendship network and the desire for strong family relationships. As we have seen, although families are important relationships in terms of support and our sense of well-being, the obligatory nature of familial relationships can become stifling at times. During these periods, we may feel more of a need to establish a stronger friendship network because of its more voluntary nature. At other times, we might feel the desire for more connection with our family members, especially if our friends fail to meet needs that are traditionally associated with the family, such as the desire for instrumental support, unconditional love, or a more involved shared history.

Moreover, there may be times during the life course when family members are not immediately available, and we may bolster our friendship network. You might be geographically separated from your family while attending college, and you may find yourself interacting more with friends as a support network. Later in life, people often find themselves in more distant relationships with friends because of life changes, such as retirement, death, or moving to an assisted-living center. Under these circumstances, family members, such as spouses, siblings, and adult children may be the primary networks with whom older people interact and rely on for support.

Patterson (1995) also suggested that, although older people may have more contact with family members than younger people, both groups tend to have a high degree of affinity toward family members. Because family

family
relationships are somewhat fixed and stable, and friendships may be harder
to maintain over time because of changing life events, older people may
tend to have more contact with family than friends.

Monsour (2002) recently completed a landmark review of the existence
and importance of cross-sex friendships across the life span. The great
majority of our social scientific knowledge concerning friendship is based
on a rich literature on same-sex friendships. Although it is true that many
barriers currently exist prohibiting the formation of cross-sex friendships,
structural changes in our society, such as the growing number of women in
the workforce and the growing popularity of online friendships, are creating a much more acceptable environment in which cross-sex friendships
can emerge. Cross-sex friendships can add significantly to the companionship and instrumental activities at all points in the life span. The extent
to which cross-sex friendships function to meet different physical, psychological, and social needs at different points in the life span has not been
researched. It is not unreasonable to speculate, however, that Monsour's
(2002) belief that cross-sex friendships play an important role in the process of successful adaptation to the many challenges of aging is valid.

Friendships From Early Childhood Through Middle Adulthood

Haslett and Samter (1997) provided an exceptional description of how
communication plays a significant role in the formation of friendship
during childhood and adolescence. Although factors such as proximity,
gender, race, and physical attractiveness determine the pool of potential
friends with whom a relationship may be formed throughout life, the ability of individuals to communicate effectively will ultimately ensure the
formation and maintenance of the friend relationship across time. Based
on research by Gottman (1983), Haslett and Samter (1997) concluded
that friendship in early childhood is based on play and the ability to coordinate play, and rarely involves conflict. Middle childhood is filled with
a much larger number of social contacts outside the home. The need to
"fit in" drives friendship at this age. Norms and rules of social behavior
are expressed and acted out, and those who do not conform may be sanctioned or at least may be the central character in gossip. Friendship in adolescence revolves around the discovery of self. "Self-disclosure dominates
the conversations of adolescent friends" (Haslett & Samter, 1995, p. 223).
Much time is spent metacommunicating in an attempt to understand the
complexities of various family and friend relationships. Friendship during

adolescence is a safe, comfortable context within which to display emotion and to discover that different perspectives do exist.

Young and middle adulthood can be a time of dramatic change in the nature of the friend relationship. Noller, Feeney, and Peterson (2001) reported that the number of friends, the amount of contact with friends, and the intimacy level within friendships decrease in young adulthood. Several factors contribute to this trend. First, the modern definition of the ideal marriage stipulates that the spouse should fill the role of best friend. This expectation, in combination with time spent parenting and in career development, prohibits much social and emotional investment in the friendship network. Gender differences also emerge in friendships during this time of life. Women tend to emphasize the emotional concerns of their friends. Men's friendships appear to be less emotional and center on work or recreational activities. As the children leave home during middle adulthood, more time can be spent with friends re-engaging the affective nature of the relationship and discussing common concerns that relate to caring for parents and preparing for retirement.

Although relatively little is known about friend relationships during the middle of the life span, common life events associated with middle age are likely to affect the nature of friendship. For example, by middle age, most individuals have decided on a career (or a long-term job), many people have entered into marriage or long-term partnerships with a significant other, and a significant proportion of middle-aged people in our society have children.

Our careers can affect friendship patterns in several ways. For example, it is quite common for people to meet friends through their jobs, and many of the friendships we develop in this context are maintained until we leave a job or we retire. Because middle age is typically associated with time devoted to a long-term job or career, it is likely that this context will have an influence on the available pool of friends. Although people certainly maintain friendships from earlier points in the life span and meet people through other activities outside of the workplace, our employment situation puts us into greater proximity to some individuals over others. People who are busy with career aspirations often find that they have little time for maintaining friendships associated with other contexts. In addition, Bruunk (1990) found that the number of coworker friends decreases after retirement, and retired individuals often turn to family members or a few close friends for social support. Although many people complain about their jobs, they can provide an important context for developing and maintaining friendships during early and middle adulthood.

Similarly, marriage and children can affect friendship patterns during young adulthood and middle age. A friend of one of the authors of this book said to him at a wedding that "weddings and funerals are a lot alike... you never see your friend again." If you have a friend who has married, you may have noticed changes in his or her communication patterns with friends. However, the effect that marriage has on friendship may also depend on communication patterns in that relationship (see chapter 5). A person's decision to have children can also affect friendship patterns in a variety of ways. The immense responsibility of raising a child might leave little time to devote to friend relationships formed prior to the child's birth or time to meet new friends. However, some individuals may rely on their friends to participate in activities with children or to help share with child rearing. Of course, careers, marriage, and raising a child can all occur at younger periods of life, and they may not occur for some individuals in midlife, yet these events tend to be highly correlated with middle age.

Another aspect that may affect friendships during the middle of the life span, particularly in terms of intergenerational friendship, is the negative stereotypes that middle-aged people have of younger individuals and vice versa. For example, Harwood and Giles (1993) argued that stereotypes of different age groups influence our perceptions of people within them. Younger people often perceive middle-aged individuals as condescending and prone to give unsolicited advice to younger people. In addition, middle-aged people sometimes have negative stereotypes of younger people, assuming that they have little ambition or lack of knowledge about the world. These stereotypes often have a negative affect on intergenerational communication between young and middle-aged adults. One context in which the young and middle-aged have an opportunity to interact is in the workplace. Although friendships certainly develop between people from different age groups in the workplace, it is likely that negative out-group stereotypes may hinder the development of some friendships between young and middle-aged individuals even in this environment.

Older Adult Friendships

Nussbaum et al. (2000) considered a network of close friends in later life to be essential in the ability to adapt to the many health and financial challenges of growing old. The egalitarian and voluntary nature of friendship serves older adults well as they rely on their friends for everything from companionship to accomplishing the everyday tasks of life. Patterson et al. (1993) uncovered a developmental trend in the way individuals define the nature of friendship across the life span. Older adults reported a much more complex and multidimensional understanding of friendship compared with younger adults. Although younger adults had difficulty establishing friendship as more than a best friend or acquaintance relationship, older adults were able to consider numerous levels and types of friends. Older adults distinguished their best friend with whom they grew up, from work friends with whom they enjoy activities, from new friends who share residence in a retirement village. Each of these different sets of friends was perceived to be close and to be an important part of a rich and full life.

Nussbaum et al. (1996) stated that the research on older adult friendship patterns is contradictory, and no clear patterns of ideal network size or optimal characteristics of older adult friendship networks for influencing psychological and physical well-being have emerged from research studies. However, the authors contended that older adult friendships likely serve a number of supportive functions, including: (a) helping older people maintain contact with larger society, (b) providing a buffer against loneliness and depression, (c) providing a secure context in which declining health can be managed, and (d) providing emotional support during times when it is unavailable from family members.

Researchers have also found that older people report that their closest friendships were those that were developed long ago (Field & Minkler, 1988; Powers & Bultena, 1976; Rawlins, 1992). Although many of these relationships may have become less vital for some older people over time, they appear to persist in their minds as reciprocal, mutually beneficial, and so forth, even in cases where friends rarely come in contact with one another. Moreover, older people may not view frequent contact with friends as important to the life of a friendship as do younger people. Cohen and Rajkowski's (1982) research suggested that friends who live close to one another are often less important than those who may live farther away. Their participants reported that best friends lived in relatively remote locations. Nussbaum (1994) contended that separation from friends is a common occurrence as a person ages, and "this separation, which at younger ages may impair a relationship, is more normal in old age and thus not perceived as a major difficulty for the relationship itself" (p. 222).

Contact with friends has been shown to both increase and decrease with age. Adams's (1987) older women subjects said that they had more friends than at any other time in their lives, whereas Cantor (1979) reported that those who live alone were likely to have more friends than those who lived with their spouses or families. Other researchers have found that in cases where family members are the primary care provider of choice, contact with friends often declines. Many older men describe their wives as their best friends and may actually have a limited number of friends outside of marital or family ties (Rawlins, 1995). In older marriages, women often assume the responsibility for maintaining important social links to friends and family members, and are more likely to have a larger network of friends than men. This can cause problems for older men if they limit their friendships outside of the marital dyad, especially if their spouses die or if their wives feel overburdened by taking on the primary role of confidant and companion.

Field and Minkler (1988) and Morgan (1988) reported an overall decrease in communication with friends in old age. Because of the nature of friend relationships, they may be more difficult to maintain, requiring considerable effort that cannot be maintained with the decrease in communication (Hays, 1988; Rawlins, 1992). Nussbaum et al. (1989) suggested that events such as poor health, loss of mobility, institutionalization, and family interference can also lead to decreases in friend relationships for older adults. Finally, because friendships are voluntary, we are generally freer to walk away from them with little cost compared with family relationships, in which there are more stringent role obligations.

Seniors and Internet Use for Friendship Purposes

Older individuals today have more resources than ever before for developing and maintaining friendships through the use of new technologies, such as the Internet. Although this is still a developing area of research, some scholars have found evidence that many older people are using the Internet to maintain old friendships as well as a means for developing new relationships (Baum & Yoder, 2002; Wright, 2000a, 2000b). Furlong (1989) found that older adults using SeniorNet, an online community for people aged 55 years and older, enjoyed "an opportunity to meet people with similar interests and to share not only information, but also communication on emotional and social issues that are particularly relevant to older adults" (p. 145).

Baum and Yoder (2002) found that older individuals are increasingly using the Internet for social support, especially when it comes to gathering health information about diseases or conditions they might be experiencing. Wright (2000a, 2000b) found that older people using SeniorNet frequently develop friendships and rely on these ties for social support for a variety of concerns. Although the degree of intimacy often varies among older SeniorNet users, participants reported enjoying both close relationships and the ability to have weak ties when disclosing sensitive information and when wishing to preserve anonymity while obtaining feedback from others. In addition, seniors reported using SeniorNet for companionship more than social support. In other words, many seniors enjoy meeting other older adults with similar interests and engaging in lively discussion with them as opposed to relying on others on the Internet to help them cope with problems.

The Internet provides the ability for older adults to circumvent problems, such as decreased mobility and health issues, that might limit their interaction with friends in the face-to-face world, as well as providing a means for convenient communication. More research is needed to establish the benefits of cyber-friendship for older adults.

SUMMARY

As we have seen, friends play an important role throughout the life span in terms of providing support and companionship. These functions of friendship appear to be important to our psychological and physical well-being. Friendship is qualitatively different from other relationships we experience in life because of its voluntary and egalitarian nature. Individuals vary in terms of their desire to maintain long-term friendships, and changing life events often influence the size and characteristics of our friendship networks. Clearly, friendship is important for young, middle-aged, and older people, although conceptions of friendship are likely to change as we age because of the greater number of experiences we have with friends. New innovations, such as the Internet, may provide older adults with additional opportunities to create and maintain long-distance friendships.

IV

The Changing Nature of the Self and Relational Networks Across the Life Span

Part III focused on communication in relational contexts across the life span. This part focuses on communicative competencies that cross a number of relational contexts and help us to define our individual identities, that is, how we think about ourselves and, therefore, how we interact with others. The issues discussed in this part have also been mentioned in the part on relational contexts, but are viewed to be so important that they need the more detailed attention provided in the following chapters. Each of these phenomena has consequences for individuals and for their network of family, friends, coworkers, and acquaintances. Although these two parts are presented separately, remember that they are inherently intertwined.

Chapter 7, Social Roles and Transitions, focuses on our development and management of identity. The roles that we play not only help define who we are to others, but also help define who we are to ourselves. Some roles are thrust on us (e.g., the role of child or grandchild), whereas other roles are taken up voluntarily (e.g., the role of parent or career roles). Whether roles are chosen or not, how we act within a role is, to some extent, within our control. We may choose to behave as a "good" daughter or not. Of course, what it means to be a good daughter may vary considerably by culture and family. Although identity is often viewed as an individual issue, our interactions with others profoundly impact the identities we choose as we receive feedback from others. Related to the roles that we enact are issues of presentation of self and impression management. When we act in certain ways, we expect others to assign labels to that behavior reflecting desired definitions of our selves. Our self-esteem may be enhanced when we are rewarded for being a good daughter or may be damaged when we are reprimanded for not being a good daughter. Because we care what other people think about us, roles and identities are inherently social processes.

Chapter 8, Interpersonal Conflict Management, examines the inevitability of conflict in relationships and the consequences of conflict for individuals and relationships. How we handle conflict can affect the nature of our relationships and how we see ourselves as individuals. The level of conflict in a relationship may reflect the depth of the relationship. After all, we usually do not bother to engage in a conflict with a person serving us a burger at a fast-food joint because we have limited need to interact with that person. On the other hand, we may have considerable conflict with a loved one because we are concerned about the consequences of that individual's behavior or we have different ideas about our obligations to each other.

Chapter 9, Social Support, Health, and Well-Being, examines the interrelationships among these factors. Health has physical, mental, and emotional components, each of which is impacted by our perceptions about whether those around us are concerned about us. Well-being refers particularly to the mental and emotional aspects of health as we feel appreciated and understood by those closest to us. The support others provide us is instrumental in these emotional aspects of health, but also affects our ability to physically recover from injury or illness.

The phenomena examined in this part are not the only communicative skills required of a competent communicator, but they do serve as examples of the importance of communication in our lives and our ability to enhance and refine our interpersonal skills across the life span.

7

Social Roles and Transitions

Human beings are not born socially competent, but by nature, they are social creatures. As social creatures, we form groups that serve a number of functions; therefore, we have expectations about the behavior of others and our selves. We not only have to learn the language of our culture, but the values, attitudes, and beliefs that are important in that culture. The values of a culture define which roles are important, how those roles are to be competently performed, and who should perform those roles. This chapter focuses on how individuals are socialized into their cultures, develop a sense of self and social identities, and learn to incorporate new roles in their role repertoire throughout the life span.

The term *socialization* is used to refer to "the comprehensive and consistent induction of an individual into the objective world of a society or a sector of it" (Berger & Luckmann, 1966, p. 130). Socialization is a complex process through which individuals acquire the social skills and knowledge required of them to be competent members of their group(s). Scholars divide the socialization process into two types: primary and secondary. Primary socialization begins at birth and results in children becoming members of their society; therefore, primary socialization occurs only once in an individual's life (Berger & Luckmann, 1966). Secondary socialization, however, occurs after primary socialization and continues to recur throughout a person's life as the individual takes up new roles (Staton, 1990). Therefore, secondary socialization continues across individuals' life spans as they move through life's stages and acquire new roles.

A *role* is: "a set of prescriptions and proscriptions for behavior— expectations about what behaviors are appropriate for a person holding a particular position within a particular social context" (Kessler & McKenna, 1978, p. 18). When children are born into a family, they are assigned a number of roles, such as son/daughter, grandson/granddaughter, brother/sister, nephew/niece, and so on. At birth, children do not know what is required of these roles, but they will acquire this knowledge during their first years (that is, during the primary socialization process). These roles, however, are not static and will continue to change as the family ages, so that, for example, the expectations for a daughter may be different during her childhood and adolescent years compared with her adult years. In addition, one role is affected by other roles that are taken up by the individual. A daughter may also be a wife and a mother as well as an attorney and a volunteer for a hospice service. These roles will influence each other, sometimes generating conflict between different roles, but always informing the nature of the interrelationships of these roles.

Individuals do not take up roles in isolation. Roles are socially constructed, defined, and negotiated. Family roles, in particular, are defined in relation to other family members. For example, a man and a woman become a husband and a wife when they get married and become parents (a father and mother, respectively) when their first child is born, and one of them becomes a widow or widower when the other one dies (O'Bryant, 1994). Although other roles, such as career roles, may not be inherently defined by a relationship to another person, these roles still reflect the expectations and meanings that others assign to the behaviors of that role.

As individuals age, they undergo a number of status passages in which they take up new roles or abandon old ones, although we are never completely "free" of old roles because they continue to affect our definition of ourselves. Whether and when events occur in our life cycle plays a significant role in the meanings that we assign to any role at any point in time (Stevenson, Paludi, Black, & Whitley, 1994). Thus, our past history affects how we take up and adapt to new roles (O'Bryant, 1994). In addition, the taking up of some roles may be more significant or occur more obviously in our lives. For example, becoming a parent for the first time, especially for women and their physical connection to the birthing process, is likely to have a more significant impact on an individual's identity than is a more mundane event, such as getting a speeding ticket for the first time.

THEORIES OF SOCIALIZATION

With the process of learning to be socially competent in a number of roles across the life span being so complex, how do individuals accomplish this task? Staton (1990) reviews a number of related theories of socialization, which can be categorized into two broad perspectives: the functionalist and the dialectical. The functionalist perspective advocates a rather deterministic view of the individual. In this perspective, socialization serves to mold people to fit into society; therefore, people are considered to be passive recipients of a variety of external socializing forces. The role of communication in this perspective reflects the position that others inform us about their expectations for our behavior.

In contrast, the dialectical model of socialization emphasizes the constant interplay between individuals and the institutions into which they are socialized. In this perspective, socialization is a complex, interactive, negotiated, provisional process in which the individual is an active agent. The role of communication in this perspective reflects the nature of mutual exchange and negotiation as others inform us about their expectations, we ask for feedback, together we redefine our expectations, and the cycle repeats itself.

Symbolic interaction and role theory have been proposed to address different elements of the socialization process (Staton, 1990). The more general theory dealing with the socialization process is symbolic interactionism (SI), which is based on the work of Mead as reported by Blumer (1969). According to SI, people become who they are based on their interactions with others. We learn not only language and cultural rules through social interaction, but also how others think we should behave. Although language gives us labels for people, things, and situations, the use of language provides us with the meaning that we should assign to those people, things, and situations. Individuals, then, begin to learn their roles in the world by examining others' responses to their behavior. When people examine their behavior in light of what they think other people expect of them, they are said to be perspective taking. That is, individuals attempt to see and evaluate their actions from the perspective of another, usually a valued, person. People care about what other people think of them and their actions. This process of perspective taking helps us to identify not only the expectations that others have of us, but to develop a set of expectations for our own behavior. Thus, we learn what roles we are expected to fill and how to successfully fulfill those roles, eventually internalizing these messages to develop our definition of our self.

Role theory is a more narrowly focused theory than SI, but builds on SI principals (Staton, 1990). Because the world is a complex place, we tend to develop a set of categories or schema that guide our behavior and knowledge. Our schema help us to identify people, things, and situations and to understand expectations for our behavior within these constraints. Having a set of schema allows us to more quickly identify what a situation "is" and what is appropriate behavior for us to enact in that situation. Based on information in our surroundings, we determine what role we should play and, usually, we act accordingly. Thus, our organization of information influences our behavior and the meanings assigned to these behaviors by others (Fagot & Leinbach, 1994). All individuals have a number of roles from which they may select a set of behaviors, depending on situational cues for what is appropriate in the setting. As a consequence, individuals have an entire set of roles that they undertake at different times and places, which all impact on individuals' definitions of themselves. Role development is a continual process, as individuals take on new roles and potentially drop old ones as different elements of family-, friend-, and work-related roles become salient. Therefore, most individuals undergo a number of role shifts as they move through the life span (O'Bryant, 1994).

Several social and biological factors influence the taking up of and comfort with new roles. For example, reproductive maturity (a biological factor) influences the age at which people may become parents and thus take up this particular role. Different cultures, however, may view becoming a parent at a given age "normal" or "abnormal" timing (a social factor), resulting in different meanings being assigned to the nature of parenthood for that individual. In addition, individuals not only have to learn a role, but continue to adapt to changes in roles across the life span. For example, the role of worker may be a consistent role throughout most of an individual's adult years. Although individuals become workers for the first time only once, they may refine the role definition with work experience, renegotiate the role definition with the addition of new family responsibilities or with a promotion or career change, and again redefine it with the approach and enactment of retirement. Across the life span, individuals may seek commonalities in the roles they select and struggle to minimize any differences that emerge in roles to maintain a consistent definition of themselves.

Probably the most commonly used system for examining socialization is a stage or phase model. In one of the earliest studies of socialization into organizations, Van Maanen (1976) proposed three phases of social- ization: anticipatory, entry or encounter, and continuance or adaptation. The anticipatory phase occurs when an individual is preparing for work and selecting a career and a particular organization to join. The entry or encounter phase occurs as the organizational newcomer confronts the oc- cupation, the job situation, and the particular organization. Newcomers may find that their previous ideas about the job or the organization may have to be adjusted as new information conflicts with expectations. The continuance or adaptation phase occurs when newcomers are accepted members of the organization and have successfully reconciled their false expectations with the reality of the situation. This last phase is seen as on- going as role conflicts are managed and individuals must renegotiate their roles and even be resocialized when status changes occur.

A major criticism of the stage approach has been that the stages tend to be treated as static and linear; however, the stages in the models are prob- ably not discrete, and attitudes and behaviors may differ more in degree than in kind over time (Jablin, 2001). Jablin (2001) pointed out that the shift from one phase to the next is not a simple chronological occurrence, even though most models posit certain kinds of behaviors or attitudes as markers indicating transitions from one phase to the next. Therefore, although we may take on a role, we are never completely "finished" with "becoming" whatever that role entails. Socialization, then, should be viewed as an ongoing process. Jablin (2001) stated that:

> assimilation involves a chain of events, activities, message exchanges, interpreta- tions, and related processes—essentially "links"—in which individuals use what they have learned in the past (the extant chain of sensemaking moments) to understand new organizational situations and contexts, and as appropriate realign, reshape, re- order, overlap, or fabricate new links so they can better adapt to their own and their organizations' requirements in the present and future. (p. 759)

This more complex view of socialization suggests that researchers need to not only collect data over an extended period of time, but also need to collect data that allows them to examine the nature of the renegotiation of roles. However, as Jablin (2001) pointed out, most studies collect data at two to three points in about 6 months of each other, so the complexity of the assimilation process is missed.

Although these phases were identified with the workplace in mind, they can be applied to any situation in which an individual is taking up a new role. Therefore, scholars can examine the nature of individuals becoming parents by examining how they prepare for the role, even before a pregnancy, adapt to that role once the baby arrives, and continue to adapt to changing demands of the parental role as the child matures.

Communication plays a critical part in role negotiation. Initially, newcomers take in information about others' expectations and attempt to enact their new roles accordingly. With time, however, they eventually begin to negotiate and coordinate differing expectations about their roles once they have attained a threshold of adaptation to the new environment. This process of role negotiation occurs as people attempt to "individualize" roles to better satisfy their own needs, values, and beliefs (Jablin, 2001).

ACQUIRING AND ADAPTING ROLES ACROSS THE LIFE SPAN

Now that we have defined and discussed key terms and examined the major theoretical underpinnings of the socialization process, we turn our attention to the research on specific public and private roles, how we learn the expectations for these roles, and how those expectations change over the life span. First, we examine the most pervasive of public and private roles—that defined by biological sex and associated social expectations. Although there are many private family roles that individuals may take up in their lives, family relationships in the changing context of our life spans are discussed in other chapters, so will not be reviewed here. Extensive research has been conducted on two public roles, that of student and worker, both of which will be reviewed in detail because these roles have received considerable attention by communication scholars.

Gender Roles

All cultures distribute roles and tasks along gender lines, and these social categories are among the most concrete and fundamental ones that children learn in developing an understanding of the world around them and of themselves (Eccles & Bryan, 1994). In a complex world, gender is one of the most salient categorizations for helping to organize and simplify that world (Fagot & Leinbach, 1994). Children fairly quickly learn that

discriminating and labeling themselves and others along sexually dimor-
phic lines is extremely important as they learn to identify the attributes
and behaviors that are considered appropriate and inappropriate for each
sex (Fagot & Leinbach, 1994):

> The life-span perspective on gender roles rests on three assumptions: (a) that being
> female or male is important in the understanding of a person's life experiences from
> birth to death, (b) that being female or male may influence people's experience in
> different ways during different life stages, in different cultures, and during different
> historical periods, and (c) that the experience of being female or male during one
> life stage may have an effect on a person during a later life stage. (Stevenson et al.,
> 1994, p. ix)

Because gender is a complex categorization system, the elements of gender are manifested on several levels. At the most fundamental level of
physiology, differences in the biological makeup of males and females are
apparent. However, because humans are social creatures who actively construct their own social reality, "every society surrounds the basic fact of sexual reproduction with a system of social rules and customs concerning what
males and females are supposed to be and do" (Fagot & Leinbach, 1994,
p. 4). As a consequence, at the psychological level, individuals' identities
are tied to their biological sex and acceptance or discomfort with the expectations their social group has regarding appropriate behaviors, personality characteristics, and preferences of their gender. At the sociological
and cultural levels, groups identify how women and men are expected to
behave toward each other and the positions they are expected or allowed
to occupy in the social system (Stevenson et al., 1994).

Gender roles, however, are not the same as roles that are taken up more
voluntarily, such as teacher or friend. Because gender reflects a basic biological manifestation, much like race, it is more complex than other roles
and influences the very nature of the other roles one plays. "Being a woman
or a man is not a social role but a pervasive identity and a set of self-feelings
that lead to the selection or the assignment by others of social roles and to
the performance in some situations of different sets of behaviors by women
and men" (Stevenson et al., 1994, p. xiii).

Considerable debate has been generated surrounding the use of the
words "sex" and "gender" when describing an individual or a role. This debate, however, has been inconsistent in its use of these terms and how they
are differentiated. Usually, sex is used to describe a biological fact, whereas
gender is used to describe the cultural expectations that are assigned to
that biological designation. The term *gender role* then is used to describe

"the public manifestation of the 'gender identity,' what refers to the sameness, unity, and persistence of one's self-awareness as male, female, or ambivalent" (Stevenson et al., 1994, p. xii). Matthews (1994) pointed out, however, that one major problem that arises when we dichotomize people and examine the differences between these two groups is that we end up ignoring or minimizing the variability that exists within gender roles. Although gender roles are social constructions used to categorize individuals into easily identifiable groups, individuals occupying each group may vary in significant ways from each other.

Gender roles exist at both the social and the individual levels. At the social level, gender roles are symbolic constructions that are defined by the values and expectations of that role (Hollos, 1994). Because gender roles are the product of social and cultural processes, they vary tremendously across cultures, not only in the nature of expectations, but also in the degree of difference expected between the roles of male and female. For example, sexuality is a part of the gender role; however, different cultures have different definitions of what is appropriate sexual behavior for males and females and may have different sanctions for the same type of behavior exhibited by a male or a female. Roles take shape within a social context; therefore, even within a culture, individuals may experience different pressures for taking up various aspects of their gender roles depending on their family configuration, such as the number, gender, and birth order of siblings (Matthews, 1994).

At the individual level, children are motivated to exhibit their social competence; therefore, they are rewarded when they pick up the traditional expectations and abilities associated with their sex (Eccles & Bryan, 1994). As children incorporate these socially sanctioned expectations into their self-schema and identity, they begin to define their identity through these gender roles. Most theories of social identity development, however, argue that individuals move through a process of at first accepting the traditional definition of their gender identity, but at some point evaluating whether and how that definition "fits" for them. This period of self-reflection may lead to a more individualized identity in which individuals continue to accept some of the traditional expectations of their gender role but will drop other expectations from their own identity. A traditional role identity, then, may reflect an immature individual who has not been self-reflective or a more mature individual who has been self-reflective, but has chosen to maintain the features of the traditional role.

In spite of the uneven process of developing a gender identity, some generalizations can be made about the process across an individual's life span.

Children are born into a social group that passes on its values and attitudes about gender roles (Fagot & Leinbach, 1994). Young children gather information regarding gender roles from their family, peers, and the media. Children as young as 7 months old demonstrate an ability to differentiate between male and female faces, although the differentiation may be based on generalized features, particularly hair length. Although children may be able to make this sex differentiation, they do not label themselves or others by sex until after 2 years, and their labeling process is somewhat inconsistent at that. By the age of 2 to 3 years, however, children are fairly consistent in their ability to correctly identify the sex of others. The process of developing the ability to label others by sex often becomes overlearned, so that by the age of 3 or 4 years, children are unaware of what factors they use in this identification process (Fagot & Leinbach, 1994).

Gender roles are particularly significant during adolescence as individuals come to define their sexual identities and their social group attempts to reinforce traditional expectations for sexual behavior. As Stevenson et al. (1994) pointed out "gender-based social relationships" are a "major component of gender roles" (p. xx) for adolescents across all cultures, although the amount of interaction may be severely limited in some cultures. The acknowledgment of sexuality leads to changing ideas of what is appropriate behavior for both males and females, and although considerable overlap may occur in male and female behavior, the same behavior may be assigned very different meanings by the adolescents' social group.

Because the cognitive development of gender roles occurs in a sociocultural environment, adolescents are not just dealing with their personal adaptation to physical changes, but must also deal with the reactions of others around them. The physical changes associated with adolescence may lead to increased pressure from others for young people to act in gender-stereotypic ways. If these pressures lead the individual to having to give up some preferred behaviors, this pressure may stimulate a gender identity crisis (Eccles & Bryan, 1994). For example, girls who are told that girls are not as good in math as boys may choose to give up their interest in math or to continue with that interest, but struggle with redefining what it means to be a girl to maintain a strong self-identity. Because socially defined gender roles impact sexuality, attitudes toward what is considered appropriate sexual behavior, particularly who one should choose as a partner, may also lead to a gender identity crisis if the individual is bisexual or homosexual. Adolescents may have particular difficulty struggling with developing their sexual identity if that identity is not socially sanctioned.

Research on gender roles in adulthood tends to focus on jobs and/or work/family divisions and the division of labor rather than the individual's cognitive development because individuals are assumed to have incorporated their culture's definitions of these roles and formed their gender identity (Stevenson et al., 1994). Because every culture distributes tasks and behaviors along gender lines (Eccles & Bryan, 1994), some jobs are seen as "men's"jobs, whereas others are seen as "women's"(Frieze & Olson, 1994). These assumptions about gender differences in relationship to work extend to differing expectations for what men and women want from work. Because women bear most of the family responsibility, they are more likely to go into jobs that require less training and time commitment so that they can tend to family needs. Men, on the other hand, value recognition and accomplishment more than women, which leads them to strive for workplace achievements.

Indeed, family responsibilities fall mainly on women across the life span, whether they are caring for children or parents, although men often become more relationally oriented in later life (Hagestad, 1994). Because of this difference in focus, family roles tend to be more important to women and nonfamily roles tend to be more important to men (Hagestad, 1994). In addition, women's sense of life course change is more strongly linked to family change, that is, to a "life of responding to the needs of others" (Hagestad, 1994, p. 235). Because women tend to have a greater focus on family, balancing work and family is more critical to women (Frieze & Olson, 1994), and women's work lives often appear more disorderly than do men's because they are more likely to take time out of the workforce to attend to family needs (Frieze & Olson, 1994; Hagestad, 1994).

Changes over time, however, have led to changing definitions of gender roles, especially with changes in women's role in the workforce (Ferree, 1994). These changes are most apparent in the division of labor in the home. Although a working couple may agree to share household chores, the salience of housework is different for men and women (Hagestad, 1994). When examining domestic work, researchers find that men with working spouses continue to do a minimal amount and that there is a limited redistribution of work (Ferree, 1994). What happens in most households is not that men do more, but that women do less, so either housework does not get done or is purchased. This pattern is influenced, however, by economic status. Couples with more equal salaries and a priority on sharing tend to exhibit more egalitarian patterns of domestic work.

With the definitions of gender roles changing, other definitions are changed as well (Ferree, 1994). For example, "breadwinner" and "homemaker" are interlocking roles with "specific sets of normative obligations to other persons" (Ferree, 1994, p. 205) and have related standards of performance. Although men and women alike agree that these definitions are changing, they define fairness in the division of labor differently. These changing definitions result in changes that have led to a redefinition, renegotiation, and restructuring of family roles.

Although most of the research on gender roles in adulthood has focused on work-related issues, some research has examined the consequences of aging in relation to gender roles. For example, women and men have different orientations to age and time (Hagestad, 1994). Aging is perceived more negatively for women. Men are considered distinguished, whereas women are considered to be over the hill. Even notions regarding the life stages of childhood and middle age have developed differently for males and females. Middle and old age start at younger ages for women than for men, and men assign women to older age categories at a younger age than women do.

On a more positive note for women, women's social support networks are larger and more multifaceted than men's (Hagestad, 1994). Women are more likely to maintain contact with family and have a larger circle of nonwork-related friends. Children often see their mothers as confidants, but rarely see fathers in this role. As a consequence of these larger networks, older women can stay in their homes longer based on the assistance they receive from this network, whereas men are more likely to become isolated.

In late adulthood, gender roles may become less salient and less well differentiated. The experience of gender in later life, however, is influenced by "developmental changes across the life span, social expectations about appropriate roles, and current life events" (O'Bryant, 1994, p. 283). Because gender roles establish life scripts and age-related norms of behavior, men and women learn different roles and develop different expectations in any culture (Hagestad, 1994). Individuals' age and gender interact with their life experiences. As a consequence, experiences of and meanings for aging may differ. In addition, women have stronger intergenerational ties, especially when nonmarried or after divorce, which may create even greater differences in experience in later life.

Later life is often examined in relation to events rather than behaviors, especially events related to widowhood and retirement, which reflect social expectations with regard to gender roles. These role changes affect the larger family system, as they also redefine their expectations of an older family member who has experienced the loss of a spouse or who no longer engages in productive paid work (Stevenson et al., 1994).

A common finding in the research on gender roles in later life is that, at least for marital couples, sex roles become less differentiated, especially after retirement (Hagestad, 1994). These findings suggest a greater level of androgyny in later life. Both men and women become more androgynous with age, as men become more passive and emotional and women become more aggressive and task-oriented (O'Bryant, 1994). Another factor that may move individuals to more androgynous behaviors is that gender-related roles become less prominent in later life; therefore social forces no longer push behaviors toward gender stereotypical extremes (O'Bryant, 1994).

O'Bryant (1994) reviewed a number of studies that revealed a shift in gender roles following widow(er)hood. These studies, however, tend to focus on task behaviors and not on individuals' attitudes or self-identity as they shift in the process of adaptation to life changes. Therefore, she interviewed widows and found that only about half of her sample took up more masculine behaviors after widowhood. Women who fell into the "no change" category either already did many "male" behaviors and continued to do these, or they did not do these activities at all and hired someone else to do them. Those women who decreased in the number of "male" behaviors hired help or had family assistance, which often followed an extended period of caregiving to an ill husband prior to his death. These findings suggest that not all individuals experience a shift toward more androgynous gender role orientations in later life.

Matthews (1994) reviewed the literature on parental caregiving and found that the nature of caregiving to an elderly parent was not solely reliant on the adult child's gender, but was also influenced by sibling relationships and support in caregiving activities. Most research in this area has focused on the primary caregiver and has ignored others' roles. Matthews (1994) found that, in families that only had sons, the sons spent less time and assumed fewer responsibilities compared with families that had daughters, although in this random sample of elders, about half indicated that a son was the primary caregiver. Several factors may contribute to these findings. One factor may be that men have been socialized into their gender roles with an expectation that they do not talk about burdens; therefore, they will respond to interview questions in a different manner than will women. Another factor is that assistance to parents is often operationalized to favor female behaviors (such as housework and personal care). These issues need further examination.

Although women and men may become more gender-neutral in their later years, Hagestad (1994) argued that women experience a life of contingency planning, which may make them more capable in managing the puzzles of later life when scripts are being developed and redefined. Because gender roles contain less clearly defined social constraints during the later years, this flexibilty may work to women's advantage as they struggle to maintain "continuity in the face of multiple changes and discontinuities" of life (Hagestad, 1994, p. 238).

The Student Role

Staton (1990) conducted one of the most thorough examinations of role transitions by focusing on the student role from kindergarten to college. Her work is particularly relevant in this review because she places communication at the center of the socialization process. As Staton (1990) argued, schools serve as the most important secondary socialization agent for young people. Although school is not the only source of knowledge regarding roles and cultural expectations, it plays a central function in transmitting and reinforcing the values, beliefs, and attitudes of the society that establishes the educational system. For example, a society that values a strong work ethic will want school to help children learn to conform to authority, conform to a schedule, and avoid wasting time, and will equate achievement with personal worth.

Staton's (1990) studies examine the process of socialization into the student role, focusing on how young people, through communication, learn the student role intitially and continue to socialize into new and different roles throughout their student careers. Several types of the student role exist across the career, including novices (first-time inhabitants of the student role), veteran newcomers (individuals who are entering a new school as a cohort moves from one level of schooling to the next), developing adolescents, serious adolescents, social outsiders (transfers at any age), and strangers (immigrants at any age). An individual is a novice only once, but later transitions (e.g., moving from elementary to middle school) bring about a need for fine-tuning socialization into slightly different roles as students move through age groups. Individuals do not inherently know how to be a student, so they must learn to think, feel, and behave as a student. A group of novices are more likely to receive messages about explicit expectations and procedural routines, so children in preschool or kindergarten receive explicit instructions about "how we behave in school." The requirements for enacting the role of student competently change as status changes, that is, the behaviors one learned in kindergarten are not necessarily still considered competent when one is in high school or college. These changing expectations reflect the fact that students are given more freedom and responsibility with age, so students must continually refine their behavior within the role.

Although several differences arise across the student career, commonalities exist as well because students continue to have behavioral, cognitive, and affective needs regarding their performance of and in this role. Throughout the student career, individuals are most likely to feel uncertain during anticipatory and entry phases of socialization as they have a greater need to gather role-specific information, especially information related to appropriate vocabularies, which includes not just language, but the meanings, tacit understandings, and affective colorations associated with these meanings. Thus, students at all ages need information about how to behave in their roles and the content areas they are supposed to be learning, and they need reassurance that they belong. Younger children, however, do not request affective information as much as older children do, which may be a developmental issue because young children may not have the cognitive awareness of this need or the ability to express this need overtly. Students have concerns regarding self and task throughout their career. These concerns may exhibit a lack of information about a particular domain or issue, a personal frustration, or a problem situation that they do not know how to resolve. Although information alone may reduce uncertainty, reducing concern also requires reassurance and support, focusing more on the affective rather than behavioral and cognitive needs of the student. Students' concerns about self are focused on the need to fit in, avoiding embarrassing situations, and face saving. This concern may be particularly salient at major transition points when a cohort worries about being the youngest group in a building and the impressions they are making on the older students. Task concern is focused on academics and the environment, although the concern is not so much about the ability to perform, but on how to accomplish the task appropriately. Again, task concerns may be particularly salient when moving into a new school, either with a cohort at a major transition or as a social stranger or immigrant. Another common feature across the student career is the taken-for-granted nature of the status passage associated with moving from grade to grade and school to school, although talk about repeating appears at times if children are potentially going to be "held back" another year. Students recognize a considerable amount of formality in passing to the next grade, even when no formal graduation event occurs.

To reduce uncertainty, a number of strategies are used, including overt means, being interpersonal, asking indirect and rhetorical questions, testing limits, observing behavior, getting around in the school on one's own, and "hanging loose." Teachers often provide information and reassurance directly by making explicit comments and using verbal imperatives, rewards, and negative sanctions, but also do so in more subtle ways by reinforcing appropriate behavior. Communication during a status passage reflects the collective nature of that passage (except for transfers and immigrants who either do not receive these messages or do so in isolation). The collective nature of the passage is emphasized by the awareness that others are making the same passage and communicating with others as the passage occurs. This social cluster of status passage is inherently communicative. Communication also serves informative, regulative, and integrative functions. The informative function is met when communication is related to the giving and seeking of information about cognitive and task dimensions, that is, academic content. The regulative function is met when communication is related to the giving and seeking of information about normative and task dimensions, that is, procedures. The integrative function is met when communication is related to the giving and seeking of information and reassurance about social or affective dimensions, that is, addressing self-concerns and affective uncertainty.

Staton (1990) concludes that socialization can be viewed as a communication process of acquiring information and gaining reassurance to reduce uncertainty and to resolve self and task concern during the passage to a new student status. For students to socialize into the classroom community, they must learn the rules of the community, interpret the context, and integrate the interactional form and academic content. The role of student exists only in relation to others, including other students, teachers, parents, and the larger social system. The concern and uncertainty expressed about the new student role and school environment are part of a universal phenomenon of student socialization, and it is through communication that they are resolved and the socialization process occurs.

The Worker Role

Jablin (2001) reviewed the literature on socialization/assimilation into organizations and the role of worker, focusing on the stages of anticipatory socialization, organizational entry and assimilation, and organizational disengagement. As Jablin (2001) pointed out, the majority of research in this area focuses on the earliest stages of socialization and assimilation into organizations and organizational life and those individuals who are entering the full-time workforce for the first time.

Anticipatory socialization starts in early childhood as children begin to develop expectations and beliefs about work and how people communicate in work-related settings. A wide variety of sources of information influence the child's developing attitudes, including family, educational institutions, part-time job experiences, peers and friends (including non-family adults), and the media. Although each source is separate from the others, they are also interconnected. Research, however, usually focuses on the influence of one source and not on if and how these different sources reinforce or contradict each other.

Family members, particularly parents, are very influential in the work attitudes and career choices of their children. A child first receives messages about work from family members related to household activities through which they establish and reinforce expectations about work habits. In the family setting, children are exposed to the gendered nature of some activities, the use of metaphors to illustrate work principles, and how to differentiate between the public and private spheres. In addition, children develop and refine their communicative skills related to justifications, accounts, and excuses in not performing tasks and how to solicit help. The rules for these behaviors may be implicitly or explicitly stated, but the family may use more explicit means for sharing information about work expectations as parents talk about their own work activities and interpersonal relationships at work.

Educational institutions also serve to socialize children into the organizational world. Schools are usually the first place outside of the family in which children learn about coordinating activities with others, status and hierarchy differences, and standards for comparison with others. In the process of becoming a student, children learn skills that they may use over and over in their lives as they encounter new organizational settings and find the need to seek information and interpret the behaviors of others in their organizational roles.

Part-time employment is considered to be anticipatory socialization for the first full-time job. Over three fourths of high school-aged individuals have part-time jobs at some time prior to graduating from high school. Depending on the job, these adolescents may have many or few opportunities to enhance their communication-related skills on the job. Although limited research has been done on the impact of these part-time jobs, they may have some influence on adolescents' attitudes toward work in general and the type of work they prefer. As a consequence, part-time jobs may affect career choices.

Children and adolescents communicate regularly in task settings through school and other activities, providing them with ample opportunity to learn "how to behave and communicate 'properly' in working with others (e.g., controlling emotions, displaying team spirit/unity, and managing impressions)" (Jablin, 2001, p. 740). These peer interactions, because they occur on a more equal footing than happens in relationships with family and adult organizational members, especially teachers, allow children and adolescents opportunities to develop their skills in managing conflict and to define the nature of organizationally based relationships, especially when having to work together, even if they do not particularly like each other and do not choose to interact voluntarily.

The media influences attitudes toward work roles, although these sources "often transmit distorted and stereotypic images of occupations and how people communicate in them" (Jablin, 2001, p. 740). The media, especially television and movies, focus on "glamour" jobs or show people spending all their time talking about other people and not working, or exhibiting high levels of conflict with authority that would not be accepted in many organizational settings. Limited research exists in this area, however; therefore just how much media influences expectations about work is still unclear.

Although young people receive both general and specific messages about work from a number of sources, at some point, they must intentionally or otherwise decide on a preferred career. This decision leads the young person to receive the education and training required to competently perform those tasks associated with this particular occupation. Because of the investment of time and energy into this training, most individuals attempt to find positions for which they have been trained. Throughout this process of education and the job search, individuals develop expectations about the positions for which they are trained and the organizations in which they are most likely to be able perform those jobs. Thus, the socialization process may shift from the more general aspects of defining the meaning of work and developing basic communicative behaviors to the more specific aspects of acquiring information about a particular organization. This information comes from two primary sources. The first source is mediated, including printed organizational literature and information available on the Internet or through other mediated sources. The second source is interpersonal interactions that occur with teachers, organizational interviewers, current employees of the organization, other applicants, and other direct and indirect social network ties. Most individuals will have access to multiple sources of information, but may receive inconsistent information from various sources. Researchers do not know how these inconsistencies are reconciled, but speculate that individuals weigh the perceived credibility of the different sources that may be filtered by other factors, such as individuals' self-esteem and demographic characteristics that may influence their perceptions of the credibility of different sources.

Once an organization has made an offer and the individual has accepted that offer, the organization and the individual begin the formal process of socializing the individual into the organization. The individual is not a passive receiver of messages from the organization, but is an active agent who also seeks and interprets information. The organization desires for newcomers to become integrated into the culture of that organization, so that the newcomer will become a productive member. While the organization is socializing newcomers into their new roles through formal, planned, and informal, possibly unintentional efforts, the newcomers are attempting to identify how this role and work environment fit their values, attitudes, and needs. Newcomers often experience surprises as they realize that differences exist between their expectations and their experience of reality in the organization. As a consequence of these surprises, newcomers will begin the process of trying to change or "individualize" the role to provide a better "fit" between the organization's values and needs and their own values and needs. The reciprocal nature of this process is central to role making as organizational roles are socially constructed and negotiated.

This initial entry phase is an important time for the newcomer to learn the behaviors, values, and beliefs associated with the job and the organization. Although many of these aspects of communication become mundane, the newcomer must learn how to address others, how to dress, the uses and functions of humor, formal and informal rules, and the appropriate media for communicating with others. This information may be gained through both implicit and explicit interactions with supervisors, peers/coworkers, and management sources. Organizations use a number of processes for providing this vital information, including orienting, training, and formal and informal mentoring.

Orienting usually occurs through formal orientation programs in which newcomers are provided with written materials designed to familiarize them with the organization and their place in it. These materials may include formal statements about the organization's history and mission, policies and procedures, and employee benefits and services. The process of orienting may actually be an ongoing process that reoccurs when the organization changes its mission, policies, and business line.

Training usually occurs through formal programs that may be held away from the work setting and formal on-the-job probation periods where aspects of the job are performed by others and the newcomer observes, or the newcomer performs tasks that are routinely checked by the supervisor or an experienced employee. Formal training may also occur throughout a person's tenure with a company as new skills are required for occupants of a particular position; however, these later sessions are rarely examined with socialization processes in mind.

Formal mentoring occurs when the organization deliberately pairs a newcomer with someone more established in the organization. These formal mentoring relationships are designed to assist the less experienced person in developing competencies and skills without the evaluative aspect of a supervisor providing feedback on performance. Mentoring performs several functions, and different functions may be more important at different stages of the protégé's career. For example, psychosocial functions of mentoring may be more important than career-related functions early in an individual's tenure with the organization. Overall, perceptions of a closer relationship (i.e., one that is more open, supportive, and helpful) have the strongest impact on outcome variables, such as socialization into and commitment to the organization. Informal mentoring occurs when an experienced person provides guidance, training, and/or support to a less experienced person. This relationship, unlike in formal mentoring, develops naturally through interactions in the workplace rather than being formally assigned.

Organizational disengagement occurs when an individual leaves the organization. The nature of the disengagement process is affected by a number of factors, with the most significant difference being whether the departure is voluntary (e.g., transfers, retirement, promotions, or new opportunities) or not voluntary (e.g., job changes because of mergers and acquisition, layoffs as a result of downsizing, or dismissal). This process is an issue not only for the individual exiting, but also for those who remain. A process of mutual withdrawal occurs as the exiting individual withdraws from the group, and the group withdraws from the individual. One difficulty that arises during the disengagement process is that this process does not proceed at the same pace and in the same manner for all parties involved. Conflicts may arise as different individuals handle

the disengagement process in different ways at different times. The disengagement process is not the same between leavers and stayers, but is
interdependent. How one party handles this process may help or hinder how another party handles the process. Using a systems analysis, a
change in one part affects the whole until a new equilibrium or home-
ostasis is reached. Thus, an individual's departure may have far-reaching
consequences for an extended period of time.

Although the disengagement process is quite complex and varies from
individual to individual, four stages are common: preannouncement, announcement, actual exit, and post-exit. Preannouncement activities are
relatively private, whether the exit is voluntary or not. If the departure
is voluntary, different members of the network may be the target of and
will take up cues about the individual's dissatisfaction. These individuals
may encourage the individual to make a change. If the departure is not
voluntary, then rumors may circulate about the possibility of downsizing
or of an individual being fired, but these discussions are kept relatively
private. The announcement and actual exit are relatively public events;
however, the formal announcement may be anticlimactic if rumors have
already spread the impending news, especially in the case of layoffs. Once
the formal announcement has been made public, the group or organization may need to save face in light of losing a valued member. As accounts
of the departure are relayed, the account may alter from time to time, as
the person recounting the departure announcement actively reinterprets
what happened and incorporates new insights into revisions of the account. This aspect of the disengagement process may be easier for groups
that have more experience with leave taking, as they may have developed
scripts for managing the departure. On the other hand, groups with little
leave-taking experience may find the process more awkward because they
cannot rely on these types of scripts. Post-exit, the amount of contact between the leaver and stayers usually decreases over time and often becomes
nonexistent at some point. Those left behind will eventually shift from a
focus on the past (why the leaver left) to a focus on the present and future
(as they discuss the qualities of the new hire and future opportunities and
challenges).

Successful socialization into the workplace is important to organizations because they find that employees who are assimilated into the organization are more committed to the success of the company. Little research
has been conducted examining the assimilation process after the first full-
time job. As more and more people are more likely to change jobs and
careers over their lifetime, these experiences must have some impact on

later experiences. What are the consequences for these efforts when an employee has prior work experience? Do employees who anticipate leaving an organization in a few years resist assimilation efforts? Are employees who have previously been laid off resistant to assimilation efforts at new organizations? How do individuals change or adapt their strategies for resisting efforts at assimilation as they develop experience? Staton's (1990) research on the refining of the student role across a student's career may provide some insight into how individuals refine the worker role, but empirical research is needed to examine those insights.

SUMMARY

We must learn the roles that are deemed appropriate in our culture. These roles are socially constructed, but we incorporate them into our definition of our self as we develop our identities. Primary socialization occurs as we learn to be competent members of our culture. Secondary socialization occurs as we learn roles across the life span. Roles often are experienced in a number of stages as we move from thinking about the possibilities associated with a new role to residing in the role and moving from a newcomer to an "old hand" and then, sometimes, to exiting the role. We continue to incorporate new roles throughout our lives. As we take up new roles, we may have to redefine prior roles, and the role set we have influences the nature of our experience of other roles. A key element of understanding roles is that different individuals may experience the same role in very different ways and may assign quite different meanings to those experiences. As examples of the socialization process, in this chapter we examined gender roles and the roles of student and worker. Although the worker role, for example, may have a focused period of explicit training, most roles must be learned through more implicit means over a more diffuse period of time. Communication plays a crucial part in the exchange of messages about the expectations for roles and in providing feedback on our performance in a role. As we age and develop more sophisticated communication skills, we develop more successful strategies for making these life transitions.

8

Interpersonal Conflict Management

"Conflict" may be defined, in the simplest terms, as "interaction between persons expressing opposing interests, views, or opinions" (Cahn, 1990, p. 1). Interpersonal conflict situations arise when interdependent people seek different outcomes, or different means to the same outcome, and feel a need to address these differences to avoid negative consequences to their relationship (Lulofs & Cahn, 2000). The depth of these conflicts may range from relatively minor to emotional and long-lasting disturbances to the relationship (Bergstrom & Nussbaum, 1996). A minor disagreement (e.g., where to go for dinner or what movie to see) may have little impact on the relationship, whereas a major difference of opinion (e.g., whether and when a marital couple should have children) may alter the nature of a relationship. In the most extreme and negative case, the conflict may escalate to one in which physical violence and psychological abuse become common. The frequency of conflict, then, is not the only important measure, but intensity, consequences (both short- and long-term), the level of affect displayed, and how the conflict is resolved should all be considered (Hartup, 1992).

Conflict is an inevitable aspect of interpersonal relationships (Canary, Cupach, & Messman, 1995; Hocker & Wilmot, 1991), but is generally viewed as a negative or undesirable aspect. Experiencing conflict, however, can have positive as well as negative consequences, helping individuals to develop cognitive and social competence (Chapman & McBride, 1992; Dunn & Slomkowski, 1992; Katz, Kramer, & Gottman, 1992) and helping relational partners to define their relationship by how they act toward one another (Lulofs & Cahn, 2000). In this chapter, issues related to interpersonal conflict management are reviewed from a life-span perspective. These issues include strategies for managing conflict and topics of conflict, focusing on changes that occur over an individual's life span as well as within relational dyads and larger social units.

STRATEGIES FOR MANAGING INTERPERSONAL CONFLICT

Research on interpersonal conflict management addresses styles, strategies, and tactics. According to Lulofs and Cahn (2000), a conflict style is the "preferred mode of dealing with conflicts" (p. 100), whereas a conflict strategy is "an overall plan for dealing with conflicts generally" (p. 100), and a conflict tactic is "a specific observable action that moves a conflict in a particular direction in line with the strategy" (p. 100). For example, individuals who have a conflict style of avoiding conflict will have a strategy to withdraw from or avoid conflict by enacting tactics such as physically withdrawing, remaining silent, or changing the topic of discussion. An individual may have a preferred conflict style, but is likely to have conflict management skills that reflect a variety of strategies and to use any number of strategies and tactics during any given conflict episode (Thomas & Kilmann, 1974).

Implicitly or explicitly, most of the research on conflict in interpersonal relationships focuses to some extent on the role of self-disclosure as individuals decide whether to avoid or engage in conflict (Sillars & Weisberg, 1987). The choice to avoid conflict results in limited self-disclosure as the individual makes circumscribed, irrelevant, or ambiguous remarks. On the other hand, the choice to engage in conflict requires some disclosure of personal feelings and perceptions. Thus, conflict strategies are conceptually related to self-disclosure, particularly to disclosure of negative feelings and perceptions, and couples who are more disclosive are more likely to use direct styles of conflict (Zietlow & Sillars, 1988). Self-disclosure, however, is not the only dimension used to label interpersonal conflict styles. Inherently, conflict requires a partner, and one's feelings regarding the other person's feelings, desires, and needs play an important role in our selection of conflict strategies.

One approach for differentiating conflict styles, as Lulofs and Cahn (2000) discussed, is based originally on the work of Blake and Mouton (1973), with modifications by Kilmann and Thomas (1977) and Rahim (1983). This approach identifies five styles that reflect a combination between individuals' concerns for their own goals and concerns for others' goals or for the relationship. These styles are labeled avoiding, smoothing (also called accommodating or obliging), forcing (also called competing or dominating), compromising, and confronting (also called collaborating or integrating). Avoidance is seen as withdrawal and reflects a low concern for one's own and others' goals. Tactics associated with avoidance include physical or emotional withdrawal or silence. Accommodating is seen as acquiescence and reflects low concern for one's own goals and high concern for others' goals. Tactics associated with accommodation include giving in to the other person. Competition is seen as aggression and reflects high concern for one's own goals and low concern for others' goals. Tactics associated with competition include arguing, confrontation without listening to the other's point of view, and coercion. Compromise is seen as trade-offs and reflects moderate concern for both one's own and others' goals. Tactics associated with compromise include give-and-take trade-offs, meeting the other party halfway, and offering exchanges. Collaboration is seen as mutual satisfaction and reflects high concern for both one's own and others' goals. Tactics associated with collaboration include sharing information, respecting the other's point of view, and problem solving.

Another approach to differentiating conflict styles is based on whether one works with, against, or away from the partner (Canary et al., 1995). In this approach, three general styles have been identified. A style that works with the partner in a cooperative manner is labeled integrative (Sillars, 1980) or solution-oriented (Putnam & Wilson, 1982). Tactics reflecting a cooperative conflict style include explicit discussion of the conflict and potential alternatives, and seeking an acceptable compromise without negative evaluations of the partner. A style that works against the partner in a competitive manner is labeled distributive (Sillars, 1980) or controlling (Putnam & Wilson, 1982). Tactics reflecting a competitive conflict style include explicit discussion and confrontation of the conflict associated with persistent argument, verbal forcing, and negative evaluations of the partner. A style that works away from the partner is labeled passive–indirect, avoidant (Sillars, 1980), or nonconfrontational (Putnam & Wilson, 1982). Tactics reflecting an avoidant conflict style include avoiding discussion of the conflict and attempts to smooth over or minimize differences of opinion.

Obviously, these two approaches to identifying conflict styles overlap to some degree, but focus on slightly different aspects of the conflict situation. The first approach, with five styles, focuses on the individual's concern for achievement of goals, whereas the second approach, with three styles, focuses on relational consequences of working with or against the partner. Whichever system is used for labeling conflict behaviors, individuals develop interpersonal conflict management skills and use different strategies at different points within a conflict episode or over the course of a relationship.

CHANGES IN THE NATURE OF
CONFLICT OVER TIME

When examining conflict styles, the unit of analysis may be the individual, the relationship, or the larger social/cultural group and how expectations regarding conflict change over time. This section first examines the role of conflict and the development of conflict management skills at the level of the individual, then shifts to relational partners, and then examines social/cultural expectations.

The Individual

Children learn about conflict and conflict management through observation of others in conflict and their own experiences involved in conflict episodes with parents, siblings, peers, friends, and others in their social network (Katz et al., 1992). Research has consistently shown that intrapersonal and interpersonal conflict affects a child's or adolescent's development (Canary et al., 1995; Chapman & McBride, 1992; Dunn & Slomkowski, 1992; Minuchin, 1992; Paikoff & Brooks-Gunn, 1991; Shantz & Hartup, 1992). Intrapersonal, or cognitive, conflict results from inconsistencies in the child's knowledge and belief structure. As a result, conflict serves as a catalyst for children to gain new knowledge and to develop rational thinking and argumentative skills, spatial perspective-taking ability, and moral reasoning. Conflict with others, on the other hand, helps a child to develop moral reasoning and an understanding of a wide range of social interaction rules (Chapman & McBride, 1992; Dunn

& Slomkowski, 1992). Young children have limited skills initially, but develop more sophisticated ones, especially as parents model such behaviors, negotiate/mediate conflict between siblings, and, ultimately, help children to transfer these skills to manage conflict between themselves and peers. This process of children developing more sophisticated skills is tied to similar processes related to children's development of a variety of cognitive, interpersonal, and communicative skills. Children who demonstrate greater ability in managing conflict also demonstrate greater ability in a wide array of social skills (Katz et al., 1992). Although these different areas of development are treated in separate chapters in this book, the reader should remember that these processes are intimately interwoven and mutually influence each other.

Although conflict is generally seen as negative, the experience of conflict during early childhood is critical for the child's development (Chapman & McBride, 1992; Dunn & Slomkowski, 1992). Children's arguments with those around them reveal their understanding of the feelings and intentions of others (Dunn & Slomkowski, 1992). In the family, children begin to confront others during their second year. Anyone who has been around a 2-year-old has heard the word "no" millions of times. During the third and fourth years, children become more verbal, develop a sense of autonomy, start to understand the importance of compliance and the consequences of noncompliance, and come to realize that they can exert influence on their parents as well as the parents and other caregivers exerting influence on them. Situations in which children this age exhibit the ability to teach others about social rules and to annoy those around them demonstrate their understanding of the feelings and knowledge of others and their ability to influence those around them. Children also demonstrate their understanding of the social rules of conflict when they ask a parent or other caregiver to intervene in a conflict with siblings or peers, when they blame others, or when they make justifications and excuses for their own behavior. Definitions and separation of self and other are refined as preschoolers begin to realize that their own transgressions are not more acceptable than are the transgressions of others, even as they develop the ability to point blame and make justifications and excuses for their behavior.

During middle childhood (ages 7 to 11 years), children become better able to read social cues of hostility or exclusion, especially as exhibited by their peers. Young children move from concepts of conflict resolution as changes from momentary and physical (e.g., simply taking a toy with which they want to play) to mutual and symbolic solutions (e.g., developing turn-taking strategies for playing with a desirable toy). By ages 6 to 7 years, children are able to demonstrate their "grasp of the emotions of others, their understanding of appropriate strategies for resolving conflict, and their ability... to use these capabilities to gain their own ends" (Dunn & Slomkowski, 1992, p. 80).

Between middle childhood and adolescence, an important developmental change occurs in social understanding in that individuals learn the distinction between conflict and support in friendships. Younger children feel that friends cannot engage in conflict and be supportive, but by adolescence, they see conflict and support as compatible in friendships. Thus, by late adolescence, children have learned that conflict can be good for relationships and that friendship is a matter of more than just sharing resources (Dunn & Slomkowski, 1992).

People often think of adolescence and conflict as synonymous. Collins and Laursen (1992) argue that an increase in conflict is a natural consequence of this age as adolescents undergo a "realignment process." The teen years are a period in which dramatic shifts in role expectations occur along with physical, cognitive, and social changes. Adolescents must balance changes in hormones, reevaluation of their view of their parents, and preparation for the impending role of "adult," and they now have sufficient knowledge to identify inconsistencies and imperfections in others. These changes result in intrapsychic conflict as adolescents redefine themselves and solidify their self-identifies, and interpersonal conflicts arise as interdependencies are renegotiated in relationships both within and outside the family. Although adolescents report having negotiation skills, can identify those skills, and say they are the best skills to use when attempting to resolve a conflict, they usually resolve a conflict episode by disengaging or asserting their power, although power assertions decline overall from early to late adolescence.

Developmental changes, however, do not end with the onset of adulthood. Although children do undergo remarkable changes in their development of social understanding and conflict management skills, individuals continue to change in their conflict management abilities and preferences as they age. In one of the rare life-span examinations of conflict at the individual level, Bergstrom and Nussbaum (1996), using a cross-sectional design, compared conflict preference styles of younger (mean age, about 21 years) and older (mean age, about 62 years) adults. Younger adults reported using a controlling style more frequently than did older adults, whereas older adults reported using a solution-oriented style more frequently than did younger adults. The groups did not differ in their reported use of a nonconfrontational style. Bergstrom and Nussbaum (1996) argued that these findings reflect an important developmental process during adulthood. Young adults' accept current societal norms that conflict should not be avoided, but should be engaged in. However, their frequent use of a controlling style demonstrates that they have not yet developed all the skills necessary for productive conflict management. The older adults demonstrated that they were not only willing to engage in conflict, but had also developed the skills characteristic of effective, productive conflict management. In addition to changing preferences in conflict styles, Bergstrom and Nussbaum (1996) examined satisfaction with conflict in relation to the depth, or importance, of the issue of conflict. Although both age groups reported decreased satisfaction as the depth of conflict increased, only the younger group increasingly preferred nonconfrontation as a strategy for managing more emotional types of conflict. The older group continued to prefer a solution-oriented style used to mutually resolve even the most difficult types of conflict.

In summary, conflict plays a critical role in children's development. The experience of conflict on the intrapsychic level allows the individual to learn to reconcile differing points of view, and to develop rational thinking and moral reasoning. On the interpersonal level, the experience of conflict allows the individual to develop an understanding that others have feelings and desires and that others can be manipulated. As children develop more sophisticated skills in managing conflict, they also develop more sophisticated skills in argumentation and compliance gaining as they adapt their strategies to take into consideration the other person. Learning to manage interpersonal conflict continues throughout life, however, as adults continue to develop additional skills and to change those skills that reflect changing priorities. Younger adults tend to be highly engaged in all types of conflict, but learn with experience to be selective about the issues that receive attention, to take the other person's goals into consideration, and to move toward more effective and productive styles of conflict management that lead to mutual satisfaction with a resolution.

The Relationship

Individual life experiences can influence and ultimately change how we manage our interpersonal conflicts, yet our individual experiences are tempered by the context of our relationships with others. At the level of the relationship, most research on interpersonal conflict has examined romantic, particularly marital, relationships; however, conflict occurs in other interpersonal relationships as well, including parent–child, sibling, and friend relationships. The nature of conflict differs somewhat in each of these relationships, however, because of differences in the power dynamic among these different kinds of relationships. Current cultural expectations for spouses, at least in the United States, are for a more egalitarian relationship. Friends also tend to have a more egalitarian relationship. Siblings may at times consider each other as peers and have a relatively egalitarian relationship, whereas at other times a considerable power dynamic, usually based on age, may come into play during their conflicts. The parent–child relationship is one that is inherently unequal in power, particularly when a child is young and in need of considerable care by the parent.

Power dynamics is not the only characteristic of relationships that may influence the nature of conflict. Another important characteristic is the voluntary versus nonvoluntary nature of the relationship (Collins & Laursen, 1992). Family relationships are nonvoluntary, being defined and constrained by kinship. Friendships, however, are voluntary, being formed and dissolved based on the participants' own choosing. Because family relationships are ongoing ones from which one cannot easily remove oneself, the management of conflict takes on a different nature compared with friend relationships, which can be dissolved should conflict become too serious of a problem.

Because of different power dynamics and voluntary status in these various types of relationships, they will be examined separately in the following discussion of interpersonal conflict management at the relational level. For individuals, relational partners with whom they first experience conflict in interpersonal relationships are parents and then siblings in the family context. At an early age, however, individuals begin to experience conflict with age-peers who may or may not be considered to be friends and, eventually, with romantic partners. The review of conflict in interpersonal relationships, while focusing on the relationship as the unit of analysis, follows the individual's life course experiences for order of presentation: the parent–child relationship, siblings, peers and friends, and then romantic partners.

Although these different relationship types will be addressed separately, dyadic conflict affects more than just the two relational partners. Any dyadic conflict, especially in the family, is likely to affect other family members (Katz et al., 1992). Early experiences of conflict between parents and children are believed to influence not only their joint experience of later conflict, but also the children's experiences with their social networks as well (Osborne & Fincham, 1994). Conflict between the parents has a number of consequences for their children (Katz et al., 1992). Individuals, regardless of gender, tend to use the same conflict strategies with marital partners as with their children, again regardless of the target child's gender, therefore, potentially teaching the child a limited range of conflict strategies (Noller, Feeney, Peterson, & Sheehan, 1995). Older siblings who have positive peer relationships have more positive relationships with their younger siblings, although having a sibling does not appear to have an impact on peer relationships. As adolescents, individuals who come from families that engage openly and constructively in disagreements are more likely to productively resolve conflict with peers (Collins & Laursen, 1992). Siblings tend to engage in conflict with each other in the same manner in which they engage in conflict with their parents (Noller et al., 1995). In addition, conflict in one relationship may provide fodder for discussion in other relationships. For example, teenagers share complaints about their parents, and individuals complain to their friends about romantic partners. Again, although these different relationship types are treated separately, they are intimately intertwined in people's lives. As a consequence, research on interpersonal conflict should take into consideration the nature of the relationship, the partners' relational history, and their social networks.

Before addressing conflict in these different relationship types, however, three common themes emerge from the research on conflict across all relationship types—relational consequences of conflict, changes in preferences over time, and patterns of conflict. First, although the frequency of conflict can affect the nature of an interpersonal relationship, of greater consequence to the relationship are the intensity of the conflict, the amount of negative affect expressed, and whether the conflict is resolved (Canary et al., 1995; Gottman, 1994; Hartup, 1992; Katz et al., 1992; Osborne & Fincham, 1994; Vandell & Bailey, 1992). Frequent minor squabbles may be unpleasant, but do not necessarily create negative consequences for a relationship, especially when compared to even a few serious arguments during which relational partners question their commitment to the relationship. When emotions are strong and negative feelings are expressed, relational partners may need to engage in more repair work to mend the relationship following such an encounter. If these repairs do not occur, the relationship can be permanently altered or dissolved. Conflicts that remain unresolved may be used when future conflicts arise as old issues get recycled, potentially creating downward spirals.

Second, because of the serious consequences that conflict can have for relationships, as relationships "mature," the members of the relationship tend to modify their conflict strategies to maintain the relationship at a reasonable level of harmony (Baruch & Barnett, 1981; Pecchioni

& Nussbaum, 2001; Zietlow & Sillars, 1988). Most relationships cannot withstand high levels of ongoing conflict; therefore, relational partners will either end the relationship or develop strategies for containing the amount of conflict in the relationship. In addition to a desire to maintain harmony in a relationship, relational partners develop an understanding of each other over time and learn to maximize the value of their conflictive interactions and to use more effective strategies for resolving conflict in mutually satisfactory ways.

Third, certain patterns of interaction are typical for conflict episodes. The two most common patterns can be differentiated based on the reciprocity of responses (Rogers, 1981). In the nonreciprocal pattern, the two partners enact different types of behavior. Most commonly, one partner "pushes" the issue, while the other attempts to avoid it; this is often labeled "demand–withdraw" (Christensen & Heavey, 1990). Therefore, one partner is engaged in the conflict and attempts to engage the other person, while the other partner is not engaged and attempts to avoid the conflict. In the reciprocal pattern, both partners demonstrate the same level of engagement and the same types of tactics (Zietlow & Sillars, 1988). For example, if one partner is confrontive, the other partner is confrontive as well, and when one partner changes tactics, the other partner changes to the same tactics (Gottman, 1979; Zietlow & Sillars, 1988). Partners may develop patterns that are flexible and move between different styles as needed (Messman & Canary, 1998; Zietlow & Sillars, 1988) or that lock them into the same pattern of interaction, which can be difficult to break when determined to be unsatisfactory (Christensen & Heavey, 1990; Messman & Canary, 1998; Zietlow & Sillars, 1988). When relational partners fail to regulate the intensity and negativity of their conflicts, a particularly destructive cycle can result—one partner voices a complaint or criticizes the other, followed by expressions of contempt, which prompt the partner to become defensive and stonewall (Gottman, 1994). A negative pattern such as this one can have a serious impact on the quality and survivability of the relationship. Although these negative patterns can be difficult to break and relational partners are influenced by each other's behaviors, those individuals with more sophisticated conflict resolution strategies are better able to deflect, minimize, manipulate, and otherwise strategically control their partners' escalation of conflict (Messman & Canary, 1998).

The Parent–Child Relationship. Research on conflict in the parent–child relationship usually focuses on the mother and child during the child's early years and the mother and daughter during the child's adult years. This bias toward mothers reflects the assumption that mothers serve as primary caregivers during the child's early years and the assumption that mothers and daughters, as females, tend to serve as family kin keepers and maintain more consistent contact after the children reach adulthood. These assumptions do not reflect changes in fathers' more active roles as caregivers and research that shows that sons remain in contact with their parents as much as daughters do. As a consequence, the dynamics of conflict between fathers and their children and between mothers and sons needs more research attention, particularly from a life span perspective.

Because the parent–child relationship plays a critical role in the child's development, and the nature of conflict changes as the child develops, research on parent–child conflict is reviewed based on the child's chronological age. Of course, this trajectory is also the one that is experienced by the parent and child as both age. A typical trajectory, then, follows the path of the child being born and growing through childhood and adolescence, passing through a number of developmental milestones that influence the child's ability to engage in conflict in more sophisticated ways. At some point, usually in late adolescence or early adulthood, the child moves out of the parents' house, although the child may still be financially dependent on the parents, for example, if the parents are paying for the child to attend college. In early adulthood, the child becomes both physically and financially independent of the parents. Children then may enter into long-term romantic relationships, become parents themselves, and experience a divorce or job change, while the parent may be contemplating retirement or have a health crisis. All of these individual transitions impact the relationship and the nature and topics of conflict for the relational partners.

Conflict in the parent–child relationship stems from the very nature of the relationship, based in both an age and a power differential. Fingerman (1995; 1996) suggested that parents and children inherently experience tension in their relationship because of developmental schisms and that these developmental discrepancies lead to tension, even as the nature of this tension changes along with these developmental changes. Because the parent is older, a power differential exists in the relationship. A difference in age, however, is not the only factor that contributes to this power differential. Parents also have the responsibility of training the child to behave in socially appropriate ways (Maccoby & Martin, 1983; Osborne & Fincham, 1994). Along with this responsibility, parents must also provide care for the child and help the child to become independent. Parental authority places limits on the child's behavior as the child struggles to achieve autonomy and self-reliance (Maccoby & Martin, 1983). As both the parent and child attempt to assert power, conflict results. Conflict, therefore, is inevitable in the parent–child relationship.

As parents and children interact, they assert power through different behaviors. Parents assert power by making demands, whereas children assert power by not complying with those demands (Osborne & Fincham, 1994). Over time and with experience, children develop more socially skilled strategies for noncompliance and, eventually, conflict resolution. These skills may be viewed as existing on a continuum, with demonstrations of anger (e.g., yelling or being destructive) or whining at the unskilled end, simple refusal and passive noncompliance in the middle ground, and negotiation (involving explanations and attempts to compromise or bargain) at the skilled end.

The topics of conflict between a parent and young child frequently focus on the child's behavior when that behavior is defined as noncompliant by the parent (Canary et al., 1995). Conflict then arises over the child not following the rules set down by the parent, such as not hitting or biting a sibling, not yelling or throwing tantrums, or not destroying objects. As the child matures, the parents' rules may change to reflect greater demands on the child, such as expecting third-graders to keep their rooms clean, clearing dishes from the table, or feeding the family pet. Around 4.5 years of age, children's conflict behaviors shift from a focus on possessions and rights to those possessions to others' behaviors, that is, whether relational partners are or are not doing what is expected by the child. As mentioned earlier in this chapter, adolescence is a period of dramatic change that impacts the teenagers' relationships with all members of the family. Parents and adolescents are likely to argue about the rules that the parents have established (e.g., setting a curfew, limiting the number of after-school activities, helping around the house), sharing family resources (e.g., use of the television, telephone, computer, or car), and interpersonal relationships (both within and outside of the family, especially in relation to friends and romantic partners). Thus, parent–child conflict at this time focuses on the adolescent's questioning the legitimacy of the parent's rights to impose behavioral restrictions on the adolescent.

Inherently, the topics of conflict between a parent and child will change after a child leaves the parental home because the topics of conflict that revolve around shared living space will be limited to those periods when the child returns to the parental home. The nature of conflict at this point may depend on whether the child continues to be financially dependent on the parents. For example, college students report that their greatest topics of conflict with their parents during their high school years were what they wore, helping around the house, and who their friends were. Now that they are in college, the greatest topics of conflict are money and grades. Once children are no longer dependent on their parents, however, conflict does not necessarily disappear. Adult children may have conflict with their parents about romantic relationships, the way they are raising their own children, and job-related decisions, as well as issues related to the parents' behaviors, such as deciding to move closer after retirement or getting a divorce or marrying someone the child does not like or distrusts. To maintain a harmonious relationship, however, adult children and their parents often develop either a solution-oriented or an avoidant strategy for managing their conflicts.

Many changes occur in the individual lives of adults, which affects the relationship between parents and children. The mother–daughter relationship has received considerable attention. Baruch and Barnett (1983) reported that conflict in the mother–daughter relationship may be greatest during the daughter's 20s as the daughter struggles for her own identity and autonomy, but these issues are usually resolved by the daughter by the time she is 35 years old and the mother and daughter have a more harmonious relationship from that point on. Fingerman (1995) found that healthy older mothers and their daughters did not have tension in their relationship because they avoided telling each other when they were upset. Pecchioni and Nussbaum (2001) examined conflict between independently living older mothers and their adult daughters as they discussed potential caregiving for the mother. The occurrence of conflict during these discussions was rather limited, although the potential for conflict was quite high in this context. The main reasons these women gave for limited conflict in their relationship were that they agree on most issues or they learned over the years not to fight by not fighting over small matters, coming to appreciate each other, and agreeing to disagree on major issues. Mothers and daughters talked about how they had learned that some issues were "just not worth fighting about." On the other hand, if an issue was important enough, they were willing to express their opinions more forcefully and were less willing to give in and meet the other person halfway. Other mothers and daughters talked about having had serious disagreements in earlier years, particularly when the daughter was a teenager. Over the years, however, they had become closer and learned to appreciate each other. Daughters commented that this change occurred particularly after they were married and started having children because they began to see their mothers as resources and friends.

In summary, parents and children experience conflict with each other. How parents manage this conflict affects their children's development, the nature of their relationship, and the nature of the children's relationship with their larger social network. Because parents have the responsibility for molding their children's behavior, conflict inevitably arises as parents make demands and children attempt to exert their own limited power by not complying with the parents' demands. As children mature, they develop more sophisticated skills at noncompliance and at resolving conflict. The issues over which parents and children experience conflict shift as different developmental tasks become important. After the child reaches adulthood, conflict changes as the pair no longer cohabitate (although the child may return home or the parent may move in with the child at some point, making shared living space a renewed issue). With maturity, both partners adapt their behaviors to maintain harmony in the relationship, which sometimes means avoiding conflict, even though this avoidance generates a different kind of tension in the relationship.

The Sibling Relationship. The majority of research on the sibling relationship focuses on the years when siblings share the parental household. Very little research has been conducted focusing on conflict between siblings following adolescence (Bedford, 1994). The lack of research on conflict between siblings leaves us with many questions about the nature of this relationship across the life span.

Compared with other interpersonal relationships, the sibling relationship contains the most frequent and intense conflict with the most negative affect, especially during the early years (Collins & Laursen, 1992; Katz et al., 1992; Vandell & Bailey, 1992). Although some siblings rarely fight, others persist in frequent episodes of conflict, including such behaviors as quarreling, fighting, resisting, opposing, refusing, denying, objecting, and protesting. Over the younger sibling's first 5 years, the number of intense conflicts remains fairly high, although the total number of conflicts peaks when the younger sibling is between the ages of 18 and 24 months (Vandell & Bailey, 1992). The frequency of less intense conflicts continues to decline throughout middle childhood, not just because the siblings are spending less time together as both are in school part of the day, but also because the younger sibling learns more constructive approaches to handling disputes.

Siblings not only engage in conflict, but also exhibit aggression toward one another. Aggression is unilateral and, therefore, is not technically conflict, as conflict requires mutual opposition (Vandell & Bailey, 1992). Because conflict and aggression are not synonymous, a complication arises in research on sibling conflict when these behaviors are not differentiated, which inflates frequency counts and fails to contrast the consequences these different interaction styles have for the relationship. In spite of this problematic area in the research, a number of reasons have been identified to explain the high levels of conflict in the sibling relationship.

The causes of conflict in the sibling relationship have been attributed to the siblings' relationship with their parents, the sibling relationship itself, the individual characteristics of each sibling, and the context in which siblings find themselves (Collins & Laursen, 1992; Katz et al., 1992; Vandell & Bailey, 1992). Parents play a role in the conflict between their children through their modeling of conflict behavior, the emotional climate they create in the family, and their treatment of the children (Vandell & Bailey, 1992). Siblings relate more positively to each other when the parental relationship is more positive (Katz et al., 1992). Children who have mothers who are punitive as disciplinarians are more likely to resolve conflict with siblings through physical means (Vandell & Bailey, 1992). Parents who refer to the feelings and needs of siblings when mediating a conflict help children develop more sophisticated perspective taking and the ability to negotiate resolutions. When children perceive inequities in parental treatment and resources, they are more likely to compete for a parent's attention, leading to sibling rivalry and conflict.

Initial conflicts between siblings may arise when the younger child first joins the family. Older siblings may feel that the new baby is receiving attention that used to be given to them. Studies find that children are three times more likely to be "naughty" when their mothers are caring for infant siblings compared with times when their mother is not involved with the baby (Vandell & Bailey, 1992). As the younger sibling becomes more capable of moving about and playing with objects, older siblings report increasing amounts of interference in their own play by the younger sibling. Most early sibling conflicts revolve around toys and objects, although the focus on these resources may actually be an attempt to garner parental attention and approval. During the second year, the younger sibling begins to actively resist the older sibling's attempts to control these resources. How parents intervene in these early disputes may set the tone for conflict throughout the life of this sibling relationship.

Asymmetries in power and dominance generate conflict between siblings (Katz et al., 1992); however, some characteristics of the sibling relationship lead to more conflict between these relational partners (Vandell & Bailey, 1992). The relative age of siblings has an impact on conflict, diff in age

with older siblings usually being more aggressive and more likely to initiate a conflict. This dynamic continues at least into college age. The age spacing between siblings also impacts conflict in the relationship. When there are at least 6 years' difference between siblings, the older sibling has a relatively positive response to the new sibling, resulting in less conflict. Siblings who are less than 2 years apart in age have more quarrels than any other age combination. The gender combination also affects conflict. Although boys have more disagreements than girls, and these disagreements are more likely to turn physical, opposite sex siblings have more frequent conflict than either same-sex combination.

Relational history and situational factors also influence the nature of conflict in the sibling relationship. Siblings with a negative interaction history, particularly those with coercive cycles in which one hits and then the other hits, have more frequent, more intense, and more negative affect displays in their conflicts (Vandell & Bailey, 1992). These repetitive interactions become reflective of multiple layers of contention that do not have a single cause, but reflect an immediate issue, an ongoing struggle for status in the family, and resentment built up over years. Situational factors that lead to conflict include times when children are bored, confined in close proximity, and engaging in competitive activities (Vandell & Bailey, 1992). Because siblings have considerable access to each other, they have many opportunities for conflict, especially when disagreeing about the distribution of resources, such as toys or space (Katz et al., 1992).

When siblings are younger, they tend to have conflict over sharing resources, such as playing with toys or deciding what game to play, and rule violation, such as name calling and hitting. Adolescent siblings continue to disagree over property and possessions, but also are likely to have disagreements over responsibilities around the house, authority issues, and the nature of the relationship itself (Vandell & Bailey, 1992). Although adolescent siblings have disagreements over control of the television, telephone, or computer, their conflicts with friends tend to be over violations of trust, reflecting a greater differentiation between the social categories of "sibling" and "friend."

How siblings manage conflict with each other varies with the age of the participants. Preschoolers are more likely to demonstrate chains of simple assertions between siblings than when in conflict with a nonfamily age-peer (Vandell & Bailey, 1992). By adolescence, siblings are less likely to actively resolve conflicts with each other than they are with their friends. Adolescent siblings are likely to either withdraw or ignore a sibling, which results in brief episodes that end when one withdraws, or the use of coercion, yelling, name calling, threats, or even physical force, which results in longer conflict episodes. In contrast, adolescent friends are more likely to discuss and compromise, demonstrating that they have the skills for other strategies for resolving conflict, but do not use them with their siblings (Vandell & Bailey, 1992). Adolescents are more likely to allow disputes with siblings to escalate, but find ways to curtail escalation with their friends (Katz et al., 1992). In addition, adolescents are more likely to make formal repair attempts after a fight with a friend than with a sibling.

Conflict in the sibling relationship has consequences for that relationship. These consequences differ depending on the nature of the conflict and how these conflicts were resolved, if at all. The frequency of unmanaged conflict (conflicts that the siblings either did not manage, were ineffective in managing, or relied on others, especially parents, to manage, i.e., those conflicts that they did not resolve between themselves) negatively influences the quality of the relationship (Katz et al., 1992). Destructive conflicts are characterized by high negative affect and often escalate to intrusive or insistent coercion (Vandell & Bailey, 1992). In contrast, constructive conflicts are more likely to be resolved by means of negotiations that are acceptable to both parties. When toddlers display intense negative affect during conflicts with their older siblings, older siblings are less likely to engage in cooperative interactions, such as helping, sharing with, or comforting the younger sibling. During middle childhood and adolescence, siblings with hostile, alienated relationships display high levels of coercion and aggression as well as low levels of warmth and support. These siblings report actively avoiding each other. Siblings with companionate-caring relationships demonstrate high levels of warmth and communication and moderately low levels of aggression and rivalry. Siblings who report having a history of escalating disputes and, therefore, difficult relationships as children continue to have less interaction with each other as adults and, when they do interact, the interactions are more negative. Destructive conflict in the sibling relationship not only has negative consequences for that relationship, but for the individuals' development as well. Children with companionate-caring sibling relationships exhibit less hostility and aggression in peer relationships and have fewer behavior problems and school difficulties (Vandell & Bailey, 1992).

Although conflict between siblings during the early years has consequences for both the individuals and the relationship, how that conflict impacts their later relationship is not clearly understood. Bedford (1994) reviewed the research on the sibling relationship in middle-aged and later years, with only a limited amount of that research focusing on conflict. Cross-sectional studies reveal that conflict between siblings decreases during early adulthood and usually continues to decrease across the life span. Several reasons are postulated for this decrease, all of which may be true. First, adult siblings usually have less contact with each other than when they were younger; therefore, they have fewer opportunities for conflict. Second, siblings who have negative (i.e., conflict-ridden) relationships may avoid each other, again, limiting opportunities for conflict to arise. Third, individuals in early and middle adulthood have other priorities than the family of origin and, therefore, are less involved with siblings. Fourth, sibling rivalry is likely to be resolved and no longer an issue that generates conflict. Fifth, siblings may invest more energy into maintaining a more harmonious relationship. Sixth, these declines in overall conflict may reflect cohort differences with older individuals reflecting different expectations for their sibling relationships, which include a less open expression of feelings.

As Bedford (1994) pointed out, life events may generate or ameliorate conflict in the adult sibling relationship. Siblings who live in closer physical proximity may have more opportunity to interact, resulting in greater potential for conflict. When siblings are sharing caregiving responsibilities (or sense an inequality in this responsibility) of a parent, differences of opinion may generate conflict. On the other hand, a sister becoming a widow may find tensions decrease with a sister who is also a widow, as they now share similar roles. The factors that influence the nature of conflict in the sibling relationship during the adult years deserve more attention. In summary, although conflict is inevitable between siblings, these experiences can provide children with important opportunities and play a critical role in the development of conflict management skills and other cognitive and social processes of young children. Because of the confines of the family relationship, conflict may be more intense and negative, allowing children to develop a better understanding of their own feelings and those of others. However, the intensity of these conflicts must be regulated for the relationship to remain within acceptable levels of hostility. Siblings with more positive relationships are more likely to continue to be sources of support for each other well into their later years.

The Friend Relationship.   Because the friend relationship is one that is based on reciprocity and commitment between more or less equals, the nature of the relationship, including conflict management, is different from family relationships (Canary et al., 1995; Hartup, 1992). Power dynamics play a less central role to conflict because the partners are nearly equal in power within the relationship. In addition, because the relationship is voluntary, too much conflict may result in termination of the relationship, whereas in family relationships, termination of the relationship is a less accessible option. Because of the potential negative consequences of extended, intense conflict in friendships, disputes with friends are usually of short duration and low intensity. For young children, joint activity continues or is quickly resumed following a conflict (Hartup, 1992). The nature of conflict in friendship, then, stands in stark contrast with family, especially sibling, conflict, which may be frequent, intense, and ongoing.

For young children, conditions that heighten social interdependence increase social conflict (Hartup, 1992). For example, whether friends or nonfriend peers, a larger number of children confined in a smaller space with fewer resources and options available tend to have more conflict. Because the main focus of behavior between young children is the coordination of play, issues related to play—sharing possessions and space and the rules of play—generate conflict (Canary et al., 1995). Thus, the issues that generate conflict among young children focus around behavioral issues (e.g., wanting the person to stop teasing, calling names, or hitting), social rules or rules of friendship, and, facts or opinions (Hartup, 1992). During middle childhood, as definitions of friendship become more complex and these relationships become more meaningful, conflict between friends becomes more salient (Canary et al., 1995). Children this age learn to not just reciprocate the other's behaviors during conflict, but to choose from an ever wider range of possible responses. With friends, conflict is more likely to occur during free time, whereas with nonfriends, conflict is more likely to occur during task-related activities, such as school or sports activities (Hartup, 1992).

By adolescence, the shift from a focus on family to peers makes peer relationships more important (Canary et al., 1995). Adolescents continue to develop more differentiated definitions of friends and to manage conflict with friends in more constructive ways. The issues that generate conflict between friends tend to focus on the friendship itself, ideas and opinions, teasing and criticism, and annoying behaviors (Hartup, 1992). Violations of trust and expectations for what friends are and do become particularly important issues for older children and adolescents. Thus, individual development is reflected in the issues that generate conflict between peers. In early childhood, conflict is about possessions, whereas in middle childhood and adolescence, conflict is about affiliation, trust, and interpersonal concerns. This shift in issues of conflict reflects a shift in primary concern from that of the individual (concerns about self) to the social realm (concerns about the relationship and social rules and roles). Thus, the issues of conflict reflect the development of the relational partners (Collins & Laursen, 1992).

Because of the nature of friendship, conflict between friends is memorable and impacts the development of the relationship (Hartup, 1992). Children as young as 7 years old can discuss what they learned from conflict with friends, but rarely reflect on lessons learned in conflict with siblings (Shantz, 1993). Depending on the stage of the friendship, conflict serves different functions (Hartup, 1992). With a peer who is not yet a friend, too much quarreling stifles relationship development. Without some conflict, however, the two individuals cannot move towards intimacy and mutual understanding. Although the occurrence of agreements predicts likelihood of becoming friends, the relational partners must have some disagreements to learn about each other and identify those areas in which they do agree. When individual relational partners see areas of agreement with their partners, they can see the relationship as workable or paying off, whereas disagreements create doubt about the workability of the relationship. As a voluntary relationship, then, friends with too much conflict question the workability of the relationship and may end a relationship that seems unworkable. Because conflict helps relational partners recognize whether they share common ground, they need agreements and disagreements in tandem to construct close relationships. Thus, a dialectic of agree–disagree is needed to develop a friendship. In established friendships, conflict is less contentious at the intense level than is conflict with a sibling or nonfriend, but there can be a considerable amount of conflict at the less intense level of quarrels, quibbles, disagreements, and misunderstandings. Therefore, because longer episodes of conflict that involve several turns and that are more intense tend to be more consequential for the relationship, these episodes are relatively infrequent because they can cause the relationship to end. Yet, friendships are terminated. By 9 or 10 years of age, children report that disloyalty and betrayal are the main causes for friendship termination. Adolescents report violations of trust as the most common reason for ending a friendship (Hartup, 1992).

Beyond adolescence, relatively little research has been conducted on the friend relationship, especially studies that focus on conflict in this relationship during the adult years (Blieszner & Adams, 1992). The research that has been conducted often focuses on college-age friends (Canary et al., 1995). The reasons for this lack of focus on friends during the adult years lie in the nature of the relationship in the larger social network. First, the underlying assumption is that friends become less important as individuals focus on romantic and new family relationships. The demands of these other relationships are believed to leave little time for friends. Second, because of this assumption about friendships being less important, conflict is believed to be less salient as individuals will not maintain friendships that require high levels of engagement to resolve conflict. What research has been conducted suggests, however, that friendships remain important and that conflict continues to play an important role in the development and maintenance of these relationships. Certainly, research on social support (see chapter 9 in this volume, which deals with social support networks) suggests that friends play a critical role in our well-being throughout the life span. Further research on this important facet of this significant relationship is needed.

One source of evidence that these relationships continue to be important is that friends can take offense at statements made by their relational partners (Healey & Bell, 1990). Although individuals can be hurt by friends during adulthood, they are likely to avoid conflict by not saying anything to the friend. As a consequence, they often build up resentment toward the friend and may say things to hurt the friend in return. Obviously, avoiding the conflict does not help the relational partners maintain a satisfactory relationship.

Argyle and Furnham (1983) compared adult friendship in a cross-sectional study of young and middle-aged adults. The younger adults reported having more frequent conflict with all relational partners compared with the middle-aged adults. The middle-aged adults reported having less frequent conflict with friends than with parents, children, siblings, and coworkers, pointing to the perception that they experience less criticism from friends than from any other relational partners. In contrast, in a study with older adults, they reported having about the same amount of conflict with friends as with family members (Dykstra, 1990). However, they also reported having a higher level of enjoyment in friendships that made the relationship worth maintaining in spite of the conflict levels and their ability to voluntarily leave the relationship.

In summary, friends experience conflict with one another. The issues that generate conflict change as the relational partners develop and the strategies that they use for managing conflict in their relationship also change as they become more competent in conflict resolution skills. Without some conflict, two individuals cannot learn about each other and develop the levels of trust and intimacy that are required to develop a close personal relationship between them. Because friendships are voluntary,

the need to maintain conflict at a manageable level may be more important than in family relationships. Ignoring issues, however, can have a negative effect on the relationship if the partners harbor resentments toward
one another.

Romantic Relationships. The vast majority of research on conflict in interpersonal relationships has focused on romantic partners. Romantic relationships may range from a couple on their first date to a couple that has
been married for 50 years. Naturally, the degree of interdependence and
the level of relational commitment vary tremendously across these different stages of romantic relationships (Canary et al., 1995). Even among
married couples, not all marriages are alike, and the same marriage experiences different stresses at different points in the life course (Zietlow &
Sillars, 1988). Therefore, the nature of conflict in romantic relationships
varies depending on the stage of the relationship and the relational history
of the partners. This research has typically examined the nature of conflict
in heterosexual romantic relationships. Whether the dynamics and nature
of conflict in romantic relationships with same-sex partners are the same
remains for future study.

Dating couples that are not yet "serious" about the relationship, generally experience relatively little conflict (Canary et al., 1995). As the
couple becomes more committed to the relationship, they experience an
increase in both the frequency and intensity of conflict. Therefore, conflict may reflect the degree of involvement the couple has with each other.
As mentioned previously, experiencing agreement and disagreement in a
relationship helps the relational partners to discover what they have in
common and to develop intimacy and mutual understanding; therefore,
conflict has positive consequences for the relationship (Hartup, 1992).
Once a dating relationship has reached a certain level of commitment,
the frequency and intensity of conflict remains relatively stable, at least
through the early stages of marriage, although the couple may cycle
through periods of relative calm versus periods of relative turmoil (Canary
et al., 1995).

Research is inconsistent regarding the consequences of conflict on dating relationships. Although relational partners who report high levels of
conflict also report lower levels of satisfaction with the relationship, high
levels of conflict do not necessarily predict that a relationship will dissolve
(Kelly, Huston, & Cate, 1985; Sprecher & Felmlee, 1993). More important to the relationship's future is how the conflict is managed. Conflict
that remains unresolved may accumulate and lead to an erosion of love

and commitment over time (Kelly et al., 1985). For married couples, the frequency and intensity of conflict also does not necessarily predict the end of the relationship, but does differentiate between distressed and nondistressed couples (Gottman, 1994). Distressed couples that seek professional assistance for their marital problems experience more frequent, more intense, more negative, and less frequently resolved conflict. These couples are more likely to engage in negative cycles in which they not only engage in conflict, but also show contempt for each other, leading to defensiveness and withdrawal, inhibiting the chances that the couple will resolve the issue at hand. Conflict issues, then, accumulate and lead to an overall sense of low satisfaction with the relationship, which may lead to divorce.

For couples in long-term committed relationships, the changing dynamics of the relationship may lead to changes in the nature of conflict in the relationship. Newly married couples tend to be highly engaged, often confrontational (Zietlow & Sillars, 1988), as they negotiate the nature of their relationship with each other (e.g., who is responsible for finances, who cooks and cleans, etc.). As issues related to learning to live together are resolved, new issues may develop, but the couple will have developed a relational culture (Wood, 1982), with expectations for how they will handle conflict. As a result, they may become less engaged in conflict. For example, they have come to know that on some issues they just will not change the other's mind, so they do not bother to argue about that issue. For less important matters, they learn not to argue, but are willing to become highly engaged when an important issue arises (Zietlow & Sillars, 1988). Recently married couples or those who have been married for some time may have to deal with issues regarding child rearing, especially in blended families where the two parents may have very different sets of rules regarding their children. Older couples may have experienced more long-term, mutual adaptation, so they are less engaged in conflict, except when an issue is highly salient. New issues continue to arise throughout life. For example, retirement issues may become salient when the wife has been in charge of the domestic sphere and now her husband is under foot all the time (Szinovacz & Ekerdt, 1994). These issues will be somewhat different than for a couple in which both partners have been wage earners and they need to negotiate mutual retirement dates. At the same time that the husband is thinking about retirement, the wife may be reaching the prime of her career because she is younger and took time out of the workforce for raising children. The wife may want to continue to work when the husband is ready to travel or move. Both types of couples must decide what to do about retirement-related issues.

In one of the few life-span studies that compared conflict styles among couples of different age cohorts, Zietlow and Sillars (1988), using a cross-sectional design, examined conversations between young, middle-aged, and retired married couples. Although Zietlow and Sillars (1988) argued that different stressors exist in marital relationships at different points in time, they found no difference in the salience of problems across age groups, although all marital issues were less salient among the older couples. The problems that were rated included: irritability, lack of communication, lack of affection, money, criticism, disagreements about leisure-time activities, housing arrangements, and division of household responsibilities. Participants responded to the list of topics and rated the importance of each one. Whether differences in salience might occur across age cohorts based on a different set of issues, which might arise at different points in the life course of a marriage, is unclear.

In spite of the lack of differences in the salience of these issues, the different age groups managed their conversations about these topics differently (Zietlow & Sillars, 1988). The young couples exhibited a relatively intense engagement style in which they alternated among analytic (i.e., statements that were descriptive, disclosive, qualifying, or explicitly solicited a response from the relational partner), confrontive, and humorous remarks regarding the topic of conflict. In contrast, the middle-aged couples were more nonconflictive and noncommittal in their discussions, but became analytic when marital problems were salient. Retired couples were the least analytic and most noncommittal in their remarks, possibly because they rated most marital problems as nonsalient. However, when an issue was identified as both salient and unresolved, they were extremely conflictive, with partners producing chains of reciprocal confrontive statements. Zietlow and Sillars (1988) also found that the older individuals and couples were less disclosive with each other, especially about negative feelings and perceptions regarding their partners' behaviors. As these older couples made decisions, they used fewer evaluative statements and were much less likely to disagree compared with the young and middle-aged couples.

Overall, a strong effect of life stage on conflict tactics was found (Zietlow & Sillars, 1988). Young couples were more engaged compared with other life-stage groups. They exhibited a higher percentage of irreverent, analytic, and confrontive statements and a lower percentage of denial, topic management, and noncommittal statements. As a result, their style of interaction was relatively intense. In contrast, the middle-aged couples exhibited a higher percentage of denial, topic management, and noncommittal statements with a lower percentage of irreverent and confrontive statements. Their style of conflict management was clearly a less engaged and intense style. The retired couples had the highest percentage of noncommittal statements and the lowest percentage of analytic codes, but also exhibited a comparatively high percentage of confrontive statements, resulting in interaction styles that were either very placid or very combative.

Although no differences in topic salience were identified among age groups, when particular middle-aged and retired couples identified a topic as a salient problem for them, their style of interaction was dramatically affected. When shifting from talking about a nonsalient to a salient issue, middle-aged couples changed from a passive style to an analytic one, whereas retired couples shifted from an extremely congenial to a very confrontive style that was relatively uncensored and undiplomatic. In contrast, the young couples' styles of interaction did not change to any large extent as they shifted from a nonsalient to a salient issue. Zietlow and Sillars (1988) suggested that these differences in interaction style reflect both changes over time in the marital relationship and the different cultural expectations about what conflict is and how it should be managed in the marital relationship at the time when each marriage was formed.

In summary, an increase in the frequency and intensity of conflict between romantic partners indicates an increase in commitment to the relationship. As the couple's lives become more intimately intertwined, the consequences of the other's actions become more important. The issues over which romantic partners have conflict change as the circumstances of their lives change. Couples without children or with grown children are not likely to have conflict over child-rearing concerns, whereas couples with small children in the home are more likely to have conflict over these issues. The frequency and intensity of conflict are not predictive of the course of the relationship. However, how conflict is managed does seem to influence relational satisfaction. Couples with unresolved conflict are less satisfied with their relationship than are couples that are able to resolve their differences. Marital couples change their style of conflict management over time, with young couples being highly engaged over any issue and older couples being less engaged, except when an issue is important.

Social/Cultural Groups. Research examining changes over time in social expectations of interpersonal conflict management have not been conducted; however, studies examining expectations for interpersonal relationships in general shed light on potential changes in conflict management as well. Interpersonal relationships, especially those in the family, are currently expected to be highly expressive compared with these relationships in earlier times (Fitzpatrick & Badzinski, 1994). Social expectations for high levels of expressivity may lead to greater potential for conflict, as everyone shares how they feel about everything. In the marital relationship, as gender roles have changed, the nature of conflict in that relationship has also changed over time. When areas of responsibility were more neatly divided based on gender, the husband, who worked outside the home for pay, was more likely to make financial decisions, whereas the wife, who worked inside the home, made decisions regarding household tasks and child rearing. With these divisions of labor, conflict could be avoided by assigning responsibility to different partners, resulting in little or no need to share decision making. As gender roles have been redefined, couples find they need to negotiate responsibilities and share decision making, resulting in greater opportunities for conflict. For homosexual couples, the relaxation of gender stereotypes in the larger society has also affected their definitions of role expectations in ongoing relationships, leading to a similar process, as is experienced by heterosexual couples as they negotiate individual roles in the relationship. Zietlow and Sillars (1988) pointed out that the cohort differences uncovered in their cross-sectional study of married couples may reflect different cultural expectations for the nature of marital relationships, especially in the areas of valuing self-disclosure and open expression of conflict.

SUMMARY

Although interpersonal conflict is often seen as negative, the experience of conflict has profound effects on the individual's development of cognitive and social skills and on the development and nature of interpersonal relationships. As individuals develop more sophisticated skills for conflict management, they are more selective in their approaches to handling conflict with significant others. In long-standing relationships, partners may avoid conflict when an issue is relatively unimportant, but will rely on solution-oriented strategies for salient issues to maintain their relationship at a satisfactory level. Whenever interpersonal conflict occurs, that conflict is to some extent defined by the various disagreements experienced by the participants and, therefore, is contextualized by their life span experiences and circumstances.

9

Social Support, Health, and Well-Being

The process of life-span development can be a rewarding physical and emotional journey (Olshansky & Carnes, 2000). The quest for a long, healthy, enjoyable life has attracted much attention from the most prominent Nobel laureates studying biological processes, to the most quirky pop-philosophers who find their messages of longevity saturating the media. The best and most recent empirical evidence from the biological and medical sciences indicates that there may be very little each of us can do "to extend the latent potential for longevity that was present at your conception. However... there are many things you can do as an individual to reduce your risk of disease, enhance your health and level of fitness, and improve the odds of achieving your longevity potential" (Olshansky & Carnes, 2000, p. 236). The goal of life should not be to simply live as long as possible, but to live a healthy, satisfying, high-quality life. We believe that communication is a key ingredient in this process of maintaining good health, satisfaction, and a high-quality long life.

The importance of health communication across the life span has been somewhat ignored in the mainstream scientific literature. Scholars who study the predictors of good health across the life span have concentrated their efforts on the biological and physical causes of optimal health. Olshansky and Carnes (2000) offer the following recipe for a long, healthy life: "daily vigorous exercise (30-60 minutes per day); plenty of fruits, vegetables, fiber, and moderate amounts of low-fat protein; a restful sleep every night; an intellectually rewarding, nonstressful job, or no job at all; sex at least once a day; and a regular indulgence in your favorite vice: chocolate, barbecue ribs, you name it" (p. 235). Absent from their recipe for good health and longevity is any mention of the significance of communication as both a direct and indirect antecedent not only to good health and longevity but as an important and essential contributor to any biological, physical, medical, or psychological process (Nussbaum et al., 2000). Health communication students and scholars question how that 60 minutes of exercise can be made more enjoyable. How are we informed as to what fruits, vegetables, and low-fat foods are affordable and available? How do we land and maintain an intellectually rewarding job? And does engaging in sex at least once a day have anything to do with relational maintenance? Communication is at the heart of each ingredient in that recipe for a long satisfying life.

This chapter emphasizes four components of effective health communication across the life span. First, we examine the role of social support as a primary contributor to well-being by helping individuals maintain healthy habits and providing for needs during a health crisis. Second, scholars from the disciplines of communication and public health are actively designing health messages to positively affect individual health behavior. An essential component of these health messages is an understanding of the target audience. Different messages are effective with different populations. Health messages directed toward individuals of different ages reflect an awareness of the life span perspective. Third, individuals directly interact with the health care community through their physicians. Research has addressed the changing nature of the physician–patient interaction across the life span and the possible consequences of the intergenerational nature of this interaction for the delivery of quality care. Finally, health institutions have been constructed in various age-segregated ways. At various points in our life span, we are faced with health care organizations that require an impressive variety of competencies to negotiate the "health system" effectively.

SOCIAL SUPPORT AND WELL-BEING

Research consistently finds that social support is the major predictor of perceived well-being (Albrecht et al., 1994; Schwarzer & Leppin, 1991). When we feel that others care for us and are willing to provide us with assistance when we need it, we feel "loved, esteemed, and valued; and [have a] sense of belonging to a reciprocal network" (Sarason, Sarason, & Pierce, 1990, p. 10). A search of an academic database revealed that over 2,000 articles on social support were published in the last 5 years. Researchers reported that people cope better (specifically, exhibit fewer depressive or posttraumatic stress symptoms) with illnesses (including athletic injuries, various types of cancer, acquired immunodeficiency syndrome/human immunodeficiency virus, stroke, cardiovascular disease, Alzheimer's disease, and eating disorders) and emotional challenges (including stressful life events, such as work stress, career change, geographic relocation, being a single mother or parent of a child who is handicapped or terminally ill, rape, divorce, and the loss of a spouse or parent) when they have a strong support network (Albrecht & Adelman, 1987a; Ames & Roltzsch, 2000; Chou & Chi, 2001; King, King, & Adams, 1998; Klocek, Oliver, & Ross, 1997; Kornblith et al., 2001; Leserman, Petitto, & Evans, 2000; Leskela et al., 2002; Michalak, Wilkinson, Hood, Dowrick, & Wilkinson, 2003; Mickelson & Kubzansky, 2003; Miller, Smerglia, & Kitson, 1998; Prince, Harwood, & Mann, 1997; Rimmerman & Muraver, 2001; Roy, Steptoe, & Kirschbaum, 1998; Wade & Kendler, 2000; Xu, 2001).

Although the concept of social support is complex, a basic definition is "the exchange of instrumental, emotional, and informational resources that assist recipients in attaining their goals" (Stephens, 1990, p. 6). Three types of support are commonly identified: instrumental, emotional, and informational (Albrecht & Adelman, 1987a, 1987d; Sarason et al., 1990). Instrumental support refers to tangible types of assistance, such as a loan of money or giving someone a ride to the doctor's office. Emotional support refers to such diverse activities as listening to someone's troubles, validating someone's feelings, offering encouraging words when someone is down, and simply "being there" during a time of need. Informational support reflects support that shares information, such as when a parent or grandparent teaches a child how to fix something around the house or if a child teaches a parent how to log on to the Internet.

Not all acts of social support are the same, depending on the intensity of the need for support and the timing of that support. Obviously, loaning someone $5.00 for lunch is a less intense act of support than is helping someone cope with the loss of a long-term romantic partner. The timing of social support can be proactive or reactive (Sarason et al., 1990). Proactive support is any type of assistance that helps an individual prevent or avoid problems, such as when a parent advises a child to avoid talking excessively in class while at school or a financial advisor helps an individual with estate planning. Reactive support is usually assistance that is provided in response to some crisis or disruption in normal events that an individual is facing. For example, when a child experiences rejection from peers or a friend breaks up with a romantic partner, the support provider responds to the event causing the emotional distress.

Social support networks are composed of individuals with strong ties, such as family members and close friends, and individuals with weak ties, such as acquaintances, clergy, neighbors, services providers (e.g., hair stylists, bartenders) or professionals (Adelman, Parks, & Albrecht, 1987a; Albrecht & Adelman, 1987a; Granovetter, 1973, 1982). Although social support from family plays a critical role in well-being, social support from friends may be perceived to be more helpful because friends have less stringent role obligations compared with family members (Adelman et al., 1987b; Nussbaum, 1994). In addition, social support from weak ties is also important because these relationships are less demanding, making it easier to try out new role definitions during life transitions and safer to discuss "scary" topics because information shared with these individuals is not likely to get back to the primary support network (Adelman et al., 1987a).

In addition to providing support during times of need, friends also have a positive effect on our mood during times when no crisis exists. This function of friendship is often associated with companionship. Companionship consists of activities such as simply spending time with friends, sharing in activities and interests, and enjoying each other's company (Rook, 1995). Companions have a positive effect on our psychological well-being through what is known as the *direct effects model* of social support by elevating our moods and reducing stress levels, even during times when no crisis or stress situation exists (Antonucci, 1990; Rook, 1987). When our moods are elevated because of positive experiences with friends, we are less likely to be negatively effected by everyday hassles and problems.

Social support, no matter who is the source, is thought to have a positive effect on an individual's psychological and physical well-being by providing a buffer against stressful situations. The *buffering model* of social support contends that stress, although not always a negative factor, can trigger the release of certain chemicals within our bodies that can have a negative effect on our health by weakening our immune system and lowering our resistance to illness (Cohen, 1988; Dean & Lin, 1977). For example, if you are sad because you have recently ended a relationship with a romantic partner, you might feel depressed and perhaps physically tired. Your friends can help reduce the stress you are experiencing from the break-up by listening to you, giving you advice about how to deal with your emotions, or by providing you with an escape from thinking about the situation (e.g., by taking you to a nightclub or movie). Friends can also help you minimize a stressful situation or avoid it all together by providing information or tangible support. However, a host of other variables are thought to mediate the relationship between social support and health outcomes, including: (a) characteristics of a person's social network; (b) how socially integrated the individual is within this network; (c) personality variables, such as self-esteem and social competence; and (d) different coping styles and physiological responses when dealing with stress (Schwarzer & Leppin, 1991).

Social Support Across the Life Span

Children undergo a long period of dependence during which their very survival requires assistance from others (Cauce, Reid, Landesman, & Gonzales, 1990). Although children develop an ability to fend for themselves, throughout the life span, life is much easier when we can rely on others to help us in times of need. Although social support is always important, different functions of social support are important at different life stages, and our perceptions of proffered support change with the changing circumstances of our lives (Sarason et al., 1990; Vaux, 1988). As we rely on others during various periods of crisis throughout our lives, we draw on these experiences when making judgments about the support we give and receive in our relationships. This section focuses on the developmental and contextual factors that influence our need for different types of support.

In most families of origin, children are primarily recipients of support from parents and extended family members. This type of exchange is largely because of the fact that older individuals in the family structure possess and control more resources, such as money, education, and experience. As a child, your family undoubtedly played an important role in helping you to achieve a variety of goals, including helping you to do well in grade school, assisting you financially when you wanted to participate in some activity or hobby, and encouraging you to stick with playing a musical instrument or a sport. Despite limited access to resources, however, children can and do provide support to parents and other family members. For example, children may provide tangible assistance by doing chores, emotional support by cheering up a parent, or informational support by telling a younger sibling not to make their mother angry by leaving dirty dishes lying around.

As children mature, the mix of sources of different types of support change, especially in the role that friends play (Cauce et al., 1990). During children's early years and through grade school, parents consistently provide emotional, informational, and tangible support, whereas siblings provide companionship early on and then emotional support as well. Teachers, as is fitting in their role in children's lives, primarily provide informational support and are rated as increasingly important to this function throughout the school years. Young children, however, report that teachers also are sources of companionship. This role diminishes with the child's increasing age. Relationships with friends demonstrate the greatest change. As children mature through grade school and into adolescence, they begin to confide more in friends with increasing intimacy in these relationships. As a consequence, friends not only provide companionship, but emotional support as well.

With increasing age, children begin to acquire more resources and they may begin to resent some types of informational support, such as unwanted advice, from parents or other family members. Support that may have been appropriate at one point in the life span of a family can eventually become inappropriate or troublesome as children become adolescents and young adults. Not all types of supportive behaviors are perceived positively in family relationships. For example, a younger child may accept parental advice without question, whereas a teenager may resent a mother's request to "be careful" when going out with peers. Some attempts to assist a family member may be perceived as an attempt to control behavior (Umberson, 1987), such as when parents try to keep a teenager from going to parties or seeing certain friends who are perceived to be a bad influence. Parents may perceive this type of behavior as being "for her own good," whereas the teenager may feel that her parents are "butting in."

Throughout adulthood, social support continues to play an important role in helping individuals to cope with stressful life events and to adapt to new roles. Members of the family of origin may take on less dominant roles in providing support as friends and new family members become more important sources, but family members continue to be available for assistance. Although any number of life transitions could be used as an example for how social support occurs during adulthood, the loss of a spouse is one of the most stressful events that can occur. Therefore, we examine the nature of social support in helping an individual to take on the role of widow(er) in some detail.

Widowhood. Widowhood has been found to be one of the most stressful life events a person can experience, requiring more psychological and behavioral adjustment than any other life transition (Thompson, Breckenridge, Gallagher, & Peterson, 1984). Widowhood is a common event in later life because women have a longer average life span, men tend to marry younger women, and marital partners are unlikely to die at the same time. The chance of becoming widowed increases with age. In the year 2000, of older adults aged 65 years and older, 32.1% were widowed, with 45.3% of women and 14.4% of men reporting that status (U.S. Census Bureau, 2000). Becoming a widow can affect a person both psychologically and socially. Social support plays an important role in helping individuals to cope with the loss and to adapt to their new role.

Although many people may have a difficult time adjusting to widowhood, such as experiencing increased depression, loneliness, and financial problems, most people eventually adapt to widowhood and do not suffer long-term negative physical or psychological outcomes (Stroebe, Hansson, Stroebe, & Shut, 2001). Although a number of factors affect the adjustment process, we focus on the role of social support. Widowed individuals who have strong social support networks have higher levels of life satisfaction and psychological well-being than widowed individuals with weak social support networks (Hershberger & Walsh, 1990), providing that they receive appropriate support from people within their social network. Friends tend to have a positive impact on the psychological well-being of widowed people because of their ability to offer companionship, emotional support, and a sense of acceptance. Family members are also an important source of social support during and after the loss of a loved one, although helping a bereaved person only out of a sense of role obligation can actually strain the relationship between a family member and the widowed person. In addition, the need to adjust family rituals after the loss of a spouse or significant other can make family gatherings more difficult as old ways of doing things must be replaced with new traditions.

Newly widowed individuals often have to cope with identity changes and changes in their interaction patterns with their support network. For the widowed person, the role of "spouse" must now be replaced with the role of "widow." For people who have lived a significant part of their lives as part of a couple, taking on the identity of a single person again can be challenging, and bereaved persons may realign their social networks or alter their social identities (Utz, Carr, Nesse, & Wortman, 2002). However, people vary in terms of how much they identify with their role as a married person or cohabitating partner. For some people, the relationship with their spouse or partner is central to their identity, and this can lead to problems when their partner dies. For others, career roles or other social roles may be just as important to a person's identity as their relationship with a spouse or significant other, and these individuals may have an easier time adjusting socially to widowhood.

The newly widowed person will also have to cope with changes in interaction patterns. Generally, those individuals who were more active socially prior to losing their spouse will maintain similar social participation patterns after their partner dies (Utz et al., 2002); however, some surviving partners report feeling like "third wheels" when interacting with couples who were friends of both partners and, therefore, avoid interactions with these members of their support network. A factor that may influence members of the support network to avoid interaction with the widow is the discomfort some people feel when talking about death. Death is not an easy subject for people to talk about in our culture. Researchers have found that members of a person's social network may actually decrease communication with a bereaved individual because of the fact that people are not comfortable communicating about death (Cluck & Cline, 1986). In some cases, members of a widowed person's social network may not want to talk about the loss of a loved one because they feel that they are overstepping boundaries or that it will make the person feel uncomfortable. Typically, people feel that it is appropriate to discuss the grieving process for an undefined period following a death (typically 1 month to a year). However, as time goes on, people are often hesitant to bring up the subject of the deceased or talk about feelings associated with the loss, and they may ignore these topics despite the need the bereaved person may have to talk about them.

Negative Aspects of Social Support

Although we have discussed the positive aspects of social support, the giving and receiving of support can have negative effects as well. Social support research has largely been biased toward the positive effects support has on an individual's well-being. However, a growing body of research has also supported the idea that not all supportive attempts within relationships are helpful or even wanted (La Gaipa, 1990; Rook, 1990, 1995; Suls, 1982). Problems arise both in seeking and giving support.

When seeking support, the individual may have concerns about self-image, losing status in the eyes of the support provider, and the relational costs of receiving more support than one is able to provide in return. We generally have a desire to present ourselves to the world as capable and competent human beings. Seeking support may challenge our self-esteem because asking for assistance may make us look weak or lacking in good judgment (Albrecht & Adelman, 1987c). Demonstrating weakness or lack of knowledge may make us feel vulnerable and too dependent on others. With cultural expectations for men to be independent, any sense of vulnerability may create a particularly strong barrier that prevents men from asking for assistance, even when needed. Some individuals may fear that asking for help on a regular basis will lead to a spiral of ever-increasing dependence, leading to learned helplessness. Older individuals, in particular, may delay asking for help because they are afraid that others will see them as no longer able to care for themselves, they may not want to acknowledge increasing dependency to themselves and the resulting loss of an independent identity, and they do not want to be in a position in which they cannot return the favor.

In relationships, we have a desire for social equity and reciprocity, that is, we want to be able to return the favor when someone helps us out during times of need (Albrecht & Adelman, 1987c). In long-term relationships, we hope that, over time, the give and take of support will be nearly equal. A problem arises when we fear that we will not be able to provide support in return. Although this problem is particularly true for frail older people, it can be true at any point in the life span. The fear of being indebted may create a barrier that makes some people reluctant to ask for help when needed. However, overdependence can also create a strain on the relationship, so people may feel a double bind of whether to ask for help or not (Albrecht & Adelman, 1987b).

Providing support has its costs, including feeling drained, generating relational conflict or strain, and fearing social contagion. Providing social support uses a variety of resources, including time and energy, tangible goods, and emotional nurturance, which may lead to emotional exhaustion and relational strain (Albrecht & Adelman, 1987c). Researchers have found that providing social support can be perceived negatively if it is associated with role obligations (Suls, 1982). For example, being a friend or family member often carries certain role obligations and expectations along with the relationship. In other words, people may feel that it is their duty to provide support to a friend or family member during a crisis period, regardless of whether they really want to do so. If you ever had to listen to a friend's problems over the telephone at 3:00 a.m. when you would rather be sleeping, you may have experienced a role obligation associated with friendship and perhaps felt negatively about it.

Providing social support can also lead to relational strain when messages of support are misinterpreted, perceived to be ineffective or unneeded, or cause conflict. Offering support may be interpreted by the receivers as a challenge to the individuals' ability and competence or may generate fears in the recipients that they are letting the support provider down. For example, a friend, intending to be supportive, might tell you not to worry about an important exam in your math class by saying, "You'll probably ace it." This statement, however, may have the unintended effect of causing you to worry both about your exam and disappointing your friend. Another example comes from scholarship athletes who have suffered an injury. When a teammate, intending to be supportive, says, "Hurry up and get well, man, we need you," the injured player may interpret this statement as "You're letting us down."

In other cases, ineffective attempts at providing support, such as providing too much empathy, may create relational strain, as the recipient questions the motives of the support provider. When the proffered support is unsolicited, it may create uncertainty and anxiety as the recipients question their self-reliance or independence in face of this support. For example, if a friend helps you study for that math test, but makes you feel as if you cannot pass it on your own, then the support will be negatively perceived.

Providing support in the nature of reframing negative perceptions, pointing out fallacious thinking, and redirecting the recipient's outlook may create resentment on the part of the recipient and may cause relational conflict and strain (Albrecht & Adelman, 1987c). Although the proffered support is intended to be helpful, the recipients may interpret this support as invalidating their perceptions, causing them to be defensive. This type of relational strain may be difficult for both relational partners to manage.

Because discussions about stressful life events, such as a diagnosis of cancer, rape, or the death of a loved one, are intense and often unpleasant, they generate emotional distress for the listener (Albrecht & Adelman, 1987c). This distress may raise the support providers' own emotions related to stressful events, therefore reducing their ability to provide support.

Potential support providers may avoid interactions with the individual in need of support, leading to damage to the relationship.

Summary

Social support has both positive and negative aspects; however, feeling supported is clearly linked to a positive sense of well-being. Managing life's events, both those events that are major and everyday, is easier when we know someone cares and when they can help us in tangible and intangible ways. Our social support network may also reinforce positive health behaviors, such as encouraging regular exercise and good nutrition, helping us to stop smoking, or helping us navigate the health care system.

HEALTH MESSAGES

We are bombarded by messages on exactly how to live a healthy life. From television to radio, to newspapers, to billboards, to teachers in each level of our schools, to health professionals, to our friends and family, a constant stream of health information is made available for each of us to consume. So much health information is disseminated from such a wide variety of sources that Mailbach and Parrot (1995) are concerned that any positive effect derived from well-designed, well-communicated health messages may be lost in all the clutter.

Designing and implementing effective health campaigns to change human behavior in a desired direction has proven to be a monumentally difficult task. Sufficient evidence exists that smoking causes significant health problems. Untold billions of dollars have been spent by the federal government, and now by the tobacco companies, in an attempt to reduce or prevent smoking. We can see and are touched by the devastating effects of long-term smoking in our daily lives. Yet, people still smoke.

Effective health messages must be designed in ways that educate, motivate, and reinforce behavioral change. The messages must be targeted to the specific characteristics of the intended audience and must reach that audience when those individuals are ready and willing to listen. The messages also must provide information on exactly what needs to be done or "given up" to maintain a healthy lifestyle. One of the major issues for health communication scholars concerns the attention paid to our health messages. Parrott (1995) offers the following guidelines to facilitate active thought about health messages from an intended audience:

- Use novel messages, settings, and media to present health messages.
- Consider discrepant and unexpected messages, settings, and media to present traditional health messages.
- Instruct the audience to pay attention to the message.
- Construct health messages in a denotatively specific manner.
- Choose spatially immediate demonstratives.
- Use temporally immediate speech.
- Avoid the use of qualifiers in relation to establishing a need to change behaviors; instead, identify the probabilities associated with specific outcomes of certain behaviors. (p. 20)

By manipulating the content and linguistic characteristics of health messages, health campaign strategists may optimize the possible positive behavioral change desired. Of interest to life-span communication students and scholars are the ways in which health messages can be designed to "grab" the attention of individuals of different ages. Constructing health messages with age-related cognitive, language, motivational, and environmental differences in mind will maximize the benefits derived from health campaigns. Parrott's (1995) guidelines must take into account the fundamental life-span changes that occur in our willingness to attend to the health message and subsequently to change our behaviors if the messages are to be effective.

Austin (1995) suggested that health campaigns directed toward children have not been well designed and often fail because of a disregard for developmental differences in the targeted population. A landmark investigation by DiFranza and McAfee (1992) provided information that public service announcements designed to reduce smoking and drinking may actually produce the opposite effects. The health messages attempting to show the negative aspects of smoking are being perceived as positive by children and adolescents and cause smoking to be even more appealing. "Campaigns based on moralizing, scare tactics, and knowledge-only approaches are beginning to be recognized as counterproductive or of limited effectiveness" (Austin, 1995, p. 115). The recognition by the planners of health campaigns that children, adolescents, and adults are influenced by age-related individual and environmental factors can lead to more effective health message design.

Austin (1995) presents four principles to guide the design of comprehensive health campaigns targeted for children and adolescents. We feel that these principles can be extended to include health campaigns targeted at individuals across the entire life span. Principle 1 is to begin prevention early. "Well before children can drive a car, swig a beer, or smooch in a movie theater, they learn how and why people do these things by observing family, peers, other individuals, and the media" (Austin, 1995, p.117). Considering children's exposure to these issues, we should not be shocked when reports of drug use or promiscuous sexual activity report that very young children are participating in these unhealthy behaviors. The environment is full of examples and models of healthy as well as unhealthy life choices. Designing health messages directed toward very young children who are just becoming aware of smoking, drinking, nutrition, or sex can expand the possibilities of influencing attitude formation and behavioral choices in positive ways. In much the same way, directing health messages to midlife adults who may need to begin to schedule a yearly prostate exam or a yearly mammogram could be directed to these individuals a few years before the actual exams are suggested.

Principle 2 concerns microtargeting to age and environmental differences. Developmentally appropriate messages need to consider the individual's cognitive, language, and communicative skills. Preschoolers (0 to 5 years of age) are becoming aware of health attitudes and behavior. Health messages need to emphasize a warm and stimulating environment within which the child can develop a positive self-image. Children of this age are active modelers of others in their environment and are easily influenced by those family members who are caring for and consistently interacting with them. Health messages need to emphasize the positive, need to concentrate on general communicative skill development, and should focus on issues related to creating a supportive, loving, and safe environment.

Early school-age children (5 to 7 years) begin to interact with the larger world of the neighborhood and school as peers, teachers, and other parents join family members in the child's interactive world. Children at this age are beginning to look at the world from different perspectives, are very interested in pictures and words, and can begin to understand simple cause–effect relationships. Health messages need to incorporate the larger interactive world of the preschooler into message design. Parents, teachers, and peers should be included in any attempt to develop positive family communication skills and knowledge about risk factors and protective factors.

Middle childhood (7 to 10 years) is the time at which children begin to "rebel" or at least to move away from parental authority. The peer group begins to emerge as a major interactive entity that can exercise great power over behavioral choice (Harris, 1998). The child continues to develop more competent communicative skills with which to express themselves and strategies with which to influence others. The media is also a major factor in the lives of these children. Health messages must account for the various influences of family, peers, and media. Successful health campaigns will use this expanding interactive world to maximize the growing influence of the peer group and the media. More complex messages can now be constructed that educate as well as persuade.

Early adolescents (10 to 13 years) are transitioning from grade school to middle or junior high school. Interactions with older and more mature adolescents are the norm. The influence of the parents within the realm of appropriate health behavior is often in conflict with the peer group. Experimentation with all aspects of risky behavior within the context of age-peers is quite likely. Adolescents are simultaneously coping with physical changes, psychological dilemmas, and interactive challenges. At this critical point in our lives, Austin (1995) stresses the importance of health messages not being too threatening or over-reactive. "Campaigns need to teach facts; correct misperceptions; and address the myriad of media, family, and peer influences faced by the adolescents" (p. 123). A key to well-designed health messages at this age is to incorporate effective decision-making skills into the overall health campaign. Decisions are made by the individual often within age-peer interactions; thus, effective health messages need to emphasize the interactive nature of the decision-making process and provide pragmatic suggestions of how to reach a healthy decision of behavioral choice when presented with numerous other options, many not so healthy, by highly influential friends.

Mid- to late adolescence (age 13 to college years) continues to be a time of extreme change, social pressure, and major life choices. Austin (1995) indicates that during this time, individuals are "developing a positive body image, developing an inner conscience, defining sex-roles and learning about cross sex relationships, preparing for future family and civic roles, and developing more sophisticated problem-solving capabilities" (p. 119). Health messages should continue to provide appropriate decision-making options and avoid preaching. Including late adolescents and their peers as active participants in any suggested behavioral alternatives to risky, unhealthy behavior is much more likely to be considered seriously.

Young adults (18 to 35 years) have often decided on an initial career choice and have responsibilities that result from independence and possibly starting a family. These new financial and social obligations begin to move this age group away from thinking only of one's own health to the health and safety of a spouse, lover, or child. Health messages need to incorporate the desires and anxieties of this generation into the campaign.

This time of life tends to be the healthiest, or at least is perceived to be the healthiest, time of our lives, and therefore many health messages are ignored. At this age, we may feel invulnerable to bad health and have no need to listen to health messages. Special attention must be given to novel methods with which to capture the attention of young adults.

Middle-aged individuals (35 to 65 years) are very busy raising their families, building a career, maintaining a healthy lifestyle, and preparing for retirement. Fingerman, Nussbaum, and Birditt (in press) describe this time of life as a complex juggling act. Intergenerational family relationships involving adolescent children as well as elderly parents can create significant stress. Health messages at this time in life are likely to be directed toward maintaining a stable, healthy lifestyle including diet and exercise. To maintain an active lifestyle, required behavioral changes need to be explained and interventions suggested. Often, preventive medical procedures, from mammography or prostate examinations to colonoscopies, will be suggested. These medical procedures are not comfortable and may reinforce negative feelings of growing old. Consistent, truthful information will be required to motivate this group of individuals not only to visit the physician for the procedure, but to engage in exercise and to change one's diet as well. These messages must also be directed toward those significant others who will provide support for middle-aged adults. Incorporating the social network in any planned health message continues to be valuable throughout the life span.

Older adults (65 years and older) are entering a time of life when significant energy needs to be exerted to remain healthy. Multiple messages are now being directed toward older adults to eat wisely, exercise daily, remain mentally active, and stay in close contact with family and friends. A lifetime of habits and comfortable behaviors may have to be altered to maintain an acceptable level of health. Caregivers and the support network of older adults may now become a primary audience of these health campaigns. Messages must be constructed not only to inform and motivate the older adult but also to inform and motivate the caregiver as well. In addition, as we age well into our 70s, the ability to see, hear, and process certain information may not be as effective and as efficient as it was during earlier times. Health messages need to be constructed so that older individuals can easily understand them.

Austin's (1995) third principle guiding the design of comprehensive health campaigns is to make sure consistent messages come from a variety of sources over a long period of time. A one-shot message from any single source will rarely produce behavioral change. Health campaigns should take advantage of multiple media outlets: radio, television, movies, magazines, family members, peer groups, and health professionals. The consistency of the message across these different sources can be quite powerful. During certain periods of our lives, the credibility of the health message source may change. Parents are powerful role models during childhood. The peer group and teachers can gain status throughout adolescence and can maintain that status until old age. Our children can be used as respected bearers of information and motivation later in life. In addition, many healthy behaviors serve us well across the entire life span. The style of delivery may need to change, but the consistency of the content from year to year encouraging healthy behavior, such as exercise and diet, can significantly reinforce the original health message.

The final principle purported by Austin (1995) involves giving control and ownership to those individuals who are being challenged to change their behavior. Whenever possible, those individuals who are designing health messages need to sample the targeted population to incorporate their feelings and desires into the campaign. In this way, age-appropriate messages can be constructed and targeted.

PHYSICIAN–PATIENT INTERACTION

The health care community is increasingly aware of the importance of competent communication between those individuals providing and those receiving care. Health communication scholars have produced an impressive amount of evidence suggesting that the quality of the health provider–patient interaction varies depending on numerous individual, relational, financial, and cultural factors. Of concern to us is the effect of age (both the health care provider's age and the patient's age) on the communication and ultimately the success of the medical encounter. We interact with numerous health professionals in our attempt to receive care within the health system. Receptionists, nurses, nurse practitioners, physician assistants, physicians, pharmacists, dentists, and numerous therapists spend their time and energy attempting to diagnose and intervene to solve our health problems. The majority of research that has addressed health care provider–patient interaction concentrates on the physician as the representative of the health industry. The research reviewed in this section focuses on the physician–patient interaction and attempts to address communication differences as a result of age and any implication for quality of care because of such differences.

Physician training and practice has become highly specialized; therefore, physicians may have a practice that is limited to patients from a relatively narrow range in the life span. Pediatrics, the study and practice of illnesses that threaten the health and lives of children, received formal recognition by the American Medical Association in 1879 when the rates of infant and child mortality were exceedingly high (Pawluch, 1986). Today, pediatricians continue to concentrate on the treatment and prevention of childhood disease, but have broadened their expertise into the mental, emotional, and social functioning of the child. Numerous subspecialties have emerged over the past few decades that specifically deal with such issues as cancer, heart problems, or broken bones in childhood. Our society, as well as the medical profession, recognizes that children have unique medical problems and have educated physicians to concentrate on this specific age group.

Geriatricians are physicians trained in the care of older adults. Geriatrics is not a recognized specialty area by the American Medical Association, but is best thought of as a subspecialty of internal medicine or family practice. In fact, to date, very few departments of geriatrics (the University of Oklahoma and the University of Arkansas are notable exceptions) exist in the formal structure of medical schools in the United States. Geriatric fellowships are available once physicians complete their residencies, usually in internal medicine or family practice, but these fellowships often go unfilled. Geriatrics, however, is becoming more popular as a subspecialty in medicine mainly because of to the increasing number of older adults in the general population.

The factors that can affect competent communication between physicians and their patients are numerous. Nussbaum (1998) and Thompson, Robinson and Beisecker (2004) have pointed to the context of the medical encounter, individual patient characteristics, individual physician characteristics such as ageism, the interactive dynamics of the medical encounter, and patient compliance with physician requests as several of the more important predictors of an effective physician–patient interaction that are linked to age. The great majority of patients must arrange for an appointment and then visit a clinic or a hospital to receive medical attention. Everything from the availability of the requested physician, to the size of the medical facility, to how the physician is being paid, to the reason for seeking medical care can affect the physician–patient interaction. Age can also play a significant part in the type of facility in which a medical encounter transpires. For instance, older adults living in assisted-care facilities or nursing homes have medical facilities in the residence.

The very nature of these institutions and the type of physicians willing to work in such facilities can dramatically affect communication (Nussbaum, 1998).

For patients who reside in rural areas, no medical facility may exist, and the medical interaction may take place via fiberoptic telephone lines (telemedicine). Rural areas tend to have a higher proportion of older adults, and such technology may present numerous obstacles to effective communication, especially for older individuals who are uncomfortable with interactions that are not face-to-face. Managed care in all of its various forms (health maintenance organizations, preferred provider organizations, etc.) is also having a dramatic impact not only on the business of care but also on the way care is provided (Nussbaum, 1998). The physician–patient interaction may differ depending on whether the patient is enrolled in Medicare (a federally funded health insurance program for older adults) or Medicaid (a federally funded health insurance program for low-income individuals), or pays privately. Some insurance companies do not cover certain procedures or prescriptions. Some health institutions may not accept Medicare or Medicaid patients. In short, the general context of the medical encounter that includes age-based factors can influence physician–patient communication.

The similarities in physician–patient interactions across the life span far surpass the possible differences as a result of age. However, numerous age-related individual differences are worth noting. Older adults visit health care facilities, present with more chronic diseases, have longer medical histories, move significantly more slowly, and are more likely to be accompanied by a companion than younger adults (Nussbaum, 1998). Manton and Suzman (1992) suggested that, as the population of older adults increases and life spans continue to extend, physician visits by older adults can be expected to double by 2040. Pritchett (2000) reports that older adults are hospitalized three times more often than younger adults and that older adults stay in the hospital nearly twice as long. Adelman, Greene, and Charon (1991) pointed to complications, such as sensory deficits, cognitive impairment, functional limitations, a lifetime of abusing tobacco or alcohol, and numerous consequences of suffering through wars or economic depressions, that affect the physician–patient interaction for older adults.

Younger patients report asking more questions, being more precise in their questioning, talking about their problems more, giving more detailed information, and being more assertive with the physician than older patients (Adelman et al., 1991). Nussbaum (1998) reported that older adults take more time in their medical interactions "getting to the point" of their visit. In other words, older patients will ask appropriate questions and disclose important information to the physician, but this information will take much longer to emerge during the health interview for older patients compared with younger patients.

For their part, physicians can behave quite differently, depending on the age of the patient. Haug and Ory (1987) reported that physicians spend less time with older adults during a medical interaction, even though older people take more time to undress and to provide information. Greene, Adelman, Charon, and Hoffman (1986) and Adelman, Greene, Charon, and Friedman (1990) found physicians to be more condescending, abrupt, and indifferent to older patients while being more egalitarian, patient, engaged, respectful, and likely to share decision making with younger patients. Greene and Adelman (1996) strongly suggested that physicians need to initiate and to interact more with older patients in the domain of psychosocial talk. Psychosocial concerns are the psychological and social aspects of patients' lives, such as depression, financial problems, family matters, bereavement, elder abuse, and neglect, that influence and are influenced by disease. "Geriatricians and other primary care providers know that effective medical diagnosis and treatment are not possible without a careful appreciation of psychosocial aspects of older patients' lives" (Greene & Adelman, 1996, p. 84). Thompson et al. (2004) concluded that physicians are not only more responsive to the physical needs of younger patients but are more responsive to the psychosocial needs as well. Physicians appear to simply be more effective communicators with younger patients.

Williams and Nussbaum (2001) provided an explanation for at least some of the difficulties and differences exhibited within physician–patient communication across the life span. Beyond the fact that neither patients nor physicians are especially competent communicators in each and every situation, the intergenerational nature of the physician–patient interaction provides an additional level of complexity, adding to the ineffectiveness of the interaction. As we age, a substantial portion of our lives is spent interacting with a physician outside of our age cohort. At first, the physician is older than the patients, then, the patients are older than the physician. The intergenerational nature of this interaction can cause individuals to over- or underaccommodate in their communicative behavior. The younger physician may use elder-speak and treat the older patient in a very ageist manner. Older patients may not respect or trust the knowledge level of such a young professional and therefore not fully describe the symptoms of their illness. In either case, the communicative problems created by the intergenerational interaction are not conducive to an effective medical encounter.

An important outcome of the physician–patient interaction is whether the patient complies with the suggestions of the physician. Ory, Abeles, and Lipman (1992) reported that older individuals are more likely to comply with treatment regimens and are more vigilant and responsive to health threats than younger adults. Compliance for all patients is related to the complexity of the treatment and to the ability of the physician to explain the treatment regimen clearly. Older adults present with more chronic conditions and are often provided with more complex treatment regimens. Salzman (1995) provides rather frightening data on how drugs are overprescribed to older adults. Many of these drugs interact in very dangerous ways and can cause reactions and problems much greater than those the drugs were meant to eliminate. The multiple medications must be taken in various ways during different times of the day, leading to confusion. The problem of multiple medications is much more prevalent in the older population.

A final factor that can complicate the communication between a physician and a patient is whether a companion accompanies the patient. Children are almost always accompanied by their parents, who often serve as the voice of the child. Pediatricians are quite good at incorporating the parents into the medical interaction. Beisecker (1996) reported that older adults are more often accompanied to the doctor by companions than are younger adults. "The companions, usually spouses or adult children, interact with physicians and influence the process and content of the medical encounter" (Beisecker, 1996, p. 15). Greene, Majerovitz, Adelman, and Rizzo (1994) found that the presence of a companion resulted in the older patient raising fewer topics during the medical encounter, were less responsive to topics raised by the physician, and were less assertive and expressive. Nussbaum (1998) reported that the patient companion is likely to ask questions on behalf of the older patient, may respond for the older patient, may wish to visit with the physician without the older patient being present, and may take up valuable time with concerns not directly related to the older patient's medical condition. The physician may be placed in the rather uncomfortable position of having to manage communication from both the patient and the companion. The typical dyadic interaction becomes a highly complex triadic interaction, and each participant may not possess the competencies to accomplish their individual goals effectively in this medical interview.

HEALTH INSTITUTIONS

As has been discussed previously in this chapter, the context within which we receive our health care can have profound effects on the communication that takes place between health care employees and the individual seeking care (Nussbaum, et al., 2000). Several health institutions have been constructed in our society that segregate ill individuals by age. Children's hospitals are located in most major metropolitan areas to care for the health and well-being of individuals up to their early 20s. These facilities are specifically designed, built, and organized to accommodate the physical and psychosocial needs of sick children and their parents. The hospitals often include comfortable "living room" conference areas so that parents and children feel at ease when interacting with hospital staff. Playrooms for the children are provided as an important part of the recovery process. In addition, bedrooms are provided for parents to stay close to their child before and after a medical procedure. The medical community has done quite well in providing for the emotional and social needs of children and their parents who must cope with their medical trauma.

Rehabilitation hospitals, extended care facilities, assisted-care residences, and nursing homes have been constructed throughout the United States to care for adult individuals who have serious health needs. The various reasons for being admitted to one of these medical facilities typically involve a rather long stay. Although older adults are the majority of residents/patients in these facilities, younger adults who have experienced a catastrophic injury or suffer from serious heart disease or cancer can also be found living and rehabilitating alongside of the older patients. In this section of the chapter, we review the literature on one particular age-related health institution, the nursing home. Nursing homes have received an impressive amount of study linking communication to quality care and serves as a rather good example of an age-related health institution that directly and indirectly affects our communicative world.

Nursing homes have evolved into medical institutions in the United States, whose main function is to care for those elderly individuals who have suffered a physical or cognitive problem that requires prolonged care. Nussbaum (1991) wrote that nursing homes in this country are, to a large extent, the creation of the federal government (the Social Security Act of 1935 and the Medicaid and Medicare legislation of the 1960s), and at the start of the new millenium, are home to nearly 2 million older adults. The typical nursing home resident is female, widowed, white, in her 80s, has a circulatory system disease, and needs assistance to bathe, dress, use the bathroom and get about. Current federal and state regulations that are meant to control the quality of nursing home care throughout the United States have made it possible for those who are not quite as ill to live in assisted-care facilities. Thus, nursing homes have evolved into a facility that cares for frail, seriously ill older adults or is a facility where long-term rehabilitation can occur. Older adults who do not need full-time nursing care can reside in an assisted-care facility or can be cared for in their own homes.

Nursing homes are built to be medically efficient. Nussbaum (1991) described the "hub and spoke design" of the majority of nursing homes built during the previous 30 years in this society. Nursing stations serve as the hub, and the resident rooms are located along the spokes of the building. Hallways are straight and kept free of obstacles, including wheelchairs. Dining facilities are generally located near the center of the building, with a well-furnished lobby near the entrance and an activity room located near the far end of one of the spokes. Settings where resident–resident interaction can occur are typically furnished with a television and cushioned chairs. Nursing homes can be quite luxurious or can be frighteningly spartan. The more residents pay for care, the more luxurious the nursing home tends to be. Most residents have roommates, although those who can afford a private room can certainly request one.

A series of studies was conducted to measure the effect of the nursing home living environment on effective communication and ultimately quality of life for both residents and staff (Downs, Javidi, & Nussbaum, 1988; Nussbaum, 1983; 1985; 1990; 1991; Nussbaum, Robinson, & Grew, 1985). The results of these studies point to the major impact nursing homes have on the communicative world of older adults. Nussbaum (1991) has labeled the nursing home environment a place of potential "interactive starvation." The challenge of coping with the move from home/hospital to the nursing home; the often secretive and confusing admissions process; the very strict schedule of dining, bathing, visiting and sleeping; the various rules that sanction interaction with staff and other residents; and the reaction of the family to the nursing home are very difficult to manage. This task is made even more difficult when one considers that the institution itself does not provide the social contingencies for the maintenance of independent and socially constructive functioning on the part of older adults (Baltes, Kinderman, Reisenzein, & Schmid, 1987).

An older resident who can reframe his or her environment into a more manageable and rewarding place can overcome the disarray caused by

SOCIAL SUPPORT, HEALTH, AND WELL-BEING 189

placement and continued living in a nursing home. The communicative needs and desires of the nursing home residents studied were similar to the needs and desires of older adults living in the community. Friendships between residents do form. In addition, Nussbaum (1991) provided evidence that both the family and the staff who care for the older adults are very interested in maintaining close contact with the residents. However, the environmental constraints inherent within the nursing home tend to restrict the communicative desires of residents, staff, and family. "The architectural design of the home, the medical model upon which the rules and policies of the home are based, and the individual disabilities which brought the elderly to the home in the first place present unique obstacles to the residents of nursing homes who attempt to maintain an active social existence" (Nussbaum, 1991, p. 161).

The health care organizations that control institutions such as nursing homes are primarily concerned with the physical health of their patients. Special effort and expense must be taken to ensure that health institutions maintain an environment that promotes effective communication. At various points in our life span, we will interface with medical facilities specializing in age-related illnesses. The health professions have been slow to recognize that our communicative needs and desires change as we age. As the health care industry incorporates a much broader conceptualization of quality care into the design and organization of health institutions, the maintenance of a stable communicative environment that promotes both physical and psychosocial well-being throughout the life span will become a priority.

HEALTH AND LIFE-SPAN COMMUNICATION

Does communication play a role in our ability to maintain physical and mental health throughout our life span? We believe that competent communicators have a much higher probability of maintaining a strong social support network and a healthy lifestyle throughout their life spans. We also believe that health care organizations and those governmental agencies and advertisers who are constructing and sending health messages to help us make healthy lifestyle choices can construct more effective health care environments and messages by understanding the process of age change throughout our lives.

The research reviewed in this chapter suggests that health communication and public health scholars are actively investigating the dynamics of linking social support, health messages, physician training, and health institutions to the life-span perspective. Social support is a primary factor in maintaining well-being, especially during a health crisis. The amount and types of support that we need change across the life span, and are directly related to life events that create stress and place demands on our ability to cope successfully with those events. Health messages directed toward individuals at different points in the life span must account for the different cognitive, language, and emotional needs and desires of the targeted group. Physicians and patients must be aware of the interactive complexities inherent in their professional relationship. Physicians attempting to conduct an effective medical interview should have communicative competencies that break down age-related barriers to information gathering. Older patients need to develop strategies to inform the physician of their physical problems in a timely manner and to ask pertinent questions if they so desire. Health institutions designed for specific age-related illnesses should not concentrate exclusively on physical or medical priorities so as to create an environment so devoid of positive social relationships that no one could possibly enjoy living or working in the facility.

Our physical and mental health needs and the way we manage those needs change as we age. Communication plays a significant role in our ability to identify and satisfy these health needs at each and every point in our life span. Health communication scholars and students who are aware of the changing nature of communication across the life span need to be actively engaged with health care professionals in designing and implementing training, interventions, and health policies. Interdisciplinary teams that include numerous health professionals are becoming the standard for geriatric assessment and care. Physicians, nurses, social workers, pharmacists, psychologists, physical therapists, and occupational therapists gather to share information and to discuss the best possible therapeutic interventions with which to serve the patient. Life-span communication scholars can add significantly to the decision-making process occurring in these teams. Placing age-appropriate and competent communication within the realm of quality care can enhance the good work of the health professionals.

Health communication differences across different age cohorts have been the focus of this chapter. Much more attention needs to be placed on the age changes in health communication across the life span. Longitudinal studies that track how health messages remain effective within cohorts as individuals age would be very informative. Persuasive strategies that worked well to convince young adults to use condoms may be similarly persuasive when these individuals once again begin dating later in life and want to engage in safe sex with a new partner. Young adults who communicate effectively with their physicians may find that the behaviors that once worked so well are no longer contributing to an effective medical interaction.

Williams and Nussbaum (2001) highlight the importance of intergenerational communication in the health care context. Throughout the middle years of our lives, we will be interacting with health professionals of somewhat similar ages and attitudes as ourselves. At the beginning and toward the end of our life span, we will be interacting with health professionals who belong to different generations. Intergenerational communication can result in a satisfying and positive transaction. However, the inability on the part of the patient, friends and family in the support network, the health care provider, the health message designer, and the health administrator, to appropriately accommodate to the communicative perceptions and abilities of a different generation can lead to less than satisfying interactions. In these cases, communication education and training can help to eliminate ageism and help to construct health environments conducive to the successful management of health for individuals of all ages.

SUMMARY

The ability to maintain a healthy lifestyle throughout our life span is dependent on the flexibility and adaptation of individuals—whether as patients, health care providers, or support providers—regarding health communication. Health messages are constructed to educate and motivate individuals in differing cohorts. Designers of health messages must take into account the age-related cognitive abilities, language development, communicative skills, and social networks of those targeted individuals. Patients of every age seek help from health care providers in various medical settings. The interaction that transpires between the health care provider and the patient is affected by the age of both provider and patient. Older patients behave differently in the medical interview with the physician than younger patients. Physicians, for their part, can change the manner in which they conduct the interaction based on stereotypical notions of different aged patients. The health institutions within which we receive our care have been constructed to accommodate patients of differing ages. Nursing homes have emerged as the medical institution in which frail, older adults are housed. Nursing homes have been found to be an environment where competent social interaction with other residents, family members, and the staff is not only difficult, but often discouraged. Health communication scholars and students can add significantly to the possibility of influencing healthy choices by joining interdisciplinary efforts to affect health message creation, health care provider–patient competencies, and health policies that control medical institutions.

V
Leisure and Media Use Throughout the Life Span

In this part, we examine the role of leisure and entertainment in society and its implications for life-long human development. In addition, we explore the influence of the mass media on our perceptions and behavior, and specific uses-and-gratifications of the media at different points in the life span. Because such a large amount of our lives is spent engaged in leisure activities and media use, an in-depth look at how these activities impact our perceptions, behaviors, and communication with others is warranted.

The mass media play an important role in influencing our cognitive development as children, and many of our perceptions of the world and behaviors are learned vicariously through media content. The mass media can be a positive influence on children in terms of language development and education, but they can also be a negative influence, particularly where violence and other negative content are concerned.

Chapter 10 focuses on our need for leisure and entertainment throughout the life span. Leisure and entertainment are important aspects of our psychological well-being throughout life, especially as these activities reinforce our social networks. As we get older, physical mobility problems, declining social networks, and other issues can limit opportunities for some leisure activities. However, leisure and entertainment are essential aspects of successful aging.

In chapter 11, we focus on the ways in which television and other mass media play a role in the socialization process, language development, and cognitive development of children. In addition, we examine how children learn to use the mass media, newer media such as video games and the Internet, and problems associated with the mass media, such as the link between violent content and aggressive behavior. Chapter 12 explores how older adults use the mass media to meet various types of personal and social needs. We also examine how consumption of television, newspapers, magazines, and other media changes throughout the life span. In addition, the chapter focuses on media stereotypes of older adults and its effects on older individuals. Finally, the chapter explores how older individuals are using new media such as the Internet. You will note that the review of the impact of media in our lives appears to "skip over" the middle years. The absence of such a review is not because the media are believed to play a less important role in our lives during our middle years, but because limited research has been conducted, so we have little information available regarding this period of our lives.

10

Leisure and Entertainment Across the Life Span

An entire chapter devoted to what many consider to be the rather "silly" topic of leisure and entertainment may not seem consistent with the serious tone of this book, which attempts to relate the life-span perspective to communication. Social scientists have all but ignored the study of leisure activities throughout the life span (Bernard & Phillipson, 1995), concentrating their research on the more "serious" matters of health, caregiving, relationship maintenance, conflict management, and many of the other topics that have thus far been presented in this book. However, a growing number of scholars have indicated that the notion of leisure and the various ways in which we spend our leisure time may have a significant effect on our ability to live a satisfying life (Bernard & Phillipson, 1995; Godbey, 1997, 2001; Nussbaum et al., 2000).

A significant part of the problem with studying leisure activity across the life span has been the difficulty of defining leisure (Sterns & Huyck, 2001). If researchers have difficulty specifically defining a concept, such as leisure, it becomes impossible to measure that concept. The concepts of leisure and leisure activity have been difficult to conceptualize because leisure is so closely related to work in our society. The separation of leisure from work is thought to be too subjective. One individual's work is another's leisure. A second problem is the very notion that serious scholars do not study frivolous topics. In much the same way that emotion received scant attention from psychologists throughout most of the last century and that women's health issues have been ignored until the last few decades by medical researchers, leisure has simply not been considered a topic worthy of serious, systematic investigation.

We obviously believe that leisure does deserve serious attention as a life-span communicative phenomenon. This chapter begins with a brief definitional discussion of leisure, followed by the way leisure may be directly and indirectly related to life-span communication and thus to quality of life. Three specific leisure activities, mass media consumption, travel, and exercise, will serve as examples of how leisure activity relates to communication across the life span. However, given the large amount of research dealing with media use, such as television, videos, books, newspapers, and the Internet, we devote two chapters in this section to mass media at different points in the life span. Chapter 11 focuses on media use and child development, whereas chapter 12 examines media consumption among older adults.

LEISURE

Although it is very true that few leisure scholars agree on one definition, McGuire, Boyd, and Barth (1996) provide an excellent starting point by defining leisure as any activity done primarily for its own sake, with an element of enjoyment, pursued during time that is not otherwise obligated. In this definition, leisure is clearly an activity performed by the individual for the sake of pleasure during times that are not dedicated to nonpleasurable work-like obligations. Although it may be true that some individuals find their careers to be highly enjoyable and very much a leisure activity, the separation of leisure from work makes the discussion of leisure a tad less complex (Bernard & Phillipson, 1995).

Godbey (2001) adds important information to our understanding of leisure through his discussion of three basic contexts of leisure: time, activities, and state of existence or state of mind. Leisure as time refers to various points in our life span in which we have comparatively greater freedom to do what we want and therefore choose to engage in leisure if we so desire. A valid argument can be made that our lives do pass through various stages of time more conducive to leisure. Our lives begin with no obligations other than learning how to become a competent interactant in a family context. Parents spend a significant portion of our childhood "entertaining" us or, at the very least, filling our time with various activities related to pure enjoyment. Once formal education begins, the amount of time and activities devoted to pure enjoyment is significantly decreased. Leisure can become part of the formal extracurricular activities organized by the school or the local community. Parents begin the process of transporting their children from soccer, to dance, to baseball practices.

Sterns and Huyck (2001) pointed out that during our middle years, "leisure activities are apt to be closely linked to career development, with skills and contacts nurtured during leisure pursuits contributing directly or subtly to greater success in current work or toward directing one's career" (p. 475). When someone goes golfing with the boss, the separation between leisure and work can become quite fuzzy. During an individual's middle years, leisure activities become increasingly related to retirement. Once retirement occurs, the time devoted to leisure can greatly increase. In a very simple model of leisure and life-span development, our lives begin and end with the possibility of significant time available for leisure. The middle years are characterized by a more complex, synergistic relationship between career and leisure.

Leisure as activity directs our attention to the behaviors and motivations an individual or group of individuals engage in while enjoying their leisure time. Individuals can choose to perform a very large number of leisure activities once professional and family obligations have been accomplished. Activities such as watching television, using the Internet, and exercising will be discussed later in this chapter. Beyond the nature of the actual activity, individuals may choose to participate in leisure activities for various reasons, such as self-amusement, increasing one's knowledge, improving certain physical skills, or performing good deeds. The extent to which leisure activities and the motivations to engage in certain activities change as we age is of significant interest to life-span communication. In addition, McGuire, Boyd, and Barth (1996) indicate that certain individuals attempt to maintain their specific leisure activities as they age, whereas others are comfortable participating in new leisure activities.

The third basic context of leisure discussed by Godbey (2001) is a bit more abstract than the first two contexts previously discussed. Leisure can be viewed as a "state of existence" or a "state of mind." Leisure is meant to be unhurried, tranquil, or without regard to time. When one is engaged in a leisure activity, one enters a different subjective world where there is no need to be occupied by the empirical world. A state of meditation or contemplation can exist. Leisure also can signify a time of complete freedom from controlling events. Leisure activities are meant to be a brief time of control over the environment rather than being controlled by the environment.

Godbey (2001) goes further in his attempt to help us understand leisure by listing several attributes of healthy leisure. Postulating that some leisure activities can be harmful, he makes an interesting distinction here. This distinction is important for those of us interested in the free communicative choices individuals make over the life span. We can choose to interact with individuals during our leisure time that ultimately does harm to our overall quality of life. If there are leisure activities that enhance the effectiveness of life-span communication, identifying these leisure activities and creating an environment to include these activities can directly improve our ability to cope with life-span changes.

The first attribute of healthy leisure advanced by Godbey (2001) is *acting*. Healthy leisure involves the individual in action. Playing volleyball is healthier than sitting and watching a volleyball game. A second attribute of healthy leisure is *meaning*. A healthy leisure activity involves the participant's constructing a significant meaning for that activity. This meaning can be related to positive feelings that emerge from simply participating. If the individual states that "bowling makes me feel good," then bowling has meaning as a leisure activity.

Healthy leisure activities are *creative*. Godbey (2001) made the point that each leisure activity does not have to be a complete novel experience. As we engage in the same activity over time, improvement is likely to occur. This improvement can create additional challenges, thus increasing the complexity and novelty of the original activity. The more creativity in the activity, the healthier the activity. Healthy leisure also involves *giving*. Giving is often verbalized as "giving back" rather than "taking" from an activity. Coaching baseball, volunteering at the local church, or maintaining a Web site can all become leisure activities that serve a greater purpose than simply being fun for the individual.

Healthy leisure involves *optimism*. An individual who engages in a specific leisure activity should be positive about this activity. Golf is a very challenging sport. If one cannot remain positive as his or her golf shot flies out of bounds and allows this shot to destroy the day, golf is not a healthy leisure activity for this person. The ability to laugh at this particular golf shot and to make fun of one's self while golfing is an additional indicator of healthy leisure. *Humor* is now universally accepted as an essential component of health and quality of life. Leisure provides an excellent opportunity for humor to become a significant part of our lives.

The final context of healthy leisure concerns *social relations*. The great majority of leisure activities bring us in contact with others. As depression and loneliness become the most significant mental health crises in our society, leisure activities can function to bring individuals together with the possibility of positive, life-enhancing human contact. However, activities that are designed to enhance interaction will not necessarily be positive for all individuals. Because quality of life is directly related to our network of family and friends (Nussbaum et al., 2000), any leisure activity that has the potential to strengthen this network of relationships is inherently significant.

Leisure occurs throughout the entirety of our life span. Significant components of leisure are the direct and indirect ways in which leisure functions to enhance communication that in turn relates to our overall well-being. How various leisure activities change as we age and the different functions that these leisure activities serve across the life-span are of interest to life-span communication scholars. Three leisure activities serve to highlight not only the life-span nature of leisure, but offer evidence that connects leisure with communication. We have chosen to briefly discuss the consumption of mass media as a leisure activity engaged in across the life span with rather significant communicative implications, although this topic is discussed in greater detail in chapters 11 and 12. Finally, travel and engaging in physical exercise across the life span will be related to communication.

MASS MEDIA CONSUMPTION

Robinson and Godbey (1999) summarized the data from a number of leisure studies investigating how Americans spend their leisure time. The number one leisure activity reported across all ages from late childhood until old age is watching television. Approximately 30% of the adult population spends on average of 40 hours per week of leisure time watching television. Other types of mass media Americans report spending significant time consuming are reading newspapers, magazines, and books; watching movies; listening to the radio; and listening to tapes and CDs. Not only do Americans spend a great deal of their leisure time using a wide range of media, they also report a high level of enjoyment from these activities. Americans spend their leisure hours consuming media because they enjoy media. We discuss television and traditional mass media consumption among children and older adults in greater detail in chapters 11 and 12.

COMPUTER AND THE INTERNET

Personal computers were first introduced to the marketplace as a tool with which to organize household tasks or to perform as a word processor, replacing the electric typewriter. The ability of private citizens to access the Internet through their personal computers dramatically changed the function of the computer. Personal computers are now marketed as the vehicle through which the Internet is brought into the home. Although valid data are very hard to find, the Internet is much more likely to be used for entertainment and communication rather than for word processing or home-organizational purposes. The question of interest becomes whether individuals of differing ages use the Internet for leisure, and if so, are the leisure activities different for different age cohorts?

An insidious myth associated with the aging process is that "you cannot teach an old dogs new tricks." In essence, older adults will never adopt new technologies. Younger adults will never be able to change their ways as they age, so why bother attempting to educate anyone beyond the youngest cohorts on any advance in technology in any area of existence? The personal computer revolution of the 1980s surely missed entire generations of older adults. The Internet revolution of the 1990s is only a tool of education and leisure for children, adolescents, and early-adopting young adults. Of course, nothing could be further from the truth!

Robinson, Skill, and Turner (2004) cited recent survey figures indicating that over 41% of all U.S. households contain a personal computer. Households with high income levels have a much higher percentage of in-home personal computers, whereas households with annual incomes of less than $20,000.00 per year have a low percentage of a personal computer in their homes. Homes with a college-educated head of household have a higher percentage of personal computers than do homes with lower levels of educational attainment. Homes headed by an individual 55 years of age or older had the smallest percentage of an in-house computer compared with any other age cohort. Regardless of one's income, education level, or age, personal computers have become easily accessed in libraries, schools, and cyber-cafes throughout our society.

To answer the question of whether adolescents and young adults use the Internet for leisure activities, one need only observe these adolescents as they return home from school. Often, the very first activity engaged in once through the door is to check the e-mail account and to immediately plan the evening's activities. The many excellent educational functions of the Internet taught to our children in school are being used in leisurely endeavors after school. By far, communication is the most frequently used Internet activity by adolescents and young adults.

Older adults have not been early adopters of the Internet. However, as we see in chapter 12, older adults are quickly gaining ground. For example, SeniorNet is a nonprofit organization with over 210 learning centers and close to 40,000 members and was originally created to help older adults gain some measure of computer literacy. SeniorNet not only provides training on how to access the Internet but also operates discussion groups on a variety of topics through America Online and the World Wide Web. In addition, SeniorNet is used as an opportunity for older adults to share social support and gather important information on numerous health issues (Wright & Query, 2004). Robinson et al. (2004) concluded that, although the Internet is an excellent place for older adults to acquire information, the primary benefits of Internet use among older adults are social in nature.

The Internet may become the leisure activity of preference in the very near future for all age cohorts for very similar reasons. The Internet can be creative, interactive, comforting, and affordable. In addition, Internet use impacts many other forms of leisure activity. Time spent reading magazines, newspapers, and books increases with Internet use, whereas television watching decreases (Robinson & Godbey, 1999). A possible additional benefit from the increased participation of all age cohorts in the Internet is the forging of intergenerational communities (Ward & Smith, 1997). The Internet offers a relatively anonymous medium for interpersonal communication. The many initial stereotypes of age that may cause difficulties in intergenerational communication quite possibly can be thwarted by this use of technology (Williams & Nussbaum, 2001).

Homes with Internet access have also increased dramatically in recent years (Robinson et al., 2004). Close to 30% of U.S. households currently have Internet access (World Almanac, 2001). Fingerman et al. (in press) combined information from various databases and reported that Internet use does vary across age. Forty-two percent of individuals between ages 20 and 24, 38% of individuals aged 45 to 54 years, and 14% of individuals over age 65 report using the Internet frequently in their daily lives. Wright and Query (2004) suggested that people over the age of 50 have been identified as one of the fastest growing segments of the population who

are accessing the Internet. Psychological as well as sociological constraints
have had an effect on access to a personal computer and the Internet.
These constraints have made it difficult for the poor, the undereducated,
and the older members of our society to log on to the Internet. However,
these embarrassing trends are quickly being eliminated. We examine the
growing trend of older Americans using the Internet and characteristics
of older Internet users in chapter 12.

TRAVEL

Americans love to travel. When given the opportunity, Americans look
forward to visiting other regions of the country or the world. The travel
industry has become a multibillion-dollar business. Vacations (or holidays
as they are known in Europe) have become extended opportunities for individuals in Western societies to leave home and seek out a good time. The
tourism and leisure industry attempts to convince us to leave our comfortable homes and travel. An indication of how leisure is perceived differently by individuals across the life span can be reflected in the marketing
and advertising that flows from the tourism industry to specifically targeted
age groups.

Ylanne-McEwen (2000) investigated British tour operators selling
packaged holidays specifically to individuals over the age of 50. Holiday
brochures were collected over a period of 7 years to identify what aspects
of the holidays are foregrounded and whether common themes could
be identified, and to capture any age-salient images and identifications
present in terms of elderly lifestyles. The cover pictures and photographs
included in the brochures typically portray active "young-old" individuals.
"The overall image and a first impression of the brochures is lively; the
holidays appear to be aimed at healthy and active travelers who seek the
company of other people of a similar age and who enjoy group activities"
(Ylanne-McEwen, 2000, p. 85).

For the tour operators to be successful, they need to define precisely
whom they are targeting for these particular holiday excursions in the
brochures. Even though age is the most important categorization device,
specific mentions of chronological age are few and typically are found
only in the introductory remarks. The age-specific audience is identified
through photographs, age-identifying labels such as "retirees," or activities
that can be shared by individuals who are of a similar age and retirement
status. The theme of "communalism" is quite prevalent in these brochures,

for example, the travel experience will be a group experience in which activities are performed with others. Subtle hints that "new friends" can be made during these planned activities are particularly appealing to older age groups, especially to those older adults whose spouses have died and may need to feel included as they attempt to meet new friends.

These brochures also attempt to sell an experience that is both different and familiar. The travel and group activities will be unique and exciting, yet all the comforts of home will be provided. Even though one may be traveling to the Mediterranean coast of Spain, English newspapers, satellite television with familiar programming, and English-language videos are available. The brochures indicate that afternoon tea will be served and will be provided for free. This continuity of lifestyle, even on vacation in a foreign environment, is obviously thought to be important for this particular age group.

The overall effect of these brochures is that travel and leisure for older adults is an active, sociable experience filled with fun. This image of older adulthood is quite positive. On the other hand, the implicit segregation based on age can be troublesome. The brochures are communicating not only a holiday away from the mundane place in which you may exist, but also a holiday from others not in your age group who make your life uneventful.

The authors of this book have collected similar advertisements and brochures attempting to sell travel and adventure directed at a much younger population during the yearly tradition of spring break in America. These advertisements and brochures were collected at several universities located in the northeastern United States during the winter months of 2001–2002. In much the same manner as Ylanne-McEwen (2000) studied her brochures, we attempted to identify common themes and age-salient identifications present in terms of college-age lifestyles. Our purpose was to search for similarities and differences in travel advertising directed at the two age cohorts.

The target audiences for the spring break advertisements are young adults, aged 18 to 25, who are available to leave rather cold or routinely uninteresting lives for an inexpensive and unforgettable week of nonstop fun. The photographs accompanying the advertisements typically depict young adults in their bathing suits, uproarishly laughing, as they enjoy a group grope with a frosty beverage. Much in the same way that age is rarely mentioned in the brochures targeted for older adults, age is rarely mentioned in the advertisements directed toward younger, college-aged adults. As a matter of fact, when age is mentioned, it is typically contextualized by the legalities surrounding alcohol consumption. The age of the target audience, however, is made very clear by the photographs, the constant references to those needing to take a break from college, and the list of possible activities using labels that are clearly age-specific. Identifying activities as "booze cruises," wet-t-shirt contests, and toga parties are certainly meant to be inclusive as well as exclusive.

The communalism identified earlier as a significant trait of the brochures targeted toward older adults is also quite significant in the advertisements directed toward younger adults. No activity is meant to be accomplished alone. Activities that may best be experienced alone, such as para-sailing or bungy jumping, are described as a team event. Spring break is constructed as a communal activity to be enjoyed by groups of males and females conducting themselves as a minitribe for group enjoyment.

A major difference between the messages directed toward different aged leisure seekers is the home-away-from-home phenomenon. Spring break is not being sold as a unique experience with all the comforts and routines of home available. A very common phrase found in these advertisements is "what happens during spring break stays at spring break." We interpret this to mean that this particular leisure activity is unlike anything back home and is meant to be an adventure with no, or at the very least new, rules. In other words, afternoon tea will not be served. The lack of the continuity-uniqueness dynamic inherent in the brochures directed toward a younger audience is an indication of an age difference. Younger adults are not trying to find "home" in their leisure but are attempting to escape "home."

A final message communicated to the young spring break crowd that is similar to the messages directed toward older holiday-makers deals with finances. The spring breakers are offered very inexpensive rooms, free drinks, free activities, and the possibility of great prizes. Older adults and younger college students are likely at a time in their life that they must survive on a low, fixed income. Therefore, free drinks, cheap rooms, and the knowledge that it is appropriate to share expenses with others during this leisure time creates a more affordable and therefore doable travel experience.

The image of young adulthood presented in these spring break advertisements is active, interactive, fun, and excessive. The more outrageous, the more communal, and the more perfect the body one has, the more one will enjoy spring break. The enjoyment, however, is once again age segregated. Travel during spring break is an escape from intergenerational communication and a time to bond and play with one's own cohort.

EXERCISE

The majority of Americans do not participate in exercise as a consistent and regular component of their leisure activities. The Greek ideal of maintaining balance between physical and mental health has traditionally only been put into practice by young, rich men. Until very recently, most jobs in Western societies demanded hard-core physical labor. Whether the jobs were located in fields, factories, or at home, strenuous physical activity was a part of the job. Since World War I, however, strenuous physical activity has been removed from a large proportion of job tasks and careers. Forty years ago, President John Kennedy realized that Americans were not maintaining a significant level of physical activity in their lives. The President's Council on Physical Fitness was created to encourage school-aged children to participate in exercise and set minimal standards for fitness. The original school children who participated in these programs are now in their 50s and have contributed to an exercise revolution in this country.

The percentage of individuals who actively exercise remains surprisingly low. Singh (2002) reports that only 23% of adults living in the United States participate in light to moderate physical activity for 30 minutes at least 5 days per week. These activities include walking, swimming, cycling, dancing, gardening, yard work, and various other domestic activities. Sixteen percent of adult Americans participate in regular, vigorous physical activity that promotes cardiorespiratory fitness at least 3 times per week. Activities such as running, skating, cycling, lap swimming, hiking, and competitive group sports are examples of vigorous physical activities. Twenty-three percent of adult Americans live a sedentary lifestyle. These individuals are inactive, sitting most of the time. Singh (2002) reports that the most sedentary of all Americans are adults over the age of 65.

Numerous reasons explain why Americans do not participate in more exercise. First, women, older adults, poor people, and the undereducated have suffered from a cultural message not to exercise in this country. For instance, federal law has only sanctioned equal access to sports facilities and college scholarships for women since the 1970s. Second, exercise is not as enjoyable for some individuals as it is for others. If exercise is not fun, exercise will not become part of a lifestyle. Third, exercise often takes a significant amount of time and can be expensive. Although it is inexpensive to walk around the block, it can be expensive to join health clubs, play tennis, join a swimming pool, or participate in competitive team sports. Fourth, a significant disconnect continues to exist between the medical profession and the benefits of exercise across the life span. To this day,

physicians are not trained in the benefits of exercise and often do not rec-
ommend exercise (especially for older adults) for fear that it may do more
harm than good (Singh, 2002). Finally, the social benefits of exercise have
never been documented or related to the comparable physical benefits. Exercise has been advanced as a solitary activity rather than a group activity.
The positive results of exercise have always been studied in the individual
rather than among individuals.

Austad (1997) noted that life-long exercise is as natural and normal
as breathing. Hayflick (1994) reported that regular exercise can post-
pone or reduce the occurrence of heart attacks, angina, non-insulin dependent diabetes mellitus, osteoporosis, and hypertension, but "does not
slow or otherwise alter normal aging processes or increase human life span"
(p. 278). Research evidence does not support the notion that college athletes live longer than nonathletes; however, a study of Harvard graduates
who exercised regularly throughout their life span did outlive the Harvard graduates who were more sedentary (Hayflick, 1994). Singh (2002)
reported that a wealth of epidemiological data links exercise to health status and optimal aging. However, experimental studies with human subjects across the life span have not as yet been conducted to reinforce
the exercise–optimal aging link. Although scientific investigations appear to offer an overwhelming amount of evidence that a well-structured
and professionally supervised exercise regimen can increase the overall
quality of our lives, Damush, Stewart, Mills, King, and Ritter (1999) indicated that physicians are not likely to offer advice to exercise, especially to older adults or those who are not contemplating an increase in
physical activity, as an important component of a healthy lifestyle. Singh
(2002) recommends that all physicians be trained in the basics of exercise
prescription for health-related and quality-of-life benefits across the life
span.

Adolescents and young adults are surrounded by opportunities to participate in organized, well-supervised exercise. Federal and state laws man-
date physical activity in our schools. Colleges often have departments of
recreation sciences or kinesiology that offer legitimate course work in various exercise activities. Community centers, such as the Family Y, have
a long history of organizing physical activities for families. U.S. News &
World Report (2001, 2002) has recently discussed the rising trend of hospitals, retirement centers, and nursing homes constructing exercise centers for their older patients and clients. Hospital-based fitness centers have
been installing Cybex® and Nautilus® exercise equipment designed for
the older population. Our society is moving toward the creation of an environment that provides opportunities for exercise across the life span.

LEISURE AND LIFE-SPAN COMMUNICATION

Our discussion of media use, travel, and exercise provides ample evidence that individuals actively participate in leisure activities throughout the life span. The evidence also suggests that the amount of our leisure time and the activities we choose to participate in during that leisure time varies as a result of age, gender, income, education level, and desire. What is not at issue is the fact that leisure can be an important contributor to our quality of life.

The great majority of research that has examined the link between leisure activity and quality of life has concentrated on the physical benefits of being an active participant in leisure (Bernard & Phillipson, 1995). We believe that an additional significant benefit of leisure is the creation of an environment conducive to human interaction throughout the life span. Leisure is a major vehicle through which people come together to share life. The possible benefits provided by this opportunity to engage in communication with family members and friends in a voluntary, non-threatening social situation can be remarkable.

One of the great advantages and direct results of living in a highly industrialized, modern society is the increased leisure time made available to a large segment of the population. The time devoted to leisure is beginning to attract social scientists looking for social links directly or indirectly relating leisure, communication, and quality of life. Future investigations need to concentrate on what individuals discuss during their leisure activities and the relationships formed as a result of this communication. Travel is being sold as a time to participate in activities with others of your age cohort. The Internet has become a massive source of group talk. Living environments for college students and for retirees are building exercise facilities as a benefit of renting or buying. Leisure activities for every age group are being created around possible communicative opportunities. The positive and negative effects of the enhanced communication that occurs during our leisure times need to be addressed. Specifically, communication researchers need to study the intra-individual differences that exist across leisure activities with increasing age. As we age, will our leisure activities and the communication that takes place during these activities remain constant with similar benefits? Of more importance are the results of constructing leisure and participating in leisure activities that specifically segregate the ages and minimize intergenerational communication. Does our society, through the creation of age-segregated travel, exercise facilities, and mass media production, contribute to intergenerational harmony or flame the fires of intergenerational conflict?

SUMMARY

Leisure can be defined as any activity performed for enjoyment during un-obligated time. Healthy leisure includes activities that are active, creative, optimistic, and involve social relations. Individuals of every age can enjoy a large variety of leisure activities, many of which are constructed to max-imize the potential for human interaction. Media use varies across the life span and is discussed in more detail in the next two chapters, which also focus on aspects of media other than leisure. Two other significant leisure activities, travel and exercise, were discussed, focusing on the enjoyment derived by large numbers of individuals for various reasons across the life span. Our leisure activities have implications for communication and the quality of life across the life span.

11

Mass Media and Children

The mass media have a profound impact on individuals in the early stages of the life span. At a time when we are witnessing the rapid adoption of technology in almost every part of our lives, never before have children been exposed to more choices for receiving information. However, even in this age of the Internet, elaborate interactive video games, and other electronic media, television has remained the most influential medium on children. The average American 19-year-old will have spent more time watching television than most people spend at a full-time job in a year (Dworetzky, 1993). Despite the pervasiveness of television in society, researchers have found its impact on a child's development to be both negative and positive. Although television exposes children to many negative things, such as violent acts and unrealistic behaviors, it also teaches children important social norms, language and communication, and important information about the world. Less is known about the impact of newer electronic media, such as the Internet and video games, but it appears that the new media may also present problems as well as benefits for children (Van Evra, 1998).

This chapter explores the role of the mass media in the cognitive and behavioral development of children, giving special attention to the role of television and new technology. The chapter also focuses on the effect these media have on the everyday communication of children and how they may shape communicative practices throughout the life span.

DEVELOPMENTAL PROCESSES AND THE MEDIA

Attention to the mass media, comprehension of material, and retention of what has been seen or heard have been identified as important variables in the process of learning to use the mass media. The media can have little effect on children if they do not pay attention to the content; yet, because of the pervasiveness of the mass media in our society, they are difficult for most children to ignore. Communication researchers have explored the ways in which children learn to use the mass media, particularly television. Most of the research suggests that children are not passive consumers of the mass media, but they increase their attention based on features of the media and content as well as their ability to comprehend the content. Difficult content is usually associated with decreased attention among very young children, but as children's comprehension of content increases, they will pay more attention to it.

Both auditory and visual information are important in terms of attracting and retaining attention. Auditory and visual features of the media, such as the pace of the content, cuts, and sound, influence a child's attention. Younger children may be more influenced by animation, sound effects, repetition, and other features than are older children. As children age, they become more discerning about media content and are more active in terms of comprehending material. Older children do not have to devote as much attention as younger children to understand television programs and the content of other media. In addition, cognitive differences among children may also influence attention to the media and understanding of the material.

Development of Media Comprehension

Children have to learn to understand the mass media just like any other aspect of life. Because watching television, listening to the radio, and reading seem like commonplace activities for adults, it is easy to forget that children must learn how to use them. The content that children see or hear has to be assimilated into developing beliefs, attitudes, and other cognitive structures that are simultaneously being influenced by interactions with family members and other people, and information from other sensory experiences encountered on a daily basis. Researchers have identified a number of important changes that occur in children's comprehension of television and other mass media as they engage in cognitive development.

Early Interaction with Media. A child's understanding of the mass media begins at a surprisingly early age. Although infants pay attention mostly to images and sound as opposed to content, by the time children are between the ages of 2 and 5 years, they will learn to separate the main content of a television show from commercials and other aspects of the medium. Younger children often do not distinguish between television shows and commercials. Researchers have criticized advertisers who attempt to sell program-related products during children's television programs. Children often do not understand the persuasive elements of commercials or their true purpose, and many parents fear that the children's programs along with program-related toys may be a subtle way of influencing the child to buy products. Parents and other family members are an important influence in teaching the child how to distinguish between content and commercials.

Learning Order and Sequence. Between the ages of 6 and 11 years, children begin to learn about time order and sequence in television programs as production techniques. Children learn to distinguish between a program story that is taking place in the present time and a "flashback" to an earlier time in the story. They also begin to learn the production norms associated with television, such as cuts between scenes, camera angles, and the use of music. With the advent of video games and personal computers, children also learn about the sequencing of events. Most video games allow the player to advance to various levels of difficulty, and a child in this age group begins to understand that one level is different from another.

Computers and video games offer more sophisticated features than television and other media, such as more interaction between the person using the medium and the content. Children learn to control action figures in video games and to help guide them through various scenarios. Learning to negotiate these types of features may be more complex than learning the production characteristics of television. The Internet offers even greater interactivity, as well as features that are very different from video games and television. With the invention of Web browsers, children who have access to a computer learn about features such as "hyperlinks," that connect you almost instantly to web sites that may be halfway around the world on a different server. This technology offers different challenges in terms of learning event sequencing and time order. Unfortunately, researchers are only beginning to examine the effects of newer media on the development of children's understanding and media usage skills.

Ability to Distinguish Between Fantasy and Reality. By about 6 years of age, children learn to distinguish between what is possible on television and other media and what is possible in the real world. Prior to that time, children may have difficulty understanding why cartoon characters can be blown apart by a stick of dynamite in the beginning of the show, emerge unharmed, and return to survive multiple adversities. Because fantasy is a popular element in many children's programs, family members often have to devote time to clarifying misunderstandings and challenging what is possible only in the media.

Development of Memory and Media. Also around this time, up to about 11 years of age, children develop the ability to remember details about media content. This skill is important to learning to understand the media because situation comedies, dramas, and even news shows often require people to recall information from a previous episode to understand what is happening in the present. Younger children often have a difficult time remembering the details of what occurred in previous programs, but by the time they approach adolescence, they may remember the details of hundreds of television programs, movies, and other media.

Adult-Like Comprehension. Finally, by age 12, a child has typically developed the ability to comprehend media similar to an adult. When this type of understanding takes place, children can begin to appreciate the subtle humor that is often part of television sitcoms, such as *Friends* or *The Drew Carey Show*. In addition, they have a better understanding of the similarities and differences between what takes place in the real world and the media. Having had a myriad of interactions with family, peers, and educators by this time, a child also begins to have the maturity to understand most of the social issues that are referred to in entertainment programs or that are discussed in detail on news programs.

Mass Media and Socialization Processes

Much of what we know about the world and how to behave in it has been influenced by the mass media. Although our family and our peers also are strong social influences, what we learn from these sources interacts with the mass media to help socialize us in very complex ways. However, the process by which the mass media influence the socialization of a child is not well understood by communication researchers.

The mass media serve a number of important socialization functions for children. First, children learn at an early age that the mass media (particularly television) can be used simply to pass time or as background to other activities. They learn that television, video games, and other media are useful for occupying time and providing stimulation in times of boredom. Children also engage in other activities, such as playing with toys or games with other children, while the television set or other media are turned on in the background.

Children learn how to develop a parasocial relationship with media early in life. Many American families use television and other media as an electronic babysitter. Parents may use media to hold the attention of children while simultaneously freeing time to engage in other activities (ranging from housework to finding a free moment to relax). Anyone who has ever witnessed the demands a 2- or 3-year-old child can place on a parent's time can understand the tendency to use media as a babysitter. Media may serve an important companionship function for children who do not have siblings or when friends are not available. With the advent of the videocassette recorder (VCR), parents often create a library of children's videotapes for their kids to watch when television programming does not offer appropriate content.

As children learn to watch television and use other media, many important socializing functions take place. Through the media, children learn important information about themselves and how to interact with others. Although the process of socialization is complex and not fully understood by researchers, the media appear to have an important effect on the social development of children. Television in particular provides a storehouse of important information about people, world events, and how to communicate with others. Although many of the perceptions we form through our exposure to television are a skewed vision of the real world, we are able to vicariously experience many different aspects of life. Children in the same age cohort are often exposed to the same programs, and this serves as a starting point for conversations with peers as well as a way to identify with certain periods when growing up. Think about the television programs that you watched growing up. Other people from your same age group, provided they are from a similar social and cultural background, remember the same shows, characters, and possibly even the same dialogue. As you talk to people who are much older or younger than your age group, it is unlikely that they will remember the same things.

Children also learn important information about society through television advertising. Because children's programs are often accompanied by numerous advertisements marketed toward this particular age group, children see other children in the advertisements and learn a great deal about popular toys, clothing, and other products. This exposure increases their awareness of these products as well as information about day-to-day life. Although advertising plays an important role in the socialization process, many researchers have been concerned with the negative aspects of commercials.

Advertising shapes children's product preferences, and it may contribute to feelings of unhappiness if children are unable to purchase the products they encounter. Parents often complain about the demands a child may make on them after hearing about a product. This situation may be exacerbated if a child interacts with other children at school or in other social settings whose parents have purchased the item. Advertising can create other problems for children and parents. Many products, such as toys, are often depicted in unrealistic ways in commercials, and they often fail to live up to a child's expectations after they are purchased.

As mentioned earlier, a more recent trend in advertising is the practice of creating products that are characters in children's television programs, and children are encouraged to buy dolls, action figures, and other products related to the programming in commercials that are run at the same time as the children's show. Popular figures such as the "Teletubbies," the "Rugrats," or "Barney the Dinosaur" have numerous counterparts in the form of dolls and other character-related products in stores, and identification with these characters while watching television may influence children's desires to obtain one of these products when parents bring them to the marketplace.

Finally, the mass media serve other social functions for children. Watching television or playing video games is often a social event for children when they get together with their peers. The use of media stimulates interaction between children, increases interpersonal contact, and facilitates social learning. Children learn sex-role behaviors from the mass media, and they often imitate these behaviors in their daily interactions with others. Some researchers are concerned with learning sex roles in this manner because of the negative stereotypes of women that are often depicted in the media. Fortunately, children may counter sex-role stereotypes and other perceptions formed through the media by talking to others. As discussed in the next section, the interaction between family members and other children while using media can create a rich learning environment for the development of language and social skills.

The Influence of Mass Media on Language Development

Researchers debate the precise role the mass media has in influencing the development of language among children. However, some evidence suggests that the mass media has either a positive or a negative effect on the development of vocabulary and the use of language, depending on other factors. Most of the research on children and language has centered on the role of television viewing. Over the past few decades, there has been an increased interest in the effect of educational programming and its effect on language development.

Many researchers argue that television is an important source of new words for children. In addition, television programs often provide a chance to see how words are used in a variety of social contexts. For example, children have the opportunity to associate words with characters and specific contexts. Meanings of words are often depicted explicitly in a variety of programming, and features such as simple dialogue and redundancy may facilitate the learning process. In addition, the audio cues allow the child to witness how people apply paralinguistic cues (how a word is said rather than what is said) to certain words and how these cues subtly change the word's meaning. For example, consider the word "great." Depending on the context, different vocal inflections when saying this word can convey happiness ("Great, I just passed the test"), or sadness ("Great, I just lost my favorite sweater"). The ability of television to convey both audio and video cues allows children to hear and see how other nonverbal communication cues are associated with the use of language.

Other factors that need to be considered when assessing the effect of television on language development include the age of the child, the amount of time spent watching television, the linguistic complexity of the program content, and the presence of parents or siblings.

Developmental changes associated with age appear to mediate the influence of television on language development. Very young children may have only limited cognitive ability to understand vocabulary from television, although some children's television programs, such as the *Teletubbies*, have attempted to reach this younger audience. This type of program often uses very simple words and a great deal of repetition of words that may help very young children to acquire them. However, little research examines the impact of this type of programming on language development among this age group. As children grow older, language development occurs much more rapidly. Children between the ages of 3 and 5 years, for example, benefit in terms of language development from watching television programs such as *Sesame Street* more than younger children, because of the increase of language development from other sources (i.e., parents, siblings, and peers) during this period. Younger children may have more difficulty understanding the content, whereas older children typically develop more sophisticated vocabularies (and sophisticated tastes) that would make the content of programs like *Sesame Street* undesirable.

Researchers interested in the relationship between the amount of television viewing and language development have found that children with limited vocabulary and linguistic skills are often heavy television viewers. However, it is unknown whether children with more sophisticated vocabularies actually spend less time watching television or if they favor programs with more complex language, whereas those with limited skills favor programs with more simplistic language. In other words, programs with more sophisticated language may attract and benefit children who are able to understand the content, whereas children with limited language abilities may avoid this type of programming and subsequently miss out on opportunities to further develop skills. In short, it is evident from the research that variables in addition to the medium itself influence the language development of children.

Mediation Theory and Child Development

One variable that influences what children learn from watching television or using other media is the amount of family member (or other adult) interaction that takes place when they are using media, or *mediation*. In our society, watching television is typically a social function for families, and children have many opportunities to interact with parents and other family members while watching. While using media with others, children have an opportunity to ask questions about words, clarify misunderstandings, and receive detailed additional information about program content. This type of interaction may provide a rich and stimulating environment for children to develop and practice their language skills, learn prosocial behaviors, and comprehend mediated content.

Family members and others with the responsibility of caring for children often differ in the ways they interact with children while watching television or using other media with them. Nathanson (2001) contends that three broad patterns of mediation can be seen in how adults interact with children while watching television. First, *active mediation* refers to active discussion or guidance that occurs when viewing television with children. Active mediation can take the form of many behaviors, such as an adult pointing out good things that a character does on a television show, commenting that a television portrayal is realistic or unrealistic, or providing clarification or supplemental information for content that the child perceives as ambiguous.

Active mediation influences learning from television in a variety of ways. In some studies, children who engaged in active mediation with adults thought more critically about television, their understanding of content improved, and they were able to make better distinctions between reality and fantasy when viewing televised content. In addition, active mediation helps children to develop positive attitudes toward nontraditional sex roles, and it reduces negative emotional responses to frightening content on television and aggressive behavior after viewing acts of aggression or violence. However, the effects of active mediation are influenced by such factors as a child's ability to learn, mediation strategies, and the age of the child.

Restrictive mediation refers to rules that parents and other adults set about the amount of television a child watches, when a child watches television, and which types of content can be viewed (Nathanson, 2001). Families often dictate times of the day when a child is allowed to watch television or use other media, and most parents have rules regarding the type of content their children can view. Some studies find that children with parents who attempt restrictive mediation tend to be less affected by televised content, such as violence and advertisements, than children with parents who do not have rules regarding watching television. However, studies of restrictive mediation in general indicate that this form of mediation has a relatively weak relationship with outcomes. Restricting a child from watching certain content can "backfire" on parents because restricting the content can raise children's curiosity about it, and they may watch forbidden content when parents or other adults are not present.

Finally, *coviewing* refers to a type of mediation that involves children and parents viewing television together, but in an unstructured manner.

Unlike active mediation, coviewing occurs when adults are simply in the same room with children as they watch television. Little, if any, conversation about the televised content takes place when parents engage in coviewing. Researchers argue that because coviewing is more passive compared with other forms of mediation, it may reinforce some of the negative effects of television, such as acceptance of aggression and stereotypical views of individuals and situations. Coviewing occurs more frequently among lower income families and families who have a positive orientation toward television and tends to increase as the age of the child increases (Nathanson, 2001).

The Influence of New Media

Some evidence suggests that media other than television, such as personal computers and video games, involve interaction between the child and other family members. Interactive features of home computers, including communicating with others via the World Wide Web or submitting queries for information on search engines, provide additional opportunities for family members to interact with a child and aid in the language development process (Salomon, 1990). The complexity that often goes along with using new technologies may stimulate the need for more interaction between children, parents, and older siblings. Younger children may require extensive interaction to learn the technology, and, in some cases, a child may learn the technology better than the adults (you probably have heard of computer "whiz kids" in the news). This knowledge allows for an opportunity for children to practice their linguistic skills by explaining relatively complex information to others.

Less is known about the interaction between children and family members with other media such as video games. However, the advent of home video game systems, such as Sega Genesis, may provide children with more opportunities to interact with siblings and parents while learning and playing these games. In addition to some vocabulary that is present in more sophisticated games, children may also learn important knowledge about story sequencing and other features of this type of medium. These games have become increasingly popular, and playing video games is often more popular than watching television among today's youth (Funk, 1993).

However, studies of children's use of video games reveal several interesting findings that have both positive and negative implications for child development. In terms of positive aspects of video games, researchers find that video games can enhance visual spatial skills and promote certain prosocial behaviors, such as cooperation and sharing (Calvert, 1999), and some researchers have used video games to teach children positive health behaviors (Dorman, 1997). However, research on the effects of video games on children has generally demonstrated little empirical support for their positive influences and focused more on negative aspects. Studies examining negative effects of video games on children indicate that popular video games may promote stereotypical images of femininity and masculinity (Calvert, 1999; Dietz, 1998) and influence the development of competitive behavior. The interactive nature of these games, or the ability of children to be an active participant in the game, is thought to have negative effects on children when playing violent types of games (Dill & Dill, 1998) because children are more involved with the mediated characters compared with older media such as television.

VIOLENT CONTENT AND THE DEVELOPMENT OF AGGRESSIVE BEHAVIOR

In recent years, more and more attention has been given to the negative influences of television and other mass media on children, such as the relationships between violent content and aggressive behavior. The majority of this research has focused on violent material on television. Researchers estimate that most children will witness 8,000 murders and 100,000 other types of violent acts on television before finishing elementary school (Donnerstein, Slaby, & Eron, 1994). Some of the first images we see on television as children are violent acts, such as the abusive behaviors between characters in popular cartoons, and we continue to witness violence as our cognitive development takes place and our preferences shift to programs such as dramas and news programs. In addition, children witness a wide variety of violent behaviors while playing video games (where children practice interacting with violence). According to Funk (1993), in a study dealing with children's favorite video games, 50% of the games in this survey contained some form of violence against human or fantasy characters. Some studies found a relationship between aggressive behavior and playing violent video games (Silvern & Willimanson, 1987), but Sherry (2001), in a review of the body of research on video games and aggression, found that video games generally have a small effect on aggression compared with violence on television.

Given the astounding amount of violence we see, it is not surprising that parents, educators, and government officials have expressed great concern over the possible influence of the media on violent behaviors among children. In fact, mass communication researchers have examined the relationship between violent content and aggression more than any other topic concerning the mass media and children. Over the last decade, we have witnessed more and more violent crimes committed by children and young adults, such as the 1999 tragedy at Columbine High School in Littleton, Colorado, where two teenagers brought weapons to school and killed 12 students and 1 teacher, and wounded 23 other people. These unfortunate situations have fueled concerns over the pervasiveness of violence depicted in the mass media and its impact on children.

Environmental and Trait Influences on Aggressive Behavior

Although violent acts in the real world are often blamed on the influence of the mass media, the relationship between exposure to violent content and behavior is complex. As we have seen, parents and peers have considerable influence over viewing habits, processing of information from media sources, and reinforcement of behaviors learned from the media. In addition, researchers have found a number of intervening variables that mediate the relationship between violence and aggression.

For example, Van Erva (1998) identified a number of viewer variables that may influence the tendency toward violent behavior after being exposed to violent content. One variable is the cognitive and emotional maturity of the child. Younger children, for instance, may be more affected by the violence they see than older children because of factors such as their limited understanding of the consequences of violent behavior, their tendency to be more involved with the content, and misunderstandings over the justification for violent acts. As children get older, they are usually able to distance themselves more from media content, they become less emotionally involved with the violent material, and they are more inclined to see media violence as less realistic and less frightening. In addition, older children have more experience with the real world and more opportunities to check their perceptions of media violence against the opinions of relatives and peers.

Another variable is the intelligence level of the child. Some studies have supported the idea that children with lower IQ scores are more likely to be affected by violent material and engage in aggressive behaviors. Children who are more developed intellectually may have a more diverse understanding of the violence they see, and they may have a more complex repertoire of behaviors they can enact in response to the material. However, other studies have found only a limited relationship between intelligence and violent behaviors, and researchers suspect that environmental factors may play a larger role than intellectual ability.

Other viewer variables include the gender of the child, the child's arousal level when confronting violence, and initial levels of aggression. Some studies suggest that boys are more effected by violence, see it as more realistic, and prefer more violent programs than girls. Some children have a tendency to be more aroused by violence than others and may be more influenced by it. Moreover, younger children may exhibit more arousal over violent material than older children. Finally, some children may have a genetic predisposition toward aggressive behaviors, whereas others do not. Studies have found that children with the combination of high trait aggression and repeated exposure to violent content may be the most likely to engage in aggressive or violent behavior.

Environmental factors, such as differences in the violent content by itself and viewing habits, also impact the relationship between exposure and aggression. The realism of television violence is an important variable in terms of how children will respond to it. Some studies found that the more children perceive violent behaviors to be realistic, the more likely they are to engage in aggressive behaviors. A related problem is that younger children may perceive violence as more realistic than older children. Therefore, younger children may be affected by a wider variety of violent material than older children.

The amount of television viewing a child is allowed and family attitudes toward violence are also important environmental factors. Families who have fewer restrictions on the amount of television a child can watch may increase the amount and type of violence a child sees. In addition, parents and siblings who are more approving of violence on television may negatively affect the attitudes and behaviors of a child more than households where family members disapprove of violent material. In short, environmental factors may interact with trait characteristics of the child and produce either a child who copes with violent material well or a child who experiences problems with aggression and violence.

Theoretical Explanations for the Relationship Between Violent Content and Aggressive Behavior

Mass media researchers have offered a number of theoretical explanations that may help to explain the complex relationship between viewing violent material and aggressive behavior in children. Each theory provides at least a partial explanation for this relationship, but there are still many unexplored factors that may contribute to an increase in aggression in some children but not others. The theories listed in this section are among some of the most influential in terms of studying children and media. Related to our interest in developmental issues, most of the following theories assume that effects of media occur over a considerable amount of time, effects are tempered by a number of intervening variables, and behavior outcomes associated with media effects typically take many years to manifest themselves.

Social Learning Theory. One theory that suggests that children will model or imitate the aggressive behaviors they see is known as social learning theory (Bandura, 1967). Researchers using this theoretical framework identified a number of factors that may influence the tendency to model, such as whether the child's imitation of the aggressive behavior is rewarded or punished, the child feels the aggressive behavior appears to be justified, the social cues provoking the aggression in the media content are similar to the cues in the child's environment, and the child has a tendency to respond to social situations in an aggressive manner. If children live in an environment where family members and peers do not offer positive alternatives to dealing with interpersonal problems, and the children view a large amount of violent content, their primary source of how to deal with social problems may be what they see others do on television programs, video games, or other media. From a social learning perspective, children may benefit from being exposed to a number of examples of how to deal with problems through observing the positive interactions of others and by being taught alternatives by members of their social network. Other theories, such as script theory and cultivation theory, pose that the mass media may bias children's understanding of the world at a time when they are developing important beliefs and attitudes about how people behave in society.

Script Theory and Selective Perception. Scripts, or schemas as they are often called, can be explained as mental structures or templates that help guide our behaviors (Reed, 1988; Schank & Abelson, 1977). Scripts are useful to us because they help to reduce the cognitive effort we exert when performing daily activities. For example, when you go to the grocery store or drive your car, you rarely think about every small detail involved in these situations. If you did, you would most likely experience cognitive overload. If you remember back to the time when you first learned how to drive, all of the simultaneous procedures that are needed to operate a vehicle probably seemed overwhelming. However, as you gained more experience, you developed a script for this activity, and today it probably seems like "second nature" to drive to work or school. As our cognitive development takes place, we form numerous scripts about other activities, people, and events.

Although scripts can be altered, they are sometimes resistant to change, and people tend to rely on their scripts to guide their behavior in many situations. Many parents are not aware of how scripts develop or how they can potentially influence a child's behavior. In terms of media violence and aggression, children may develop scripts about dealing with social problems based on behaviors witnessed while viewing television, and they may learn to follow these scripts in their own lives (Huesmann & Miller, 1994). Obviously, children can learn more positive scripts for dealing with problems at an early age (especially through positive role models, such as parents, siblings, and peers), but some children, especially those who witness a substantial amount of aggressive content on television or through other media, can be at a higher risk for developing scripts that influence negative behaviors.

Scripts are far from powerful mental blueprints that strongly dictate behavior. Processes such as *selective perception*, or the tendency to pay attention to only certain types of stimuli or to process and remember information in ways that are consistent with preexisting attitudes, beliefs, and values, play an important role in the development of scripts and the ways in which they are altered. For example, children who are less aggressive may not be attracted to violent content in the same way aggressive children are, and this may influence whether or not a child pays attention to the content. Moreover, some children may interpret violent content as inappropriate, whereas others see it as a viable option. Other processes, such as the concept of mediation that we discussed earlier also influence script development.

Cultivation Theory. Cultivation theory is the idea that the reality portrayed in the mass media influences our perceptions of the real world. Gerbner, Gross, Morgan, and Signorelli (1986) developed cultivation theory when they began to notice that people who watched a lot of television in their studies often believed "facts" from the world of television about society rather than actual facts about issues such as violence, social groups, and day-to-day life. For example, when asked about the number of violent crimes in cities across the country, heavy television viewers were more likely than light viewers to overestimate statistics about the number of murders, rapes, and other violent crimes. Children who spend a great deal of their time watching television may develop a skewed perception of the world, and they may begin to believe that people are much more violent and aggressive than is really the case. Such perceptions may influence the tendency to respond to social situations in an aggressive manner or they may cause excessive fear or anxiety about interacting with others.

Desensitization Theory. Finally, many researchers suspect that violent content may have a desensitizing effect on children by promoting the idea that violence is a normal and acceptable way to react to problems in life (Sparks, 2002; Van der Voort, 1986). Given the number of violent acts a child can potentially witness through the mass media, it is not surprising that violence may come to be viewed as a commonplace activity by children over time. Even if a child does not engage in violent or aggressive behavior, there is concern among researchers studying desensitization that children might learn to become indifferent about violence or more accepting of inappropriate aggressive behavior toward other members of society later in life.

Uses and Gratifications Theory. Uses and gratifications theory (Katz, Blumler, & Gurevitch, 1974) assumes that individuals vary in terms of their motivations for using media, and the way in which they use media influences the effects media has on them. Unlike the other theoretical perspectives of media influence we have seen, uses and gratifications theory suggests that people use television and other media in a variety of ways to fulfill certain needs. The needs that are fulfilled by media depend on the specific desires and motives of each individual, but they include informational, aesthetic, and diversional needs. Children frequently use television for entertainment or educational content depending on their motives or the motives of their parents. For some children, the Internet may be an important educational tool, whereas for others it may be used only to play video games. As we have seen, television and other media have been linked to aggressive behavior in children, but according to Van Erva (1998), media can also have positive developmental influences on children, including the resolution of life-stage issues (such as adolescence) or they can provide learning opportunities or content for social interaction with other children.

SUMMARY

The mass media are an important influence on a child's cognitive and behavioral development, and they continue to influence our perceptions and communication throughout the life span. Never before in history have children been influenced by so many different types of media. The development of new technologies and the pervasiveness of older media, such as film and television, offer challenges to researchers interested in their effect on children. Violence in the various forms of media and its effect on aggressive behavior continues to be a chief concern for parents and social scientists. Children must learn to understand and develop the skills to interact with more and more sophisticated media, and there is a great need for research on the impact of these media on language development, understanding, and communication behaviors. In the future, we are sure to see more developments in mass media technology, and society will not cease to be fascinated by the influence of these media on human beings.

12

Mass Media and the Elderly

Older adults, like other age groups, spend a significant amount of their time using the mass media, including television, radio, magazines, newspapers, and books. The mass media are extremely influential in our society because of their popularity and cultural influence, and they can affect the amount of time people spend engaging in other activities, relationships, and perceptions of self and others. Like many other behaviors we have seen, mass media use patterns often develop at earlier points in the life span and can remain relatively consistent over time. However, life events, such as retirement, widowhood, and decreased mobility, may lead to an increased use of mass media by many older individuals. Unfortunately, the area of older adult media use has been relatively understudied compared with other areas of communication research. This chapter examines patterns of media use among older adults, representation and portrayals of older people in the media, use of the Internet by older individuals, and how older people use media from a uses and gratifications theory perspective.

OLDER ADULT USE OF TRADITIONAL MEDIA

Television

Television viewing typically increases with age in our society, despite relatively high levels of viewing at earlier points in the life span (Davis & Davis, 1985; Robinson & Skill, 1995). Individuals of differing ages consume media differently. Robinson et al. (2004) surveyed the existing literature on media consumption and concluded that older adults watch more television than any other age cohort, including children. Kubey (1980) provided evidence that viewing television is the highest for older adults who are widowed or retired. However, time spent watching television may vary, depending on the older individual. For example, Robinson et al. (2004) reported that television viewing varies by both age and gender. Women over the age of 55 report viewing the most television per week (up to 42 hours). Men between the ages of 18 and 24 report watching an average of 20 hours per week. Increases in television viewing among older adults may also be related to reallocation of time because of factors such as retirement rather than because of age itself. In addition, television is a popular medium among older people because of its capability of supporting both visual and audio channels, and the redundancy of information through these channels is thought to help older people gain a better understanding of content over purely audio or visual media (Roy & Harwood, 1997).

Over the past few decades, older adults tended to be less likely to subscribe to cable television or satellite television than younger people. However, the number of older individuals with cable and satellite television has increased in recent years because of the growing popularity of these technologies and the fact that many baby boomers, who tend to be heavier users of these services, are reaching age 65 and older.

Content preferences of older adults often differ from those of younger individuals, especially in terms of the tendency for older people to prefer information-oriented content over entertainment-oriented content (Robinson & Skill, 1995). Older people are also more likely than younger age groups to watch news, documentaries, and public affairs programming than other types of shows. Older adults tend to rate news and public affairs programming as their favorite type of television content. Older females tend to favor television dramas over older male viewers, and more affluent older adults prefer public television, cable news, and premium cable programming, whereas less affluent older adults watch more prime-time movies, reruns, and sporting events (Burnett, 1991).

Mares and Cantor (1992) found that subjects in their experiments preferred television programs with characters about their own age. Goodman (1990), using self-report measures, discovered that older age cohorts rated news programs and public affairs programming much higher than younger cohorts. The Simmons Market Research Bureau (1991) reported that older adults watched more syndicated quiz shows, more daytime quiz shows, and more general variety shows than younger cohorts. The younger cohorts reported watching more syndicated and prime time situation comedies, true crime shows, and police dramas than older cohorts. The top seven weekly television programs in 1997 reflected these age differences across television programming. For instance, the #1 most watched program for 18- to 34-year-olds in 1997 was *Seinfeld*. The #1 most watched program for adults over age 65 was *60 Minutes*. *Seinfeld* did not appear in the top seven rankings for older adults.

Current Trends in Television Programming.   Commercial television programming is largely geared toward younger audiences because of the belief that younger audiences will spend the most money on advertised goods, and despite its rapid growth and affluence, the older adult audience has been largely ignored by marketers and advertisers (Balazs, 1995). According to Grossman (1999), "any time of the day or night, virtually all there is to be seen are programs aimed at young people, ages eighteen to forty-nine, or even nineteen to thirty-five, the group that is most sought after because it is most prized by advertisers" (p. 232). Grossman (1999) goes on to say that this "accounts for the relentless sameness of commercial television, no matter how many channels there are" (p. 232).

However, this pattern of programming continues to hold true at a time in which younger audiences are shrinking while viewership among individuals aged 35 to 65 is increasing (Grossman, 1999; Roy & Harwood, 1997). However, over 76 million baby boomers, an age cohort who grew up watching television, are becoming older, and population growth among children and young adults is expected to stagnate in the United States in the coming decades. In addition, by the year 2005, half of the U. S. labor force will be over the age of 45, and the number of older consumers will expand. Older Americans currently purchase a substantial proportion of "big ticket" items, such as new cars and trucks, which have a major impact on the economy. According to Grossman (1999), "The demand for products

and services is being redefined by older people in every area, affecting the
nature of travel and leisure, education and jobs, entertainment, information and industry" (p. 237). These trends may lead to changes in the target audience for advertisers, and this change may lead to an increase in
the number of programs and advertisements featuring older individuals or
content that would appeal to this age group.

Radio

More than 99% of households in the United States have at least one radio,
and listening to the radio remains a relatively important activity for most
Americans despite the influence of other technologies. Most radio use occurs outside of the home, particularly while driving in the car, or at times
when people are engaged in another activity (e.g., housework). However,
radio use typically decreases as we age (Robinson et al., 2004), probably
because of the preponderance of youth-oriented programs, such as top-40
radio. For those older adults who do listen to the radio, the content that
they prefer listening to is as diverse as the older adult population itself.
However, Robinson et al. (2004) found that older adults prefer listening
to news/talk/sports, country music, nostalgia, and religious programming.
Younger adults are much more likely to listen to popular music (e.g., rap,
jazz, rock, or hip-hop). Some evidence suggests that more affluent older
adults are more likely to listen to easy listening programs, whereas less affluent older adults are more likely to listen to country and western music
and religious and sports programs (Burnett, 1991).

In addition, older adults are more likely than younger individuals to
listen to nostalgia radio programs, such as rebroadcasts of popular radio
shows from previous eras or recordings of big band music. Older adults
who are from the age cohort that grew up listening to radio programs in
the pretelevision era may have a certain affinity for radio and radio programming over age groups who did not have this experience.

Reading

Older adults read more newspapers than younger age cohorts, and, although the average age of newspaper subscribers continues to climb, fewer
younger individuals are in the habit of reading newspapers, which could be
because of factors such as the rise of cable television news and online news
sources. Sommerville (2001) reviewed a series of very large demographic

studies designed to trace newspaper reading across the life span. He concluded that older Americans spend more time reading newspapers each day than younger cohorts do. This trend appears to remain stable within each cohort. In other words, reading a newspaper each day of their lives since adulthood is a consistent pattern for older adults. Failing eyesight significantly cuts into newspaper readership for older adults past the age of 70. Younger cohorts, however, do not read newspapers and continue not to read newspapers as they age. The number of younger adults reading a daily newspaper is estimated to be as low as 30% of the total cohort, whereas, as much as 60% of the older adult cohort read a daily newspaper. The tendency to read newspapers is also influenced by socioeconomic status, particularly in terms of education and income level, and this may contribute to the variability of who reads newspapers among older adults.

Unlike newspapers, magazine readership tends to decline with age (Robinson & Skill, 1995). Grossman (1999) argues that magazines in our culture have a tendency to be youth-oriented, with the exception of magazines such as *Modern Maturity*, which is published by the American Association for Retired Persons (AARP). Similar to newspapers, magazine readership is influenced by education and income level. The type of magazines that older Americans subscribe to reflects the large number of women in this age cohort and the average increase in leisure time on retirement. For example, Robinson and Skill (1995) found that older individuals (aged 55 and older) are more likely to subscribe to magazines such as *Reader's Digest, TV Guide, Better Homes and Gardens*, and *Ladies Home Journal* than are younger people. Reading novels also show age differences across the life span. Older adults read more books, whereas adolescents and younger adults attend more movies (Nussbaum et al., 2000). These age trends in the consumption of mass media reflect inter-individual change. Because the studies reviewed were not longitudinal, intra-individual change was unexamined.

OLDER ADULTS AND INTERNET USE

Although the current number of seniors (aged 65 and older) using the Internet for interpersonal relationships represents a relatively small percentage of this segment of the population (about 5% of all Internet users), people over the age of 50 have been identified as one of the fastest growing segments of the population who are accessing the Internet. Moreover, the number of these individuals is projected to grow significantly over the next 5 to 10 years (National Telecommunications and Information Administration, 2000). Researchers predict that a so-called "gray tsunami" phenomenon will likely take place during this period, as younger cohorts, who are already using the Internet for interpersonal relationships, make the transition into older adulthood (Fox et al., 2001). Several arguments support this prediction. First, Internet users between the ages of 50 and 64 are currently one of the largest groups of individuals using this technology. However, because most surveys of Internet use define seniors as 65 and older, many of the statistics appear to be influenced by a cohort effect. The majority of individuals in recent surveys report being introduced to computer technology at work, and the Internet has only seen widespread use for about a decade (Fox et al., 2001). Many seniors who entered retirement in the late 1980s and early 1990s missed the rapid growth of the Internet in the workplace while they were actively involved in their careers.

Second, computer ownership among older adults has significantly increased in the past few years. According to a 1998 survey of older computer users, one fourth of the respondents mentioned that they had bought a computer within the last year, and 60% of the sample reported they used their computer on a daily basis (Charles Schwab, Inc., 1998). In addition, innovations such as *WebTV* allow older adults access to the Internet through their television (along with a Web browser program) without the need for them to purchase a computer.

Third, although some older people experience cognitive changes, such as a decline in working memory and a slower pace of processing information, older adults working with computers in a self-paced environment tend to have few problems learning how to use the Internet, and computer apprehension is not predictive of actual ability to learn how to use a computer (White et al., 1999). Moreover, learning to use Internet navigation programs is often easier for older adults than learning other types of computer programs and applications, and therefore may attract older adults to the Internet who are resistant to learning other aspects of computers (White et al., 1999).

Finally, because activities such as "surfing the Net" are social phenomena more ingrained into the popular culture and lifestyles of younger generations, and many older people are living on fixed incomes, it is not surprising that there are only a small number of seniors using computer-mediated communication. However, given the rapid growth of computer technology and numbers of baby boomers who will soon reach age 65, the upcoming cohort of seniors is expected to become the heaviest users of the Internet and computer-mediated communication (Fox et al., 2001).

Characteristics of Older Adult Internet Users

According to Fox et al. (2001), older adults who are currently using the Internet tend to be well educated, affluent, and male. Seventy-six percent of the seniors in the Fox et al. (2001) study had at least some college education, and one fourth of respondents had an annual household income of over $75,000. Adler (1996), in a survey of 700 older computer users, found that 7% of individuals with less than a high school education had a computer, whereas 53% of people with a college degree had a computer. In addition, Adler (1996) found that older men were more likely to use the Internet for communication than older women.

Although older men may have been the first to adopt the Internet, more recent data indicate that the number of older women using this technology may be increasing. More than half of all senior citizens who obtained access to the Internet from March 2000 to December 2000 were female (Goldman-Sachs, 1999). Moreover, in terms of all Internet users, women are more likely than men to search for health-related information, including the use of online support groups (Goldman-Sachs, 1999).

Senior Internet users tend to differ from their non-Internet using peers in other ways. Sixty-eight percent of current users say they would miss the Internet if they could no longer use it, whereas 81% of nonusers say they have no intention of going online. In addition, among nonusers, the oldest segments of the aging population appear to be the most resistant to adopting this technology (Fox et al., 2001). Older adults who are more experienced with the Internet are more likely than less experienced peers to engage in a variety of online activities, spend more time online each day, and have visited state, local, and federal Web sites (Fox et al., 2001).

Although seniors who currently use the Internet represent a relatively small share of users, they are more likely to spend time online each day, use the Internet for non–work-related purposes, and use this technology to maintain interpersonal relationships than other groups (Fox et al., 2001). In terms of specific uses of the Internet, the most popular activity among seniors is e-mail and using the Internet as a research tool (Charles Schwab, Inc., 1998; Fox et al., 2001). More than half of the seniors who use the Internet frequently access search engines for conducting online research on a variety of topics (Charles Schwab, Inc., 1998). The most popular activities, however, appear to be seeking information about hobbies, health, and news (Fox et al., 2001).

Online Communities for Older Adults

Although there have been relatively few studies of online communities specifically for older adults, several researchers have examined SeniorNet, one of the first online communities for this segment of the population (established in 1986). Furlong (1989) found that SeniorNet participants enjoyed "an opportunity to meet people with similar interests and to share not only information, but also communication on emotional and social issues that are particularly relevant to older adults" (p. 145). SeniorNet members also reported engaging in companionship relationships centered around mutually shared interests, including health-related issues.

A more recent SeniorNet member survey found that the majority of participants (1,001 respondents aged 50 and older) reported using the Internet primarily as a means to keep in touch with family and friends and to access information about various topics of interest. Most people said they used the Internet (including SeniorNet) between 10 and 19 hours a week and that most of the respondents were female (SeniorNet, 2000).

Ito, Adler, Linde, Mynatt, and O'Day (2001) examined the role Senior-Net plays in the everyday lives of older adults. Older adults reported that they used SeniorNet as a place for social interaction, gaining information, recreation, and entertainment. Wright (2000a) found that SeniorNet participants frequently promote the SeniorNet Web site as a useful source of social support in messages posted on a variety of discussion group bulletin boards. Many participants in SeniorNet groups reported that other group members served as "surrogate family," and that they found it easier to discuss some sensitive topics with their friends on SeniorNet than with close friends or family members. In a related study, Wright (2000b) found that SeniorNet members who spent more time communicating with others online were more satisfied with their online support network, whereas those individuals who spent less time communicating with others online were more satisfied with their face-to-face support network.

Although SeniorNet is one of the more popular Internet Web sites exclusively tailored for older adults, there are many other Web sites and Internet relay chat rooms available to seniors, including: Baby Boomer Bistro (http://www.babyboomerbistro.org.uk/), and the AARP Web site (http://www.aarp.org/), to name a few. These communities offer people access to large numbers of seniors who currently use the Internet. However, there are probably many older adults who are members of other types of online communities dealing with issues regarding almost every imaginable interest other than age-related concerns specifically. For example, most online newsgroup portals and health-related Web sites include a forum dealing with senior issues as well as topics that may attract people from multiple age groups.

MEDIA REPRESENTATION AND STEREOTYPES OF OLDER ADULTS

Representation of Older Individuals on Television

Older people generally tend to be underrepresented on television compared with the number of older adults in the current U.S. population. Robinson and Skill (1995) concluded "the elderly remain a relatively invisible generation on TV, comprising just 2.4% of all characters" (p. 383). If you watch many popular prime-time television shows, such as *Friends*, *Will & Grace*, and *E.R.*, you may have noticed that older individuals are almost nonexistent. In other programs, older people appear, but they are typically cast as supporting rather than main characters. Older characters are cast as main characters less than 10% of the time (Robinson & Skill, 1995). Some shows, such as *Fraiser* and *Everybody Loves Raymond* do have older characters playing relatively central, but supporting, roles, and these individuals are often the target of humor about aging or they are portrayed in stereotypical ways.

Researchers also found that older adults are generally underrepresented in television advertisements. Roy and Harwood (1997) found that older adults appeared in only 6.9% of a sample of almost 800 television commercials broadcast during a 6-week period on the three major networks during a time when older people represented almost 17% of the U.S. population. In addition, these researchers found that the television commercials were primarily targeted toward men, despite the fact older women greatly outnumber older men.

Older women are generally underrepresented on television, and studies have found that they are rarely cast into primary roles on television shows (Grossman, 1999). Decades of research on television have consistently found older men to outnumber older women on prime-time television (Greenberg, Korzenny, & Atkin, 1980; Northcott, 1975; Robinson & Skill, 1995), and in some cases, the number of older men appearing on television actually overrepresent the numbers of older men in the population (Robinson & Skill, 1995).

Older characters on television are not representative of the aging population in terms of race and socioeconomic status, and the majority of older characters tend to be White and relatively affluent. Robinson and Skill (1995), in a random sample of 100 prime-time programs, found that 88% of characters over the age of 65 were White, whereas other racial and ethnic groups appeared somewhat infrequently. Although nearly 12% of characters were African American in this study, only a few African American characters were female, and there were no elderly Hispanic characters. In terms of socioeconomic status, Robinson and Skill (1995) found that most characters aged 65 and older were depicted as upper middle class or higher, whereas only a small percentage were portrayed as working class or lower. In addition, older male characters were more likely to be portrayed as being financially successful than female characters.

Media Stereotypes of Older Adults

Media portrayals of older individuals have been found to be predominantly negative (Thomas & Wolfe, 1995). Older people are often presented as feeble, inept, declining in physical activity, and needing health aids, and they are placed in scenes involving little social interaction (Miller, Miller, McKibbin, & Pettys, 1999; Roberts & Zhou, 1997; Swayne & Greco, 1987). In this section, we examine some of the research on how older adults are portrayed in the media.

Studies of television content find that older individuals tend to be portrayed negatively on television (Swayne & Greco, 1987). Riggs (1998) painted a bleak picture of how television has dealt with older adults:

> Most often, though, elders are merely absent from television. NBC's "Must See TV"—prime time Thursdays—has overwhelmingly ignored older figures or at least made them the butt of humor. And although they are a substantial component of the news audience, elders receive scant attention on these programs. Much of the network news that mentions older people frames them as victims or dependents through stories about topics such as health or economic worries. (p. 8)

However, other studies provide evidence for positive representations of older individuals on television. Roy and Harwood (1997) found that older adults were presented in a predominantly positive light in a study of commercials on prime-time network television. According to this study, older adults were portrayed as strong, active, happy, and mentally lucid. Dail (1988) found that individuals on prime-time television aged 55 and older were portrayed more positively than individuals under the age of 55. Other studies have found that older individuals on television tend to be portrayed as powerful, affluent, and active physically, mentally, and socially (Bell, 1992; Robinson & Skill, 1995), although older men tend to be associated with affluence more than older women.

In short, the picture of how older individuals are portrayed on television is somewhat unclear. This disparity is largely because of the fact that most studies of older adults on television have used relatively small samples of television content in recent years, and analyzing the large number of television programs now available on network television and cable is difficult. In addition, television programs are constantly being added and dropped in an effort to win shares of viewers, and this dynamic presents a methodological challenge to communication researchers. Moreover, the fact that older individuals are underrepresented on television may say more about how we value older individuals in society than whether they are portrayed in a positive or negative manner.

Portrayals of the elderly in media may be influenced, in part, by the type of media in which the portrayal appears or the intended audience of the program or message. Roberts and Zhou (1997) found that advertisements in the AARP magazine *Modern Maturity* were predominantly positive. Unlike the majority of television programs and advertisements, older characters were portrayed as capable, important, healthy, and socially active. However, the advertisements were tailored mostly to White seniors, and other racial groups were generally underrepresented. In addition, older individuals were portrayed as spending a disproportionate amount of time at home or engaging in sedentary lifestyles.

Magazines tailored to a wider audience tend to be similar to television and other media in terms of presenting largely negative or unrealistic images of aging. Miller et al. (1999) found that older adults were portrayed both negatively and positively in a study of magazine advertisements over a 40-year period. In general, we typically have both positive and negative stereotypes of individuals in society, including older people (Hummert, Garstka, Shaner, & Strahm, 1994; Schmidt & Boland, 1986). For example, some common positive stereotypes of older people include the Golden Ager, Perfect Grandparent, and John Wayne Conservative. These stereotypes conjure up images of older individuals living out a leisure-filled existence, living for their grandchildren, and becoming more patriotic as they age. However, these positive stereotypes tend to be associated with inaccurate beliefs about older people, especially because people vary considerably in terms of the amount of leisure time they have, how they treat their grandchildren, and their political views. Both positive and negative stereotypes of older adults tend to be oversimplified generalizations that skew our perceptions of them and may influence the way we communicate with them (or the decision not to communicate with them).

Miller et al. (1999) found that positive and negative stereotypes of older people in magazine advertisements tended to correspond with whether the older individual in the advertisement looked relatively young or old. These authors found that negative stereotypes of older individuals being cognitively impaired tended to be associated with older-looking elderly individuals, whereas the Golden Ager and Perfect Grandparent stereotypes tended to be associated with younger-looking older adults. In addition, the study indicated that severe negative stereotypes of older individuals were not the norm in magazine advertisements. However, advertisements with the negative stereotype of older individuals having mild cognitive impairment have increased over the 40 years, whereas positive stereotypes have tended to decrease.

Violent Content and Its Effects on Older Adults

As we saw in chapter 11, there is a link between violent content on television and aggressive behavior in children. Television violence also affects the behavior of older adults. Nussbaum et al. (2000) reported that the heaviest viewing older Americans feel less safe and report inflated estimates of real-life violence than older Americans who spend much less time watching television. Watching violence in programs that are either news or fictional depictions of violence appears to be related to perceptions of living in a more dangerous world. This inflated sense of danger in the real world may prevent older adults from venturing far from their homes and engaging in interactive activities with the larger community.

OLDER ADULT MEDIA USE AND USES AND GRATIFICATIONS THEORY

One mass communication theory that is helpful in explaining some of the reasons people choose certain types of media content or why they prefer one medium over another is the uses and gratifications theory. This theory proposes that the effects of media are tempered by the ways in which people use them. Specifically, the theory posits that people actively choose certain types of media and media content to gratify various psychological and social needs or to accomplish certain goals (Katz et al., 1974). For example, people may use television in a variety of ways. Some people use television as their primary source of information about the world, whereas others may use it for entertainment or diversion from the realities of everyday life. For other individuals, radio and newspapers may be more important sources of news and information than television. Mass media fill other important functions, including providing us with content that we can talk about with members of our social network, fostering a sense of connection with others (or literally connecting us in the case of the Internet), and the ability to provide us with aesthetically pleasing experiences.

Reasons individuals choose one type of media over another or choose specific media content are as diverse as people themselves, but what we choose to view, read, and listen to mediates the influence of the mass media. For example, older individuals who prefer to read newspapers or get news information from the Internet rather than obtaining this information from television are probably less likely to see ageist commercials than are heavy television viewers. Older people who only watch documentaries on cable television or who listen to "oldies" programs on the radio may be less likely to notice the preponderance of youth-oriented programming that fills prime-time television and top-40 radio formats. Today people have more choices than ever over which media they use. VCR and digital video disc (DVD) players allow people to rent and own movies and television programs that reflect their specific interests, and these choices likely reduce the negative impact of specific ageist content. However, this is not to say that the media do not play an important role in terms of shaping perceptions of aging, and ageist content in the media may contribute to overall societal stereotypes of aging over time.

Needs of Older Adults Fulfilled by Mass Media

The mass media fulfill a number of different needs for older individuals. Like other age groups, older adults tend to be heterogeneous in terms of the reasons they use media. In many ways, older adults are similar to other age cohorts in terms of their motives for using media. The motivations older adults have for watching television has not been well investigated by mass communication scholars, although there is evidence that motivations for using television may change across the life span. For example, Nussbaum et al. (2000) and Robinson et al. (2004) surveyed the literature

and reported that all age cohorts over 18 years most often report watching television to be entertained, whereas older adults watch more news
and community affairs programming, thus indicating a motivation to be
current with world and local events. However, there is relatively little
research that specifically examines motivations for using television and
other media from a life-span perspective. This section discusses some of
the findings from research on the motives of older people for using television and related media from a uses and gratifications theory perspective.

Information-Seeking and Intellectual Stimulation. Media fulfill the need
for information about the world or specific interests. Given the rapid
changes we have experienced in society in recent years, with the advent
of terrorist attacks, quickly spreading diseases, and periods of economic
and social uncertainty, most people desire up-to-date news and accurate
information about these events. The mass media help to fulfill our desire
to reduce uncertainty about our world by gathering information that will
help us to make better choices over how we should respond to daily events.
Older adults are similar to other age groups in terms of their desire to gather
information, and they often use the media to keep up with current events.
In addition, older adults rely on media advertisements for product-related
information (Roy & Harwood, 1997).

Older adults also use the media for intellectual stimulation and personal
growth (Bleise, 1986). All human beings need intellectual stimulation or
else we quickly become bored, and we often turn to the media to fulfill
these needs. Life events, such as retirement, can lead to an increase in
leisure time, and older people may find themselves with more hours in
the day in which they desire new forms of mental stimulation. Although
many of us dislike being at work, jobs can provide us with many mental
challenges and intellectual stimulation. Older individuals who are retired
often use the media to keep themselves mentally active. Staying mentally
active as an older adult is thought to promote good mental health and may
reduce the risk for some types of degenerative cognitive impairment. In
fact, studies indicate that cognitive decline is not inevitable as we age, and
life-long learning is important to cognitive maintenance and development
as we become older (Schaie, 1990).

News programs, documentaries, books, magazines, and the Internet can
also provide older individuals with opportunities to learn new information
and to learn new skills. Acquiring new knowledge and skills can be intellectually challenging for older people, but it can lead to personal growth
and a sense of accomplishment. The media provide multiple opportunities

for learning, including distance education programs offered by universities through cable television, self-paced reading materials, and the Internet.

Media Use and Effects on Interpersonal Relationships.   Watching television may provide content for future face-to-face interactions. Individuals discuss the latest *Friends* episode or the latest political scandal as reported on the numerous all-news channels when they meet in various social activities. Television can be used as a vehicle to bring individuals together as well. Super Bowl parties or *Survivor*-watching parties serve as a vehicle to entertain a social gathering. Television and other mass media provide people with the substance for conversations with members of their social network.

Stories from news programs and the lives of characters on entertainment programs, such as dramas and situation comedies, give older people things to talk about when interacting with friends and family. Being up to date on current news stories, the latest developments in the lives of television characters, or information about technology and other current trends based on books and magazines may fulfill what Katz, Gurevitch, and Hass (1973) referred to as a *personal integrative function*. The personal integrative function of media occurs when our knowledge about the world that we gain from the media, knowledge of current events, or happenings in the lives of media characters helps to enhance our credibility and status in conversations with others. For example, you may have experienced a situation when you perceived a friend to be more knowledgeable or interpersonally attractive if he or she was up to date on current world events or the latest episode of *The Sopranos.* Older people who demonstrate knowledge of current events or the latest popular culture trends that they learn through the media may be perceived more positively by individuals from younger age groups. The media can help older individuals keep up with an ever-changing society. In short, the mass media give older people things to talk about with their peers and other members of their social network.

The mass media also affect interpersonal relationships by providing a venue for social comparison with others. Characters on television often serve as role models for the ways older individuals are expected to behave in their day-to-day interactions. According to social comparison theory (Festinger, 1957), individuals compare themselves with other individuals in society and make a variety of judgments about their own lives, such as their abilities, opinions, and behaviors. When comparing ourselves with others, we can make a variety of judgments about ourselves. For example, sometimes we make *lateral comparisons,* in which we view others as being similar to ourselves. At other times, we may make *downward comparisons*, in which we view ourselves as functioning better than the person with whom we are comparing ourselves, or we engage in *upward comparisons*, in which we view others as doing better than us. A downward comparison can make people feel better about themselves, such as when older people who are physically active view a television show in which elderly characters are confined to a nursing home, and they feel more fortunate by comparison. Also, watching the monumental problems that people have on shows like *Jerry Springer* can make people feel better about relatively minor concerns they may be facing. Conversely, an upward comparison can make people feel worse about their situation. For example, if older individuals have limited financial means or are socially isolated, they might become depressed when viewing television shows in which elderly characters are affluent and have many family members or friends. In our youth-oriented culture, older people may be negatively affected if they perceive that they are unhealthy or unattractive by comparison to youthful characters in the media. Mares and Cantor (1992) found that older television viewers prefer watching programs with characters similar in age to themselves, and older people appear to use the mass media to learn age-appropriate behaviors as well as appropriate behaviors for other groups in society (Bleise, 1986).

Finally, as we have seen elsewhere in this book, interpersonal relationships are good for us in terms of promoting mental and physical health as well as quality of life. New technologies, such as the Internet, may enhance connections with family and friends, and they can be an important means for supplementing social networks and acquiring social support. Older individuals with disabilities or mobility problems may feel cut off from others, and the Internet can provide a means for keeping in touch with others (White et al., 1999).

Media as a Substitute for Interpersonal Relationships. Television and other mass media are important in terms of helping older individuals feel a sense of connection with the world. Although many people remain socially involved as they grow older, there is a tendency for individuals to reduce the number of people in their social network following events such as retirement or if they become less mobile (and unable to engage in as many social activities) because of physical problems (e.g., hip replacements). Also, living on a fixed income may force some seniors to forego more expensive social activities (e.g., vacations) where they might have the opportunity to meet others. Traditional media, such as television and radio, may serve as a window to the outside world for older people who have limited social networks. These media can provide comfort for older people, even if it just helps them to see that there are other people in society who experience similar feelings, interests, and values.

In addition, researchers have argued that *parasocial relationships*, or imagined relationships with familiar characters on television, may partially compensate for the decline in relational networks for many older adults (Nussbaum et al., 2000), and they can provide a means by which older adults can remain engaged with society. For example, older people might develop imaginary relationships with characters from their favorite television shows, or at least identify or feel comforted when watching or listening to television or radio. Media personalities often provide people with a sense of familiarity and stability, and often, unlike members of a person's real social network, they are dependable because they are consistently there for people on a daily or weekly basis. Media such as television can also provide a sense of connection with others despite the fact that we are not truly interacting with others. Perhaps you have had the experience of being by yourself at night and turning on the television or hearing another person's voice on the radio, which helped you feel better about being alone or more secure. This feeling gives you a sense of how parasocial relationships can affect us.

Convenience. New technologies, such as the Internet, have the advantage of conveniently increasing levels of interaction among people in an older person's social network because they can connect older people to relatives and friends who are geographically dispersed via e-mail and Web chat applications (White et al., 1999). E-mail attachments allow grandparents to conveniently see pictures of grandchildren or other aspects of family life when families live across the country. In addition, online communities can provide older individuals with a common site where they can frequently and easily interact with other people. Television and other broadcast media also fulfill convenience needs because news and information can be acquired quickly and easily through programs such as *CNN Headline News* (as opposed to reading *Time* magazine). Entertainment on television is cheaper and easier than going to the movies or leaving the house to find other forms of entertainment.

Affective Needs, Diversion, and Tension Release. The media also provide us with content that can help us fulfill various affective needs. Similar to intellectual stimulation, we also desire emotional stimulation as human beings, including the need to appreciate aesthetic, emotional, and pleasant experiences. The media provide us with entertainment that makes us laugh, frightens us, and makes us happy or sad. Books, magazines, television, and movies provide us with actual or imaginary images of beautiful places or exciting people. Listening to the radio or compact discs (CDs) can elevate our mood or inspire us as we go about our daily lives. If we fail to fulfill emotional needs, our lives can become as boring or stagnant as when we ignore our needs for intellectual stimulation. Reduced social networks among older individuals can affect opportunities for emotional stimulation, and the media can provide emotionally fulfilling content.

Related to aesthetic and general emotional stimulation needs are the needs for diversion and tension release. The difficulties of life often lead to stress, and the media can fulfill diversion needs by helping us to shift our attention elsewhere or by providing us with opportunities to release tension. Certainly, you have used the media at some point in your life to help you laugh when you were feeling down or to keep your mind occupied with something besides thinking about some stressful situation that you were facing. Older adults are similar to other age groups in terms of their needs for tension release and diversion. Older people who may be confined to a nursing home or who are socially isolated may have greater needs for tension release and diversion than people who are more socially active, and this may lead to greater use of the mass media.

Connection to parasocial

SUMMARY

Older adults generally use the mass media in ways similar to other age groups, yet some age-related patterns of use have been identified. Gender and socioeconomic differences among older adults appear to be more influential over media use than age. Older adults tend to be underrepresented in the mass media, and although they are not necessarily portrayed in a negative light, older people tend to be presented in stereotypical ways in media content. With the advent of the Internet, older adults tend to lag behind other age groups in terms of their use of new technologies, yet age in itself does not appear to inhibit the adoption of these technologies and the number of older people using the Internet is expected to grow exponentially in the coming years. Finally, older individuals use media to fulfill a variety of needs, including for intellectual stimulation, to supplement interpersonal relationships, and for emotional stimulation and diversion.

VI

Summary: Implications of Life-Span Communication

13

Life-Span Communication: Implications and Issues for Research

In the first chapter of this book, we reviewed the basic assertions of life-span development and set forth several propositions for the application of the life-span perspective to communication. In the bulk of this text, we reviewed the nature of communication from a life-span perspective, first laying the foundation for communication through cognitive processing and language development, then examining the role of communication in our social worlds and a number of communicative competencies, followed by the impact of the media and leisure activities. In this chapter, we return to the basic assertions and propositions of the life-span perspective of communication, then discuss the implications of this perspective for understanding and investigating communication throughout the entirety of our lives.

THE LIFE-SPAN PERSPECTIVE

The first chapter outlined the life-span perspective as initially developed in psychology and sociology. This perspective assumes that people

continue to develop in their cognitive and social abilities across their entire lives, even though the rates of development may vary from time to
time and certain developmental tasks may be closely linked to particular
periods of life. One of the most important aspects of this view of human
behavior is that important and interesting events occur throughout the entirety of our lives. In the life-span perspective, then, life is always changing
and offers continuing possibilities for growth as well as inevitable declines.

Now that a number of aspects of communication from the life-span perspective have been reviewed, the assertions of the life-span perspective
that were laid out in the first chapter may have a deeper meaning for you.
Once again, the assertions were:

- positive development occurs throughout the life span,
- diversity and pluralism occur in the changes throughout life,
- development is best viewed as a gain–loss dynamic,
- inter- and intra-individual diversity exists as we progress through the
  life span, and
- a person–environment interaction cannot be ignored in our explanations of development.

The first assertion focuses on the misconception that maturation is only
a physical process. When the physical aspects of maturation are the focus,
then aging may be seen as inevitable decline, although, as we have seen, a
significant proportion of our physical abilities, such as cognitive processing, do not decline in meaningful ways until very old age or until poor
health occurs. Humans, however, are social creatures and maturation also
involves socioemotional elements. Our socioemotional development can
and does continue throughout the life span. Life experiences and events
help us build on our repertoire of communicative resources so that we have
the capacity to successfully manage our relationships, successfully access
our support networks, and enjoy our leisure activities in ways that add to
our overall quality of life.

The second assertion claims that all aspects of development do not occur in sync with one another so that we may experience declines in one
area while also experiencing increases in others. For example, hearing loss
may make it difficult to hear conversations; however, our understanding
of the structure of conversations may make it possible to "fill in" what
we are missing and successfully manage conversations, even when we do
not hear everything that is being said. Cognitive processing declines and
word-finding difficulties may make conversation difficult, but our adaptive

abilities help us to find alternative strategies for managing conversations and maintaining relationships at the levels with which we are most comfortable.

The third assertion focuses on the nature of gains and losses across the life span. As mentioned previously, some physical and cognitive abilities can and do decline with age; however, other abilities continue to increase. A common example relates to the ability to access our support network to help ameliorate physical declines. For example, older people may have difficulty driving. If they have developed successful relationships with others, they can tap into that network to help provide transportation to go shopping or to doctor's appointments. Our ability to successfully adapt to changing life events requires a willingness to ask for support, the competency to construct helping messages, and having individuals in our lives who will respond to those requests. As we have seen in earlier chapters, our ability to become more competent as a relational partner as we age is an important aspect of development. Clearly, communication plays a central role in our ability to maintain stability across numerous areas of decline and to accentuate the areas of positive growth across the life span.

The fourth assertion claims that maturation is a complex process with considerable variability within and between individuals. This aspect of change is particularly reflective of the social nature of humans. Within individuals, changes occur as they age. The meanings assigned to those changes may be altered over time as new events alter the interpretation of prior events. Thus, an individual may have different expectations on entering a second marriage when compared with the expectations of a first marriage, and events in the first marriage may take on new meanings based on events in the second marriage.

Although the differences within individuals are important and deserve study, the differences among individuals may be even greater. For example, the experience of marriage may be quite different depending on when a person gets married, who his or her partner is, the quality of their relationship, and the changes that occur within their relationship, their larger social network, and the cultural milieu of their times. One problem that occurs in the research is that the differences found between individuals of differing ages are usually attributed to age. These differences, however, may reflect differences in cohorts who grew up in different historical contexts and related expectations that are not inherently reflective of age differences.

The fifth assertion focuses on the interaction between people and their environment. Our environment is not limited to the physical aspects of our world but also consists of our social environment. Therefore, when examining communicative processes and the mutual influence of the individual and the environment, we must incorporate individual influences, such as cognition, social cognition, language, communication skills, and environmental influences, such as culture, existing relationships, and the physical environment. The social aspects of our environment create a need to examine the meanings that individuals and their social networks assign to life events, including the timing and sequencing of these events. Many life events are considered to have "normative" periods for their occurrence. For example, becoming a widow or having a heart attack is assigned different meanings when the individual concerned is 25 compared with 65 years old. The sequencing of events may also impact the meanings that are assigned. For example, if an ex-husband dies, most people would find it odd that an ex-wife would label herself as a widow, especially if they have been divorced for a number of years. The assumption is that a widow is created when a spouse dies, not when an ex-spouse dies. These issues remind us that humans are active organisms, making sense of the world around them and making choices about plans of action, and that the meanings assigned to events are affected by our prior history and our plans for the future.

Although some environmental constraints cannot be controlled as we age, we have more influence on our environment, including our physical environment, than is commonly believed. Our genetic makeup is impacted by our environment and our genes interact with one another in complex ways across the life span. In addition, our behaviors may impact which genes are activated or suppressed at different points in the life span. Psychologists and sociologists have long pointed to the environment, especially our culture, historical times, and social networks, as having a significant effect on our perceptions and behavior. These environmental influences are often not predictable nor do they affect each of us in the same way. Our environment consists of changing, dynamic patterns of interaction that occur in our families as new brothers or sisters are added to the mix or in our social networks as friendships are developed or changed. The direction and intensity of our numerous relationships are far from linear and predictable as we progress throughout our lives. Although this complexity may seemingly make any complete understanding of communication impossible, an understanding of the diversity inherent in development should help us to capture the reality of our interactive lives and the meanings people assign to their life experiences.

In summary, the life-span perspective claims that change should be viewed as a constant in our lives and as a factor that must be traced across time. Development occurs at any point in our life span; however, the rate of change may vary, but is certainly not limited to the first few years of our existence. Gains and losses in various human abilities occur throughout our life spans with a remarkable amount of variability both within and among individuals. The changes that we experience do not occur in a linear fashion, but are highly complex. Differences found between cohorts of different aged individuals should not be automatically attributed to age. Finally, the interaction between the person and the environment must be accounted for in any developmental explanation of human perception and behavior.

LIFE-SPAN COMMUNICATION

With the only constant in our lives being change, our ability to cope with and manage those changes reflects our ability to learn from and adapt to experiences. Life is always changing and offers continuing possibilities for growth. This growth occurs through communicative processes as we have external dialogues with others or have internal dialogues with ourselves. Because communication is a complex process, when studying communication we must account for a number of important individual (e.g., intelligence, memory, age, gender) and social (e.g., language, culture, historical period) variables. Before discussing these complexities in detail, remember the propositions from the first chapter regarding life-span communication:

- the nature of communication is fundamentally developmental,
- a complete understanding of human communication is dependent on multiple levels of knowledge that occur simultaneously,
- change can be quantitative and qualitative,
- life-span communication scholars and students can incorporate all current theories of communication into this perspective as long as the theories are testable and the results are useful, and
- unique methodologies are required to capture communication change across the life span.

The first proposition, that the nature of human communication is fundamentally developmental, implies that communication is not a static event, but part of an ongoing flow of events. In a particular interaction, time is needed for communication to be developed, transmitted, interpreted, reflected on, and responded to. However, even with the element of time within an interaction, this particular event is also influenced by the individual and relational history of the participants, including their cultural and historical settings. Thus, in the life-span communication perspective, communication is viewed as a flow of events and is not static. Communication is action, not a stagnant object.

Thinking of communication as developmental implies that communicative events are continuously unfolding and impacted by a wide range of individual characteristics and factors as well as the previous experiences of those involved in the event. Therefore, a competent communicator must be able to not only adapt during an interaction, but to adapt to changing interactive experiences across the life span. What is considered to be appropriate and effective communication at one age or in one situation may not be considered to be so at another age or in another situation. An individual's capacity to communicate must continuously develop for that individual to master his or her environment and to interact effectively throughout the transitions, adaptations and new challenges that arise over the life span.

This dynamic view of communication requires attention to numerous influences on any communicative event. For example, understanding interpersonal conflict requires that we examine how individuals change strategies during any given conflict episode, their preferences for conflict strategies, their past history together and in other relationships, the cultural and social expectations for conflict behaviors, and many other influences. Even after attending to all these factors, we must remember that what these individuals do in any given conflict episode is not likely to be repeated when they are interacting with other individuals in other settings or in the future when their own relationship may have changed in ways that makes the current behaviors ineffective.

The second proposition focuses on the multiple levels of knowledge that occur simultaneously during communication. The view that life-span communication is multilayered draws attention to the many influences that exist in any message exchange. Although the individual is, at a minimum, coordinating cognitive processes, language skills, and interpersonal skills, the interaction is influenced by the participants' individual characteristics, their relational history, and social and cultural characteristics that dictate expectations for appropriate behavior. Therefore, thinking of communication as developmental and multilayered implies that communicative events are continuously unfolding and impacted by a wide range individual characteristics and factors as well as the previous experiences of those involved in the event. Because change is constant, competent communicators must be able to adapt to the changing demands of life to manage their changing roles and identities. Pressures to change may occur on a number of levels, and these levels interact with each other. For example, becoming a parent for the first time requires the acquisition of considerable knowledge, but key aspects of that knowledge change with the child's maturation. Raising a 2-year-old competently is different from raising a 12-year-old. Becoming a parent inevitably affects the parent's other roles, such as spouse, friend, and worker. In addition to these individual and relational changes, what society defines as a fit parent changes over time, and parents may have to reevaluate their actions based on these changing expectations. Life-span communication, then, is a dynamic process. What we say affects what happens and what happens affects what we say. What we say and what happens mutually influence each other as meanings are assigned, discussed, and, potentially, reevaluated over time.

The third proposition, that change can be quantitative and qualitative, focuses on the nature of change. Although we may be able to rather objectively measure changes in behavior, the meanings assigned to those changes are more difficult to capture with quantitative measures. The experience of change is not necessarily a linear process. The pressures leading to a change may build for some time or may occur relatively quickly, but we can often point to a "breaking point" when "things changed." In physics, measuring the tensile strength of a material can be graphed as a curvilinear process in which the material becomes more and more stressed until it fails. The material has very different qualities before and after reaching that breaking point. Complexity and chaos theory discuss a similar process and point to bifurcation points as the moments when systems undergoing stress move from one state to another state. In family communication and therapy, we often discuss family stress in similar terms, talking about the pressures on families that build until a crisis point in reached. When the pressures build to such a point, some event must occur (e.g., a violent episode or a decision to separate or divorce) to relieve the pressure, and then the family must develop a new definition of itself in its new situation.

The same change may have qualitative and quantitative aspects. For example, when an individual is sick, physicians can run tests and point to numbers that indicate a healthy or ill status, but for the patient, the nature of being healthy one day and sick the next is difficult to capture as quantitative change. The meanings that are assigned are reflective of a more qualitative kind of change, a change of kind rather than degree.

What it means to me to have arthritis and the impact it has on my view of my self in an aging body is as, or more, important as any objective measure of the level of pain or decrease in flexibility that I experience.

The fourth proposition claims that we can incorporate all current theories of communication into the life-span perspective. This proposition seeks to be inclusive rather than exclusive by acknowledging the dynamics of change in any theory about communication. Several theoretical paradigms have provided the basis for communication theories. Whatever tradition has provided the foundations, whether scientific, interpretive, or critical, each theory has helped to build our knowledge base concerning human communication. However, much of the research that has been conducted to test a theory or that has used a theory to frame the interpretation of data has relied on limited samples over limited time frames. A particular problem in quantitative studies has been the collection of data from college sophomores. Although the perspectives and behaviors of college sophomores are not unimportant, these findings do not necessarily generalize to individuals of other ages with a different educational status. The implications of this proposition are discussed in more detail in the next section as examples of communication theories are reviewed and extended by the life-span communication perspective.

The fifth proposition claims that unique research methodologies are required to capture the nature of change across the life span. The study of communication change across the life span necessitates an understanding of research methodology that enables the observation of that change. Because communication is influenced by a number of levels and factors, life-span communication scholars who are searching for change across time need to look for their explanations of change in numerous places simultaneously, including interactions among the various levels of influence. At least since the 1970s, considerable research in interpersonal communication has been conducted from a scientific perspective using experimental methods. One of the hallmarks of good experimental design is controlling for influences through design or statistical methods. Any attempt to control all confounding variables is doomed to fail and misses the interaction among levels of influence. We are not saying that experimental methods are not useful for communication research. This research has provided many insights into the communicative process. We do want to make it clear, however, that life-span communication scholars need to be aware of the multiple influences that affect each communicative act and to be prepared to expand their investigations to capture all possible contributors to change. Because of the numerous factors that impact the study of communication across the life span, we discuss these issues in more detail in a later section of this chapter.

In summary, the life-span communication perspective views communication as a complex process in which the nature of change plays an influential role, with humans continuing to develop throughout their lives. Understanding human communication requires an understanding of the multiple levels that influence that activity as well as how the different levels influence each other. Although change is constant, change is not a linear process and has both quantitative and qualitative elements. By taking a life-span communication perspective, we can incorporate communication theories into this perspective, extending our understanding of communication in the process. To accomplish the goal of understanding communication from the life-span perspective, we must design studies that allow us to capture the nature of that change.

Hopefully, this review of the life-span perspective and its application to communication has reinforced the arguments that we made in the first chapter. After reading the intervening chapters, you should have a greater understanding of how this perspective helps to extend our understanding of the dynamic nature of communication across the life span.

INCORPORATING THE LIFE-SPAN PERSPECTIVE INTO COMMUNICATION THEORIES

Different theoretical paradigms have different goals for theories and the research derived from that paradigm. The scientific paradigm assumes that there is one truth "out there," and the goal of research is to discover that truth. The interpretive paradigm reflects a range of theoretical perspectives, but each one assumes that humans may interpret the same experience in many different ways, and the goal of research is to discover the meanings of events as people experience them as well as the factors that influence differences in experiences. Critical theories assume that power dynamics drive human interaction, and the goal of research is to reveal the use of power to control others. The life-span communication perspective, which is a systems-based approach, can incorporate any of these paradigms into its search for greater understanding about human behavior across the life span.

Interpersonal communication research conducted over the last 40 years or so has largely been based in theories that are derived from a scientific perspective, with rigorous requirements for design and assumptions about generalizing findings from a study to an entire population. The charge we made earlier that research conducted with college sophomores as participants should not be generalized across the life span is directed primarily at scientific research projects because of the consequences of that generalization. Just because a study provides us with some understanding of the communicative behaviors of one group included in that study does not necessarily mean that individuals with different characteristics would behave in the same way. Generalizability is always at issue and must be considered seriously. Theories developed from the scientific paradigm can benefit greatly by applying the life-span communication perspective so that issues of change over time can be incorporated into these theories. The nature of interpretive and critical theories requires less "effort" for incorporating the life-span communication perspective. Because these theories are designed from assumptions based on the variability of experiences, they "naturally" leave room for developmental differences, although research conducted within these perspectives may not address those particular types of differences. Therefore, we first briefly discuss the incorporation of the life-span perspective into interpretive and critical theories and then discuss this incorporation into scientific theories at greater length.

Interpretive theories, such as Fisher's (1987, 1989) narrative paradigm, Goffman's (1959, 1963, 1967) social approach, or Pearce and Cronen's (1980; Cronen, Pearce, & Harris, 1982; Pearce, 1976) coordinated management of meaning, attempt to explain experiences and the motivations that drive people's behaviors in their interactions with others. The methodologies used by interpretivists include participant-observation, in-depth interviews, ethnomethodology, and related activities designed to help researchers learn from their subjects about their perceptions of life and its events. The researcher may present the findings as an individual case study or develop categories that, hopefully, reflect the factors that influence those behaviors or the variability that exists within that phenomenon.

Obviously, the life-span communication perspective is compatible with interpretive theories. To develop a full understanding of people's experiences, researchers must also understand the many factors that influence people's interpretation of their experiences. For example, understanding why some members of a support network are successful when others fail may include learning whether members of the network have prior experience with the particular obstacle confronting the person they are trying to support. People who have experienced the death of a loved one are often more successful at providing comfort to an individual who has just lost a loved one than are people who have not had that experience. Learning from our experiences is inherently a developmental process.

Critical theories, such as cultural studies (Agger, 1992; Hall, Hobson, Lowe, & Willis, 1981), feminism (Foss, Foss, & Griffin, 1998; Kramerae, 1989), or studies of power and language (Ardener, 1975, 1978; Kramerae, 1981) attempt to expose power differentials and how the use of power is exercised. Critical theorists' primary methodology is textual analysis, with the term "text" being defined as everything from written documents to cultural icons to examples of everyday talk. These approaches may be supplemented, however, with interviews and participant-observation of people in natural settings. Researchers may examine a number of texts and use a combination of methodologies to develop an understanding of the example of power under consideration.

The life-span communication perspective is compatible with the critical perspective. On the individual or relational level, examining the acquisition and use of power relates to developmental processes. On the cultural level, the critical perspective can be useful when examining the relative status of different age groups. What factors influence whether a social group is "heard" in the larger arena? Young children and older individuals often seem to have less power in the political arena. Why are their voices silenced or muted? In the critical perspective, an important goal beyond identifying the distribution of power in the status quo is to work for the redistribution of power. Studies of this type lead to action. How does a group that has been disenfranchised become empowered? Learning to wield power is a developmental process.

Scientific theories, such as Giles' (Barker, Giles, & Harwood, 2004; Giles, Coupland, & Coupland, 1991) communication accommodation, Burgoon's (1994; Burgoon & Hale, 1988) expectancy violations, or Hirokawa's (Hirokawa & Poole, 1986; Hirokawa, Salazar, Erbert, & Ice, 1996) functional approach to organizational decision making, attempt to discover the universal aspects of communicative behavior. The guiding principle to uncover or discover truth is the scientific method. Although most social scientists acknowledge that human behavior cannot be predicted to the same degree as physicists and chemists can predict physical processes, they do attempt to control for a number of variables in a given study and to accumulate knowledge about human behavior over a number of such studies. The goal is to design a study that controls as many variables as possible and that has a random sample from the population so that findings from the study can be generalized to the population of interest. As we have mentioned before, often the participants in such studies are college students, to whom researchers have easy access. Findings from such a study do not necessarily reflect the behaviors and attitudes of humans in general, but of those humans who are similar to the ones who participated in the study.

The life-span communication perspective is not only compatible with scientifically based theories of communication, but to develop a greater understanding of communicative behaviors, its incorporation into these theories is also a desirable integration. Because of the dominance of scientific theories in interpersonal communication and the benefit of integrating these theories with the life-span communication approach, we examine three of these theories in some detail. The first, communication accommodation theory, has already benefited from that integration; therefore, we discuss those successes first. The second, expectancy violations theory, and third, the functional approach to organizational decision making, represent communication theories from different contexts that have not been integrated with the life-span communication approach, but would benefit from such a process.

Communication accommodation theory, originally called speech accommodation theory, focuses on how individuals interact when they perceive themselves to be from similar or different groups (Barker et al., 2004; Giles et al., 1991). If other people are perceived to be from a different, but more powerful, group, we attempt to behave the same as they do, that is, we accommodate to them. If the other people are from a different, but less powerful, group, we attempt to distance ourselves from them, that is, we underaccommodate to their behaviors. The earliest studies conducted from the CAT perspective examined display of accents, speech rate, and the like among people in the United Kingdom, where accents rather strongly mark an individual's social status.

Beginning to apply the life-span perspective to communication accommodation theory, age was identified as a group marker, and in the last 10 to 15 years, a number of studies were conducted examining intergenerational communication and the consequences for the participants. Findings from this line of research led to the development of the communication predicament of aging model, which illustrates the downward spiral that can occur when older people have negative interactions with younger people (Ryan, Giles, Bartolucci, & Henwood, 1986; Ryan, Hummert, & Boich, 1995). If members of the two groups do not appropriately accommodate each other, both participants leave the interaction dissatisfied. Younger people develop or reinforce already held negative stereotypes of aging. Older people feel devalued, may suffer from poor self-esteem, and may begin to avoid interactions with other young people, reducing their interactive circle.

Related to these studies is the work of Hummert and colleagues, mentioned in chapter 12. Hummert's work reflects the incorporation of the life-span perspective in the development of cognitive schema about aging and intergenerational interaction (Hummert, 1990, 1994b; Hummert et al., 1994). Of particular note here are the findings that, as we age, we develop more sophisticated stereotypes of aging. Although individuals of all ages have both positive and negative stereotypes of aging, as we age, the number and complexity of positive stereotypes regarding aging increases. That is, young adults have more negative than positive stereotypes, whereas older adults have a complex array of stereotypes, and middle-aged individuals fall in between the other age groups. Life experience seems to provide older individuals with opportunities to develop more positive attitudes toward their own and others' aging.

Applying the life-span perspective to CAT and its related developments led to an explosion of research into the nature of intergenerational communication and the communicative lives of older individuals. Life-span communication, however, is not just about communication by and with older individuals. Life-span communication is about the developmental processes related to getting older, whatever age period happens to be the focus of any given study.

The second theory we examine in some detail is expectancy violations theory (Burgoon, 1994; Burgoon & Hale, 1988). The primary claims of this theory are that we have expectations for others' behaviors, and when these expectations are violated, we may react positively or negatively to that violation, based on a number of factors, including whether we find the violation to be desired or not. For example, the rules on entering an elevator are to turn around and face the door and to distribute ourselves within the space of the elevator, usually attempting to divide the space evenly among all parties in the space. If you are the only person on an elevator, when another person enters the elevator and stands close to you while facing you, you will probably feel a heightened sense of awareness of that person's presence. If this person is a classmate who has made "weird" or "scary" comments in class, you will probably feel quite uncomfortable. However, if this classmate is someone to whom you are attracted, you may be quite pleased by the violation and see it as an opportunity to get to know each other better.

Many of the studies on expectancy violations theory have been conducted in a laboratory setting with college students as the participants. A number of useful insights into human communication have been developed; however, by applying a life-span communication perspective to this theory, we begin to see opportunities for a number of interesting questions. For example, do our expectations change over time? If so, what drives these changes? Even if our expectations remain relatively stable over time, our reactions may change. What is the nature of that change? Based on an individual's experiences, an older adult may be more or less rigid than a younger adult in evaluating these violations. For example, changing cultural expectations have led to more informality in interactions between strangers and acquaintances. Older adults who were raised when elders were addressed with terms of respect may be offended when called by their first names by young acquaintances. On the other, an older adult may have found over time that many violations of expectations are relatively unimportant and do not lead to serious consequences, so may laugh off these behaviors.

The third theory, the functional approach to organizational decision making, moves us from an interpersonal context to a group context. In organizational settings, groups of individuals are often formally involved in decision making. Communication scholars interested in studying group processes have been particularly interested in understanding decision making and the factors that lead to poor or good outcomes. The functional approach identifies the major functions that must be accomplished during this process: The group needs to identify and assess the problem, gather and evaluate information, generate possible solutions, and evaluate the strengths and weaknesses of each solution (Hirokawa & Poole, 1986; Hirokawa et al., 1996). Much of this research has been conducted in the laboratory with groups that have no history with each other.

Applying the life-span communication perspective to the functional approach to organizational decision making raises a number of interesting questions. First, what is the nature of learning in the group when an intact group works together over a period of time? Does the group start to make assumptions about members' contributions based on their prior history with each other? Do groups become more efficient over time or do they hasten their decision making based on faulty assumptions so that they have poorer quality outcomes? Second, as discussed in chapter 2, younger and older adults have different decision-making styles and different requirements for information and processing of that information. How do these differences affect the nature of decision making in groups with members of different ages? Are the members aware of these differences, and do they use that knowledge to generate better-informed decisions? If the members are unaware of these differences, do they generate conflict to the point that groups become dysfunctional? What are the consequences for stereotypes of aging based on these types of organizational interactions?

In summary, applying the life-span perspective to theories of communication generally opens up the theory to new questions and helps us to develop a broader understanding of the communicative process. Any attempts to understand the nature of change over time will help to develop more sophisticated theories that address human communicative behavior in more complex ways that more accurately reflect the way we live our lives.

CAPTURING COMMUNICATION CHANGE ACROSS THE LIFE SPAN: RESEARCH AGENDA

Incorporating the life-span communication perspective into communication theories demands that we study and attempt to capture the nature of change across the life span. The methodologies traditionally used in the field of communication are not designed for, and therefore usually not successful at, capturing change. Unique research methodologies are required. Designing such studies will require incorporating those new methodologies into the design, integrating the findings from a number of methodologies, and, perhaps the most difficult to accomplish, taking the time to conduct studies and reevaluate findings over time.

The traditional methodologies being taught to undergraduate and graduate students are not necessarily sensitive to documenting change over time, nor do they generally account for the numerous levels of influence that exist in any communicative event. Our first proposition regarding life span communication—communication is developmental—leads to the idea that any communicative event or series of events is made clearer when studied as a progression of events rather than as an isolated event. By this we mean that a communicative event is often given meaning by the communicative events that have occurred previously. A richer understanding of communication can be achieved by studying how the communication emerged in a conversation or a relationship over time. Thus, communication is both impacted by and creates our social worlds, with the individuals involved actively being influenced by and influencing their environment. Put simply, past experiences shape current experiences. Experimental or quasiexperimental designs usually attempt to limit the influence of these

CHAPTER 13

experiences by controlling their influence through the design or statistical analysis. More interpretive designs may fail to ask critical questions about what prior experiences may have affected the interpretation of current events. Even if these issues are addressed, these studies may be conducted with data collected over a brief period, so that the true nature of change cannot be evaluated.

A hallmark of studies that attempt to control the variables under consideration is that they focus on one level of analysis. These attempts to remove other levels of influence may mask the most significant and most interesting components of the communication process. We must acknowledge that changes occur at the individual, relational, social, and cultural levels. Even when focusing on one level, we cannot ignore the changes that are occurring on the other levels as well. Thus, although the individual may be the focus of study, the relational history of individuals as well as their historical place and times must also be examined to fully understand the changes that occur and the meanings that are assigned to those changes. As a consequence, to address these shortcomings, we need to incorporate longitudinal designs in our studies and use SEM and systems analysis to understand the data collected through these designs.

The complexity of the communicative process requires that multiple methods be applied to fully understand these processes. Experimental and quasiexperimental studies provide us with one kind of information, whereas interpretive and critical studies provide us with other kinds of information. In all likelihood, no one study can provide us with all the data necessary for a complete understanding; therefore, we need more synthesis of the findings across studies, much as we have attempted to begin to do in this text. Unfortunately, our review is hampered by the fact that the studies analyzed here are not part of a coherent plan of study, but reflect the areas that have happened to receive attention. Charting a clear course of what we still need to learn and designing a number of lines of research to address those needs would lead to a more comprehensive synthesis and a deeper understanding of how and why the communicative process occurs as it does. Such a plan acknowledges that we are not looking for "an" answer, but are looking to understand the multitude of possible answers and the criteria for evaluating communicative effectiveness in an ever-changing environment.

A plan as ambitious as the one just proposed will require that single studies not only occur over an extended period, but that we periodically plan to review the accumulation of knowledge and synthesize the knowledge garnered to that point. Just as we argue that any communicative event should be viewed as part of a series of events, any research report should be viewed as part of a series of studies that lead to greater and greater knowledge. As life-span communication scholars, our work is never done because of the changing demands and complexity of the communication process. Although we may come to some understanding for a context at a given time, that context changes as age cohorts move through that context; therefore, we will need to continually reevaluate our knowledge and test its applicability to current conditions.

Such a quest may seem overwhelming. If the answer is never found, then why bother? From a practical standpoint, a better current understanding in a given circumstance may be useful for managing change as it occurs. Hopefully, a greater ability to understand the dynamics of a given change leads to a better ability to adapt to those changes. From a theoretical standpoint, however, any attempt to create a better understanding of all the factors that potentially impact the nature of change and the related communicative processes is helpful so that we can develop more complex theories of communication that address these issues and help us to prepare for ongoing change.

CONCLUDING REMARKS

Hopefully, you have found something of interest in this text. Even if you do not become a communication scholar, you will be a communicator the rest of your life. If you have developed a greater sensitivity to the complexity of communication and to the nature of change across the life span, then we have accomplished our goal. If we have helped you to look forward to opportunities to continue to grow in your abilities for the rest of your life, then we have accomplished our goal. If we have sparked your imagination to ask questions and seek answers, we have accomplished even more.

References

Adams, R. G. (1987). Patterns of network change: A longitudinal study of friendships of elderly women. *The Gerontologist, 27*, 222–227.

Adelman, M. B., Parks, M. R., & Albrecht, T. L. (1987a). Beyond close relationships: Support in weak ties. In T. L. Albrecht & M. B. Adelman (Eds.), *Communicating social support* (pp. 126–147). Newbury Park, CA: Sage.

Adelman, M. B., Parks, M. R., & Albrecht, T. L. (1987b). Supporting friends in need. In T. L. Albrecht & M. B. Adelman (Eds.), *Communicating social support* (pp. 105–125). Newbury Park, CA: Sage.

Adelman, R. D., Greene, M. G., & Charon, R. (1991). Issues in physician-elderly patient interaction. *Ageing and Society, 2*, 127–148.

Adelman, R. D., Greene, M. G., Charon, R., & Friedman, E. (1990). Issues in the physician-geriatric patient relationship. In H. Giles, N. Coupland, & J. Wiemann (Eds.), *Communication, health, and the elderly* (pp. 126–134). London: Manchester University Press.

Adler, J. (1996). *Older adults and computer use.* Retrieved from http://www.seniornet.org/research/survey2.html [Accessed November 10, 1999]

Agger, B. (1992). *Cultural studies as critical theory.* London: Falmer.

Ahrons, C. R., & Rodgers, R. H. (1987). *Divorced families: A multidisciplinary developmental view.* New York: Norton.

Albrecht, T. L., & Adelman, M. B. (1987a). Communicating social support: A theoretical perspective. In T. L. Albrecht & M. B. Adelman (Eds.), *Communicating social support* (pp. 18–39). Newbury Park, CA: Sage.

Albrecht, T. L., & Adelman, M. B. (1987b). Communication networks as structures of social support. In T. L. Albrecht & M. B. Adelman (Eds.), *Communicating social support* (pp. 40–63). Newbury Park, CA: Sage.

Albrecht, T. L., & Adelman, M. B. (1987c). Dilemmas of supportive communication. In T. L. Albrecht & M. B. Adelman (Eds.), *Communicating social support* (pp. 240–254). Newbury Park, CA: Sage.

Albrecht, T. L., & Adelman, M. B. (1987d). Measurement issues in the study of support. In T. L. Albrecht & M. B. Adelman (Eds.), *Communicating social support* (pp. 64–78). Newbury Park, CA: Sage.

Albrecht, T. L., Burleson, B. R., & Goldsmith, D. (1994). Supportive communication. In M. L. Knapp & G. R. Miller (Eds.), *Handbook of interpersonal communication* (2nd ed., pp. 419–449). Newbury Park, CA: Sage.

Allan, G. A. (1979). *A sociology of friendship and kinship.* London: Allen & Unwin.

Ames, S. C., & Roltzsch, J. C. (2000). The impact of minor stressful life events and social support on cravings: A study of inpatients receiving treatment for substance dependence. *Addictive Behaviors*, 25, 539–545.

Antonucci, T. C. (1990). Social supports and social relationships. In R. H. Binstock & L. K. George (Eds.), *Handbook of aging and the social sciences* (pp. 205–226). New York: Academic Press.

Ardener, E. (1975). The "problem" revisited. In S. Ardener (Ed.), *Perceiving women* (pp. 19–27). London: Malaby.

Ardener, S. (1978). *Defining females: The nature of women.* New York: Wiley.

Argyle, M., & Furnham, A. (1983). Sources of satisfaction and conflict in long-term relationships. *Journal of Marriage and the Family*, 45, 481–493.

Atchley, R. C. (1977). *The social forces in later life*, 2nd ed. Belmont, CA: Wadsworth.

Atkinson, M. (1989). Conceptualizations of the parent-child relationship: Solidarity, attachment, crescive bonds, and identity salience. In J. A. Mancini (Ed.), *Aging parents and adult children* (pp. 81–98). Lexington, MA: D. C. Heath.

Austad, S. N. (1997). *Why we age: What science is discovering about the body's journey through life.* New York: Wiley.

Austin, E. W. (1995). Reaching your audiences: Developmental considerations in designing health messages. In E. Mailbach & R. L. Parrott (Eds.), *Designing health messages: Approaches from the communication theory and public health practice* (pp. 114–144). Thousand Oaks, CA: Sage.

Balazs, A. L. (1995). Marketing to the elderly. In J. F. Nussbaum & J. Coupland (Eds.), *Handbook of communication and aging research* (pp. 263–284). Mahwah, NJ: Lawrence Erlbaum Associates.

Baltes, P. B. (1987). Theoretical propositions of life-span developmental psychology: On the dynamics between growth and decline. *Developmental Psychology*, 23, 611–626.

Baltes, M. M., Kinderman, T., Reisenzein, R., & Schmid, U. (1987). Further observational data on the behavioral and social world of institutions for the aged. *Psychology and Aging*, 2, 390–403.

Baltes, P. B., Reese, H. W., & Nesselroade, J. R. (1988). *Life-span developmental psychology: Introduction to research methods.* Hillsdale, NJ: Lawrence Erlbaum Associates.

Baltes, P. B., Smith, J., & Studinger, U. M. (1992). Wisdom and successful aging. In T. B. Sonderegger (Ed.), *Nebraska symposium on motivation: Psychology and aging* (pp. 123–167). Lincoln: University of Nebraska Press.

Bandura, A. (1967). The role of modeling processes in personality development. In W. W. Hartup & N. L. Smothergill (Eds.), *The young child: Reviews of research* (pp. 42–58). Washington, DC: National Association for the Education of Young Children.

Bandura, A. (1977). *Social learning theory.* Englewood Cliffs, NJ: Prentice-Hall.

Barbee, A. P. (1990). Interactive coping: The cheering-up process in close relationships. In S. Duck & R. Silver (Eds.), *Personal relationships and social support* (pp. 46–65). Newbury Park, CA: Sage.

Barker, V., Giles, H., & Harwood, J. (2004). Inter- and intragroup perspectives on intergenerational communication. In J. F. Nussbaum & J. Coupland (Eds.), *Handbook of communication and aging research* 2nd ed. (pp. 139–165). Mahwah, NJ: Lawrence Erlbaum Associates.

Barnett, R. C., Kibria, N., Baruch, G. K., & Pleck, J. H. (1991). Adult daughter-parent relationships and their associations with daughters' subjective well-being and psychological distress. *Journal of Marriage and the Family, 53*, 29–42.

Baruch, G., & Barnett, R. C. (1983). Adult daughters' relationships with their mothers. *Journal of Marriage and the Family, 45*, 601–606.

Baum, E. E., & Yoder, C. (2002). Senior support on-line. In R. W. Morrell (Ed.), *Older adults, health information, and the world wide web* (pp. 187–199). Mahwah, NJ: Lawrence Erlbaum Associates.

Baumrind, D. (1991). Parenting styles and adolescent development. In R. M. Leder, A. C. Peterson, & J. Brooks-Gunn (Eds.), *Encyclopedia of adolescence* (Vol. 2, pp. 746–758). New York: Garland.

Baxter, L. A. (1988). A dialectical perspective on communication strategies in relationship development. In S. Duck (Ed.), *Handbook of personal relationships* (pp. 257–273). New York: Wiley.

Baxter, L. A., Braithwaite, D. O., & Nicholson, J. H. (1999). Turning points in the development of blended families. *Journal of Social and Personal Relationships, 16*, 291–313.

Baxter, L. A., & Clark, C. L. (1996). Perceptions of family communication patterns and the enactment of family rituals. *Western Journal of Communication, 60*, 254–268.

Baxter, L. A., & Montgomery, B. M. (1996). *Relating: Dialogues and dialectics.* New York: Guilford.

Beal, C. R. (1994). *Boys and girls: The development of gender roles.* New York: McGraw-Hill.

Bedford, V. H. (1994). Sibling relationships in middle and old age. In R. Blieszner & V. H. Bedford (Eds.), *Aging and the family: Theory and research* (pp. 201–222). New York: Praeger.

Beisecker, A. E. (1996). Older persons' medical encounters and their outcomes. *Research on Aging, 18*, 9–31.

Bell, J. (1992). In search of a discourse on aging: The elderly on television. *Gerontologist, 32*, 305–311.

Bengston, V. L., & Robertson, J. F. (1985). *Grandparenthood.* Beverly Hills, CA: Sage.

Berger, C. R. (1985). Social power and interpersonal communication. In M. L. Knapp & G. R. Miller (Eds.), *Handbook of interpersonal communication* (pp. 439–499). Beverly Hills, CA: Sage.

Berger, C. R., & Calabrese, R. J. (1975). Some explorations in initial interaction and beyond: Toward a developmental theory of interpersonal communication. *Human Communication Research, 1*, 99–112.

Berger, P. L., & Luckmann, T. (1966). *The social construction of reality.* NY: Anchor.

Bergstrom, M. J., & Nussbaum, J. F. (1996). Cohort differences in interpersonal conflict: Implications for the older patient—younger care provider interaction. *Health Communication, 8*, 233–248.

Bernard, M., & Phillipson, C. (1995). Retirement and leisure. In J. F. Nussbaum and J. Coupland (Eds.), *Handbook of communication and aging research* (pp. 285–311). Mahwah, NJ: Lawrence Erlbaum Associates.

Bethea, L. S. (2002). The impact of an older adult parent on communicative satisfaction and dyadic adjustment in the long-term marital relationship: Adult-children and spouses' retrospective accounts. *Journal of Applied Communication Research, 30*, 107–125.

Bigner, J. J. (1994). *Individual and family development: A life-span interdisciplinary approach.* Englewood Cliffs, NJ: Prentice-Hall.

Blake, R. R., & Mouton, J. S. (1973). The fifth achievement. In F. E. Jandt (Ed.), *Conflict resolution through communication* (pp. 27–46). New York: Harper & Row.

Blanchard-Fields, F., & Abeles, R. P. (1996). *Individual and family development: A life-span interdisciplinary approach.* Englewood Cliffs, NJ: Prentice-Hall.

Bleise, N. W. (1986). Media in the rocking chair: Media uses and functions among the elderly. In G. Gumpert & R. Cathcart (Eds.), *Intermedia: Interpersonal communication in a media world* (pp. 573–582). New York: Oxford University Press.

Blieszner, R., & Adams, R. G. (1992). *Adult friendship.* Newbury Park, CA: Sage.

Blumer, H. (1969). *Symbolic interactionism: Perspectives and methods.* Englewood Cliffs, NJ: Prentice-Hall.

Bochner, A. P. (1976). Conceptual frontiers in the study of communication in families: An introduction to the literature. *Human Communication Research, 2*, 381–397.

Bowlby, J. (1979). *The making and breaking of affectional bonds.* London: Tavistock Publications.

Bowlby, J. (1988). *A secure base: Parent-child attachment and health human development.* New York: Basic Books.

Bramlett, M. D., & Mosher, W. D. (2002). Cohabitation, marriage, divorce, and remarriage in the United States. National Center for Health Statistics. *Vital Health Statistics, 23*(22), 1–103.

Brugha, T. S., Bebbington, P. E., & Wykes, T. (1997). Predicting the short-term outcome of first episodes and recurrence of clinical depression: A prospective study of life events, difficulties, and social support networks. *Journal of Clinical Psychiatry, 58*, 298–307.

Bruunk, B. (1990). Affiliation and helping interactions within organizations: A critical analysis of the role of social support with regard to occupational stress. In W. Stroebe & M. Hewstone (Eds.), *European review of social psychology* (Vol. 1, pp. 293–322). New York: Wiley.

Burgoon, J. K. (1994). Nonverbal signals. In M. L. Knapp & G. R. Miller (Eds.), *Handbook of interpersonal communication* (pp. 253–255). Thousand Oaks, CA: Sage.

Burgoon, J. K., & Hale, J. L. (1988). Nonverbal expectancy violations: Model elaboration and application. *Communication Monographs, 55*, 58–79.

Burleson, B. (1987). Cognitive complexity. In J. C. McCroskey & J. A. Daly (Eds.), *Personality and interpersonal communication* (pp. 305–349). Newbury Park, CA: Sage.

Burleson, B. (1994). Comforting messages: Significance, approaches, and effects. In B. Burleson, T. Albrecht, & I. Sarason (Eds.), *Communication of social support* (pp. 3–28). Thousand Oaks, CA: Sage.

Burleson, B., & Samter, W. (1994). A social skills approach to relationship maintenance. In D. Canary & L. Stafford (Eds.), *Communication and relationship maintenance* (pp. 61–90). San Diego, CA: Academic Press.

Burnett, J. J. (1991). Examining the media habits of the affluent elderly. *Journal of Advertising Research, 31*, 33–41.

Byrne, D. (1998). *Complexity theory and the social sciences: An introduction.* New York: Routledge.

Cahn, D. D. (1990). Intimates in conflict: A research review. In D. D. Cahn (Ed.), *Intimates in conflict: A communication perspective* (pp. 1–22). Hillsdale, NJ: Lawrence Erlbaum Associates.

Calvert, S. L. (1999). *Children's journeys through the information age.* New York: McGraw-Hill.

Campbell, D. T., & Stanley, J. C. (1963). *Experimental and quasi-experimental designs for research.* Chicago: Rand McNally.

Canary, D. J., Cupach, W. R., & Messman, S. J. (1995). *Relationship conflict: Conflict in parent-child, friendship, and romantic relationships.* Thousand Oaks, CA: Sage.

Canary, D. J., & Stafford, L. (1994). Maintaining relationships through strategic and routine interaction. In D. J. Canary & L. Stafford (Eds.), *Communication and relational maintenance* (pp. 3–22). New York: Academic Press.

Canary, D., Stafford, L., Hause, K., & Wallace, L. (1993). An inductive analysis of relational maintenance strategies: A comparison among young lovers, relatives, friends, and others. *Communication Research Reports, 10,* 5–14.

Cantor, M. H. (1979). Neighbors and friends: An overlooked resource in the informal support system. *Research on Aging, 1,* 434–463.

Carter, B., & McGoldrick, M. (1989). Overview: The changing family life cycle—a framework for family therapy. In B. Carter & M. McGoldrick (Eds.), *The changing family life cycle* (2nd ed.). Boston: Allyn & Bacon.

Carter, D. B., & Levy, G. D. (1988). Cognitive aspects of children's early sex-role development: The influence of gender schemas on preschoolers' memories and preference for sex-typed toys and activities. *Child Development, 59,* 782–793.

Cauce, A. M., Reid, M., Landesman, S., & Gonzales, N. (1990). Social support in young children: Measurement, structure, and behavioral impact. In B. R. Sarason, I. G. Sarason, & G. R. Pierce (Eds.), *Social support: An interactional view* (pp. 64–94). New York: John Wiley & Sons.

Chapman, M., & McBride, M. L. (1992). The education of reason: Cognitive conflict and its role in intellectual development. In C. U. Shantz & W. W. Hartup (Eds.), *Conflict in child and adolescent development* (pp. 36–69). Cambridge, UK: Cambridge University Press.

Charles Schwab, Inc. (1998). *Research on seniors' computer and Internet usage: A report of a national survey.* Retrieved from http://www.seniornet.org/php/default.php?PageID=5474&Version=0&Font=0 [Accessed June 12, 2002].

Chou, K.-L., & Chi, I. (2001). Stressful life events and depressive symptoms: Social support and sense of control as mediators or moderators? *International Journal of Ageing and Human Development, 52,* 155–171.

Christensen, A., & Heavey, C. L. (1990). Gender and social structure in the demand/withdrawal pattern of marital conflict. *Journal of Personality and Social Psychology, 59,* 73–81.

Cicirelli, V. G. (1980). Sibling relationships in adulthood: A life span perspective. In L. W. Poon (Ed.), *Aging in the 1980's* (pp. 455–462). Washington, DC: American Psychological Association.

Cicirelli, V. G. (1983). Adult children and their elderly parents. In T. H. Brubaker (Ed.), *Family relationships in later life* (pp. 47–62). Beverly Hills, CA: Sage.

Cicirelli, V. G. (1989). Feelings of attachment to siblings and well-being in later life. *Psychology and Aging, 4,* 211–216.

Cicirelli, V. G. (1994). Sibling relationships in cross-cultural perspective. *Journal of Marriage and the Family, 56,* 7–20.

Clark, R. A., & Delia, J. (1977). Cognitive complexity, social perspective-taking, and functional persuasive skills in second-to-ninth-grade students. *Human Communication Research, 3*, 128–134.

Cluck, G. G., & Cline, R. J. (1986). The circle of others: Self-help groups for the bereaved. *Communication Quarterly, 34*, 306–325.

Cohen, C. E. (1981). Goals and schemata in person perception: Making sense from the stream of behavior. In N. Cantor & J. F. Kihlstrom (Eds.), *Personality, cognition, and social interaction.* Hillsdale, NJ: Lawrence Erlbaum Associates.

Cohen, C. I., & Rajkowski, H. (1982). What's in a friend? Substantive and theoretical issues. *The Gerontologist, 22*, 261–266.

Cohen, S. (1988). Psychosocial models of the role of support in the etiology of physical disease. *Health Psychology, 7*, 269–297.

Cohen, S. H., & Reese, H. W. (Eds.). (1994). *Life-span developmental psychology: Methodological contributions.* Hillsdale, NJ: Lawrence Erlbaum Associates.

Coleman, M., & Ganong, L. H. (1990). Remarriage and stepfamily research in the 1980's: Increased interest in an old form. *Journal of Marriage and the Family, 52*, 925–939.

Collins, W. A., & Laursen, B. (1992). Conflict and relationships during adolescence. In C. U. Shantz & W. W. Hartup (Eds.), *Conflict in child and adolescent development* (pp. 216–241). Cambridge, UK: Cambridge University Press.

Coupland, N., Coupland, J., & Giles, H. (1991). *Language, society and the elderly: Discourse, identity and aging.* Oxford, UK: Blackwell.

Cronen, V., Pearce, W. B., & Harris, L. (1982). The coordinated management of meaning. In F. E. X. Dance (Ed.), *Comparative human communication theory* (pp. 61–89). New York: Harper & Row.

Dail, P. (1988). Prime-time television portrayals of older adults in the context of family life. *Gerontologist, 28*, 700–706.

Damon, W. (1977). *The social world of children.* San Francisco: Jossey-Bass.

Damush, T., Stewart, A., Mills, K., King, A., & Ritter, P. (1999). *Journal of Gerontology: Medical Sciences, 54A*, M423–M427.

Davis, R. H., & Davis, J. A. (1985). *TV's image of the elderly: A practical guide for change.* Lexington, MA: Lexington.

Dean, A., Kolody, B., Wood, P., & Ensel, W. M. (1989). Measuring the communication of social support from adult children. *Journal of Gerontology: Social Sciences, 44*, S71–S79.

Dean, A., & Lin, N. (1977). The stress buffering role of social support: Problems and prospects for systematic investigation. *Journal of Health and Social Behavior, 32*, 321–341.

Delia, J. G., & Clark, R. (1977). Cognitive complexity, social perception, and the development of listener-adapted communication in six-, eight-, ten- and twelve-year-old boys. *Communication Monographs, 44*, 326–345.

Delia, J., Kline, S., & Burleson, B. (1979). The development of persuasive communication strategies in kindergartners through twelfth-graders. *Communication Monographs, 46*, 241–256.

Dietz, T. L. (1998). An examination of violence and gender role portrayals in video games: Implications for gender socialization and aggressive behavior. *Sex Roles, 38*, 425–442.

DiFranza, J. R., & McAfee, T. (1992). The tobacco institute: Helping youth say 'yes' to tobacco. *Journal of Family Practice, 34*, 694–696.

Dill, K. E., & Dill, J. C. (1998). Video game violence: A review of the empirical literature. *Aggressive and Violent Behavior, 3*, 407–482.

Dindia, K., & Canary, D. J. (1993). Definitions and theoretical perspectives on relational maintenance. *Journal of Social and Personal Relationships, 10,* 163–173.

Donnerstein, E., Slaby, R. G., & Eron, L. D. (1994). The mass media and youth aggression. In L. D. Eron, J. H. Gentry, & P. Schlegel (Eds.), *Reason to hope: A psychological perspective on violence and youth* (pp. 219–250). Washington, DC: American Psychological Association.

Dorman, S. M. (1997). Video and computer games: Effects on children and implications for health education. *Journal of School Health, 67,* 133–137.

Downs, V. C., Javidi, M., & Nussbaum, J. F. (1988). A comparative analysis of the relationship between communication apprehension and loneliness for elderly nursing home and non-nursing home residents. *Western Journal of Speech Communication, 52,* 308–320.

Duck, S. W. (1994). Steady as (s)he goes: Relational maintenance as a shared meaning system. In D. Canary & L. Stafford (Eds.), *Communication and relational maintenance* (pp. 45–60). New York: Academic Press.

Dumlao, R., & Botta, R. E. (2000). Family communication patterns and conflict styles young adults use with their fathers. *Communication Quarterly, 48,* 174–189.

Dunn, J., & Slomkowski, C. (1992). Conflict and the development of social understanding. In C. U. Shantz & W. W. Hartup (Eds.), *Conflict in child and adolescent development* (pp. 70–92). Cambridge, UK: Cambridge University Press.

Dworetzky, J. P. (1993). *Introduction to child development* (5th ed.). St. Paul, MN: West.

Dykstra, P. A. (1990). *Next of (non)kin.* The Netherlands: Swets & Zeitlinger.

Eccles, J. S., & Bryan, J. (1994). Adolescence: Critical crossroad in the path of gender-role development. In M. R. Stevenson (Ed.), *Gender roles through the life span: A multidisciplinary perspective* (pp. 111–147). Muncie, IN: Ball State University.

Fagot, B. I., & Leinbach, M. D. (1994). Gender-role development in young children. In M. R. Stevenson (Ed.), *Gender roles through the life span: A multidisciplinary perspective* (pp. 3–24). Muncie, IN: Ball State University.

Ferree, M. M. (1994). Negotiating household roles and responsibilities: Resistance, conflict, and change. In M. R. Stevenson (Ed.), *Gender roles through the life span: A multidisciplinary perspective* (pp. 203–221). Muncie, IN: Ball State University.

Festinger, L. (1957). *A theory of cognitive dissonance.* Stanford, CA: Stanford University Press.

Field, D., & Minkler, M. (1988). Continuity and change in social support between young-old, old-old or very-old age. *Journal of Gerontology, 43,* 100–106.

Fields, J., & Casper, L. M. (2000). *America's families and living arrangements.* (p20-537). Washington, DC: U.S. Census Bureau.

Fine, M. A., Coleman, M., & Ganong, L. H. (1998). Consistency in perceptions of the step-parent role among step-parents, parents, and stepchildren. *Journal of Social and Personal Relationships, 15,* 810–828.

Fingerman, K. L. (1995). Aging mothers' and their adult daughters' perceptions of conflict behaviors. *Psychology and Aging, 10,* 639–649.

Fingerman, K. L. (1996). Sources of tension in the aging mother and adult daughter relationship. *Psychology and Aging, 11,* 591–606.

Fingerman, K. L., Nussbaum, J., & Birditt, K. S. (in press). Keeping all five balls in the air: Juggling family communication at midlife. In A. Vangelisti (Ed.), *Handbook of Family Communication* (pp. 135–152). Mahwah, NJ: Lawrence Erlbaum Association.

Fisher, W. R. (1987). *Human communication as narration: Toward a philosophy of reason, value, and action.* Columbia: University of South Carolina Press.

Fisher, W. R. (1989). Clarifying the narrative paradigm. *Communication Monographs, 56,* 55–58.

Fitzpatrick, M. A., & Badzinski, D. M. (1994). All in the family: Interpersonal communication in kin relationships. In M. L. Knapp & G. R. Miller (Eds.), *Handbook of interpersonal communication* (2nd ed., pp. 726–771). Thousand Oaks, CA: Sage.

Fitzpatrick, M. A., & Ritchie, L. D. (1994). Communication schemata within the family: Multiple perspectives on family interaction. *Human Communication Research, 20,* 275–301.

Folwell, A., Chung, L., Nussbaum, J., Bethea, L., & Grant, J. (1997). Differential accounts of closeness in older adult sibling relationships. *Journal of Social and Personal Relationships, 14,* 843–849.

Folwell, A. L., & Grant, J. (1999, February). *Accounts of closeness and expectancy of role behaviors in grandchild-grandparent relationships.* Paper presented at the meeting of the Western States Communication Association, Vancouver, Canada.

Forrester, M. (1993). Affording social-cognitive skills in young children: The overhearing context. In D. Messer & G. Turner (Eds.), *Critical influences on child language acquisition and development* (pp. 40–61). NY: St. Martin's Press.

Foss, K. A., Foss, S., & Griffin, C. L. (1998). *Re-visioning rhetorics: Feminist transformations of rhetorical theory.* Thousand Oaks, CA: Sage.

Fox, S., Rainie, L., Larsen, E., Horrigan, J., Lenhart, A., Spooner, T., & Carter, C. (2001). *The Pew Internet and American life project.* Retrieved from http://www.perinternet.org/ [Accessed June 12, 2002].

Frieze, I. H., & Olson, J. E. (1994). Understanding the characteristics and experiences of women in male- and female-dominated fields. In M. R. Stevenson (Ed.), *Gender roles through the life span: A multidisciplinary perspective* (pp. 151–178). Muncie, IN: Ball State University.

Funk, J. B. (1993). Reevaluating the impact of video games. *Clinical Pediatrics, 32,* 86–90.

Furlong, M. S. (1989). An electronic community for older adults: The SeniorNet network. *Journal of Communication, 39,* 145–153.

Galvin, K. M., & Brommel, B. J. (2000). *Family communication: Cohesion and change* (5th ed.). New York: Addison-Wesley Longman.

Ganong, L., & Coleman, M. (1994). *Remarried family relationships.* Thousand Oaks, CA: Sage.

Gerbner, G., Gross, L., Morgan, M., & Signorelli, N. (1986). Living with television: The dynamics of the cultivation process. In J. Bryant & D. Zillman (Eds.), *Perspectives on media effects* (pp. 17–40). Hillsdale, NJ: Lawrence Erlbaum Associates.

Giles, H., Coupland, J., & Coupland, N. (1991). Accommodation theory: Communication, context, and consequence. In H. Giles, J. Coupland, & N. Coupland (Eds.), *Contexts of accommodation: Developments in applied sociolinguistics* (pp. 1–68). Cambridge, UK: Cambridge University Press.

Giles, H., & Williams, A. (1994). Patronizing the young: Forms and evaluation. *International Journal of Aging and Human Development, 39,* 33–53.

Glick, P. (1990). Marriage and family trends. In D. Olson & M. K. Hanson (Eds.), *2001: Preparing families for the future* (pp. 2–3). Minneapolis: National Council on Family Relations.

Godbey, G. (1997). *Time for life-The surprising ways Americans use their leisure time.* University Park: Penn State Press.

Godbey, G. (2001, November). *The role of leisure behavior in health of older adults: Theories, models, findings and questions.* Paper presented at the Gerontology Colloquium, University Park, PA.

Goffman, E. (1959). *The presentation of self in everyday life.* Garden City, NY: Doubleday.

Goffman, E. (1963). *Behavior in public places.* New York: Free Press.

Goffman, E. (1967). *Interaction ritual: Essays on face-to-face behavior.* Garden City, NY: Doubleday.

Goldman-Sachs. (1999, November 11). Health-e opportunities in ehealth? *Technology: Internet/Ehealth.* New York: Author.

Goodman, R. I. (1990). Television news viewing by older adults. *Journalism Quarterly, 67*(1), 137–141.

Gottman, J. M. (1979). *Marital interaction: Empirical investigations.* New York: Academic Press.

Gottman, J. M. (1983). How children become friends. *Monographs of the Society of for Research in Child Development, 48,* (Serial No. 201).

Gottman, J. M. (1994). *What predicts divorce? The relationship between marital processes and marital outcomes.* Hillsdale, NJ: Lawrence Erlbaum Associates.

Granovetter, M. S. (1973). The strength of weak ties. *American Journal of Sociology, 78,* 1360–1380.

Granovetter, M. S. (1982). The strength of weak ties: A network theory revisited. In P. V. Marsden & N. Lin (Eds.), *Social structure and network analysis* (pp. 105–130). Newbury Park, CA: Sage.

Greenberg, B. S., Korzenny, F., & Atkin, C. K. (1980). Trends in the portrayal of the elderly. In B. S. Greenberg (Ed.), *Life on television: Content analysis of U.S. TV drama* (pp. 23–33). Norwood, NJ: Ablex.

Greene, M. G., & Adelman, R. (1996). Psychosocial factors in older patient's medical encounters. *Research on Aging, 18,* 84–102.

Greene, M. G., Adelman, R., Charon, R., & Hoffman, S. (1986). Ageism in the medical encounter: An exploratory study of the doctor-elderly patient relationship. *Language and Communication, 6,* 113–124.

Greene, M. G., Majerovitz, D., Adelman, R. D., & Rizzo, C. (1994). The effects of the presence of a third person on the physician-older patient medical interview. *Journal of the American Geriatrics Society, 42,* 413–419.

Grossman, L. K. (1999). The media's role: Life in an older America. In R. N. Butler, L. K. Grossman, & M. R. Oberlink (Eds.). *Life in an older America* (pp. 231–238). New York: Century Foundation Press.

Hagestad, G. O. (1985). Continuity and connectedness. In V. L. Bengston & J. F. Robertson (Eds.), *Grandparenthood* (pp. 31–48). Beverly Hills, CA: Sage.

Hagestad, G. O. (1994). The social meanings of age for men and women. In M. R. Stevenson (Ed.), *Gender roles through the life span: A multidisciplinary perspective* (pp. 225–243). Muncie, IN: Ball State University.

Hall, S., Hobson, D., Lowe, A., & Willis, P. (Eds.). (1981). *Culture, media, and language.* London: Hutchison.

Halpern, J. (1994). The sandwich generation: Conflicts between adult children and their aging parents. In D. D. Cahn (Ed.), *Conflict in personal relationships* (pp. 143–160). Hillsdale, NJ: Lawrence Erlbaum Associates.

Hareven, T. K. (1978). Introduction: The historical study of the life course. In T. K. Hareven (Ed.), *Transitions: The family and the life course in historical perspective* (pp. 1–16). New York: Academic Press.

Harris, J. R. (1998). *The nurture assumption: Why children turn out the way they do, parents matter less than you think and peers matter more*. New York: Free Press.

Hartup, W. W. (1992). Conflict and friendship relations. In C. U. Shantz & W. W. Hartup (Eds.), *Conflict in child and adolescent development* (pp. 186–215). Cambridge, UK: Cambridge University Press.

Harwood, J., & Giles, H. (1993). Creating intergenerational distance: Language, communication, and middle-age. *Language Sciences, 15,* 1–24.

Harwood, J., Giles, H., & Ryan, E. B. (1995). Aging, communication, and intergroup theory: Social identity and intergenerational communication. In J. F. Nussbaum & J. Coupland (Eds.), *Handbook of communication and aging research* (pp. 133–159). Mahwah, NJ: Lawrence Erlbaum Associates.

Harwood, J., & Lin, M. (2000). Affiliation, pride, exchange, and distance in grandparents' accounts of relationships with their college-aged grandchildren. *Journal of Communication, 50,* 31–47.

Haslett, B. B., & Samter, W. (1997). *Children communicating: The first 5 years*. Mahwah, NJ: Lawrence Erlbaum Associates.

Haug, M. R., & Ory, M. G. (1987). Issues in elderly patient-provider interactions. *Research on Aging, 9,* 3–44.

Hayflick, L. (1994). *How and why we age*. New York: Ballantine.

Hays, R. B. (1988). Friendship. In S. W. Duck (Ed.), *Handbook of personal relationships* (pp. 391–408). New York: John Wiley & Sons.

Healey, J. G., & Bell, R. A. (1990). Effects of social networks on individual's responses to conflicts in friendship. In D. D. Cahn (Ed.), *Intimates in conflict: A communication perspective* (pp. 121–152). Hillsdale, NJ: Lawrence Erlbaum Associates.

Henderson, S. H., Hetherington, E. M., Mekos, D., & Reiss, D. (1996). Stress, parenting, and adolescent psychopathology in nondivorced and stepfamilies: A within family perspective. In E. M. Hetherington & E. A. Blechman (Eds.), *Stress, coping, and resiliency in children and families* (pp. 31–48). Hillsdale, NJ: Lawrence Erlbaum Associates.

Henwood, K. L. (1995). Adult parent-child relationships: A view from feminist and discursive social psychology. In J. F. Nussbaum & J. Coupland (Eds.), *Handbook of communication and aging research* (pp. 167–183). Mahwah, NJ: Lawrence Erlbaum Associates.

Henwood, K. L., & Coughlan, G. (1993). The construction of "closeness" in mother-daughter relationships across the lifespan. In N. Coupland & J. F. Nussbaum (Eds.), *Discourse and lifespan identity* (pp. 191–214). Newbury Park, CA: Sage.

Hershberger, P. J., & Walsh, W. B. (1990). Multiple role involvements and the adjustment to conjugal bereavement: An exploratory study. *Omega, 21,* 91–102.

Hetherington, E. M. (1989). Coping with family transitions: Winners, losers, and survivors. *Child Development, 60,* 1–14.

Hetherington, E. M., & Stanley-Hagan, M. M. (1995). Parenting in divorced and remarried families. In M. H. Bornstein (Ed.), *Children and parenting* (Vol. 4, pp. 97–114). Hillsdale, NJ: Lawrence Erlbaum Associates.

Hirokawa, R. Y., & Poole, M. S. (Eds.). (1986). *Communication and group decision-making*. Beverly Hills, CA: Sage.

Hirokawa, R. Y., Salazar, A. J., Erbert, L., & Ice, R. J. (1996). Small group communication. In M. B. Salwen & D. W. Stacks (Eds.), *An integrated approach to communication theory and research* (pp. 359–382). Mahwah, NJ: Lawrence Erlbaum Associates.

Hocker, J. L., & Wilmot, W. W. (1991). *Interpersonal conflict* (3rd ed.). Dubuque, IA: Brown.

Hollos, M. (1994). The management of adolescent sexuality in four societies: The past and the present. In M. R. Stevenson (Ed.), *Gender roles through the life span: A multidisciplinary perspective* (pp. 65–88). Muncie, IN: Ball State University.

Huesmann, L. R., & Miller, L. S. (1994). Long-term effects of repeated exposure to media violence in childhood. In L. R. Huessman (ed.), *Aggressive behavior: Current perspectives* (pp. 153–186). New York: Plenum.

Hummert, M. L. (1990). Multiple stereotypes of elderly and young adults: A comparison of structure and evaluations. *Psychology and Aging, 5,* 182–193.

Hummert, M. L. (1994a). Physiognomic cues to age and the activation of stereotypes of the elderly in interaction. *International Journal of Aging and Human Development, 39,* 5–20.

Hummert, M. L. (1994b). Stereotypes of the elderly and patronizing speech. In M. L. Hummert, J. M. Wiemann, & J. F. Nussbaum (Eds.), *Interpersonal communication in older adulthood: Interdisciplinary theory and research* (pp. 162–184). Thousand Oaks, CA: Sage.

Hummert, M. L., Garstka, T. A., Shaner, J. L., & Strahm, S. (1994). Stereotypes of the elderly held by young, middle-aged, and elderly adults. *Journal of Gerontology, 49,* 240–249.

Ito, M., Adler, A., Linde, C., Mynatt, E., & O'Day, V. (2001). *Final report: Broadening access: Research for diverse network communities* (NSF #9712414). Retrieved from http://www.seniornet.org/research/9911.shtml [Accessed June 18, 2002].

Jablin, F. M. (2001). Organizational entry, assimilation, and disengagement/exit. In F. M. Jablin & L. L. Putnam (Eds.), *The new handbook of organizational communication: Advances in theory, research, and methods* (pp. 732–818). Thousand Oaks, CA: Sage.

Jacobs, S. (1994). Language and interpersonal communication. In M. L. Knapp & G. R. Miller (Eds.), *Handbook of interpersonal communication,* 2nd ed. (pp. 199–228). Thousand Oaks, CA: Sage.

Johnson, C. L., & Catalano, D. J. (1983). A longitudinal study of family supports to impaired elderly. *The Gerontologist, 23,* 612–618.

Johnson, J. R. (1996). Risk factors associated with negative interactions between family caregivers and elderly care-receivers. *International Journal of Aging and Human Development, 43,* 7–20.

Katz, E., Blumler, J. G., & Gurevitch, M. (1974). Utilization of mass communication by the individual. In J. G. Blumler & E. Katz (Eds.), *The uses of mass communication: Current perspectives on gratifications research* (pp. 19–32). Beverly Hills, CA: Sage.

Katz, E., Gurevitch, M., & Hass, H. (1973). On the use of the mass media for important things. *American Sociological Review, 38,* 164–181.

Katz, L. F., Kramer, L., & Gottman, J. M. (1992). Conflict and emotions in marital, sibling, and peer relationships. In C. U. Shantz & W. W. Hartup (Eds.), *Conflict in child and adolescent development* (pp. 122–149). Cambridge, UK: Cambridge University Press.

Kelly, C., Huston, T. L., & Cate, R. M. (1985). Premarital relationship correlates of the erosion of satisfaction in marriage. *Journal of Social and Personal Relationships, 2,* 167–178.

Kemper, S., Greiner, L. H., Marquis, J. G., Prenovost, K., & Mitzner, T. L. (2001). Language decline across the life span: Findings from the Nun Study. *Psychology and Aging, 16,* 227–239.

Kemper, S., & Lyons, K. (1994). The effects of Alzheimer's dementia on language and communcation. In M. L. Hummert, J. M. Wiemann, & J. F. Nussbaum (Eds.), *Interpersonal communication in older adulthood: Interdisciplinary theory and research* (pp. 58–82). Thousand Oaks, CA: Sage.

Kessler, S. J., & McKenna, W. (1978). *Gender: An ethnomethodological approach.* New York: Wiley.

Kiel, L. D., & Elliott, E. W. (1996). *Chaos theory in the social sciences: Foundations and applications.* Ann Arbor: University of Michigan Press.

Kilmann, R. H., & Thomas, K. W. (1977). Developing a forced-choice measure of conflict-handling behavior: The mode instrument. *Educational and Psychological Measurement, 37,* 309–325.

King, L. A., King, D. W., & Adams, G. A. (1998). Resilience-recovery factors in post-traumatic stress disorder among female and male Vietnam Veterans: Hardiness, postwar social support, and additional stressful life events. *Journal of Personality and Social Psychology, 74,* 420.

Kivett, V. R., & Atkinson, M. P. (1984). Filial expectations, associations and helping as a function of number of children among older rural-transitional parents. *Journal of Gerontology, 39,* 499–503.

Kivnick, H. Q. (1983). Dimensions of grandparenthood meaning: Deductive conceptualization and empirical derivation. *Journal of Personality and Social Psychology, 44,* 1056–1068.

Kivnick, H. Q., & Sinclair, H. M. (1996). Grandparenthood. In J. E. Birren (Ed.), *Encyclopedia of gerontology* (Vol. 1, pp. 611–624). San Diego, CA: Academic Press.

Klocek, J. W., Oliver, J. M., & Ross, M. J. (1997). The role of dysfunctional attitudes, negative life events, and social support in the prediction of depressive dysphoria: A prospective longitudinal study. *Social Behavior and Personality, 1997,* 123–137.

Knapp, M. L. (1978). *Social intercourse: From greetings to goodbye.* Boston: Allyn Bacon.

Knapp, M. L., & Miller, G. R. (Eds.) (1994). *Handbook of interpersonal communication.* Thousand Oaks, CA: Sage.

Koerner, A. F., & Fitzpatrick, M. A. (1997). Family type and conflict: The impact of conversation orientation and conformity orientation on conflict in the family. *Communication Studies, 48,* 59–78.

Kohlberg, L. (1966). A cognitive-developmental analysis of children's sex-role concepts and attitudes. In E. E. Maccoby (Ed.), *The development of sex differences.* Palo Alto, CA: Stanford University Press.

Kornblith, A. B., Herdon, J. E., Zuckerman, E., Viscoli, C. M., Horwitz, R. I., Cooper, M. R., Harris, L., Tkaczuk, K. H., Perry, M. C., & Budman, D. (2001). *Cancer Cytopathology, 92,* 443–454.

Kramerae, C. (1981). *Women and men speaking: Frameworks for analysis.* Rowley, MA: Newbury House.

Kramerae, C. (1989). Feminist theories in communication. In E. Barnouw and others (Eds.), *International encyclopedia of communications* (Vol. 2, pp. 157–160). New York: Oxford University Press.

Krause, N. (1990). Stress, support, and well-being in later life: Focusing on salient social roles. In M. A. Stephens, J. H. Crowther, S. E. Hobfoll, & D. L. Tennenbaum (Eds.), *Stress and coping in later-life families* (pp. 71–97). Washington, DC: Hemisphere.

Kubey, R. (1980). Television and aging: Past, present, & future. *The Gerontologist, 20,* 16–35.

Kuhl, P. K. (2000). A new view of language acquisition. *Proceedings of the National Academy of Sciences, 97,* 11850–11857.

Lacayo, R. (1995, June 12). Violent reaction, *Time,* 25–30.

La Gaipa, J. J. (1990). The negative effects of informal support systems. In S. Duck & R. C. Silver (Eds.), *Personal relationships and social support* (pp. 122–139). Newbury Park, CA: Sage.

Lee, T. R., Mancini, J. A., & Maxwell, J. W. (1990). Sibling relationships in adulthood: Contact patterns and motivations. *Journal of Marriage and the Family, 52,* 431–440.

Leserman, J., Petitto, J. M., & Evans, D. L. (2000). Impact of stressful life events, depression, social support, coping, and Cortisol on progression to AIDS. *American Journal of Psychiatry, 157,* 1221–1224.

Leskela, U. S., Melartin, T. K., Lestela-Mielonen, P. S., Rytsala, H. J., Sokero, T. P., Heikkinen, M. E., & Isometsa, E. T. (2002). Life events, social support and the onset of major depressive episode. *European Psychiatry, 17,* 175–182.

Levinson, D. J. in collaboration with Darrow C. N., Klein, E. B., Levinson, M. H., & McKee, B. (1978). *The season's of a man's life.* New York: Knopf.

Levy, B. (1996). Improving memory in old age through implicit self-stereotyping. *Journal of Personality and Social Psychology, 71,* 1092–1107.

Lulofs, R. S., & Cahn, D. D. (2000). *Conflict: From theory to action* (2nd ed.). Boston: Allyn and Bacon.

Maccoby, E. E. (1992). The role of parents in the socialization of children: An historical overview. *Developmental Psychology, 28,* 1006–1018.

Maccoby, E. E., & Martin, J. A. (1983). Socialization in the context of the family: Parent-child interaction. In E. M. Hetherington (Ed.), *Handbook of child psychology: Vol. 4, Socialization, personality, and social development* (4th ed., pp. 26–47). New York: Wiley.

Mailbach, E., & Parrott, R. L. (1995). *Designing health messages: Approaches from the communication theory and public health practice.* Thousand Oaks, CA: Sage.

Mancini, J., & Blieszner, R. (1989). Aging parents and adult children: Research themes in intergenerational relations. *Journal of Marriage and the Family, 51,* 275–290.

Manton, K. G., & Suzman, R. (1992). Forecasting health and functioning in aging societies; Implications for health care and staffing needs. In M. G. Ory, R. P. Abeles, & P. D. Lipman (Eds.), *Aging, health, and behavior* (pp. 327–357). Newbury Park, CA: Sage.

Mares, M., & Cantor, J. (1992). Elderly viewers' responses to televised portrayals of old age: Empathy and mood management versus social comparison. *Communication Research, 19,* 459–478.

Mathews, K. M., White, M. C., & Long, R. G. (1999). Why study the complexity sciences in the social sciences. *Human Relations, 52,* 439–448.

Matthews, S. H. (1986). *Friendships through the life course: Oral biographies in old age.* Beverly Hills, CA: Sage.

Matthews, S. H. (1994). Gender-roles and filial responsibility. In M. R. Stevenson (Ed.), *Gender roles through the life span: A multidisciplinary perspective* (pp. 245–258). Muncie, IN: Ball State University.

McArdle, J. J. (1998). Modeling longitudinal data by latent growth curve methods. In G. A. Marcoulides (Ed.), *Modern methods for business research: Methodology for business and management* (pp. 359–406). Mahwah, NJ: Lawrence Erlbaum Associates.

McArdle, J. J., & Nesselroade, J. R. (1994). Using multivariate data to structure developmental change. In S. H. Cohen & H. W. Reese (Eds.), *Life-span developmental psychology: Methodological contributions* (pp. 223–267). Hillsdale, NJ: Lawrence Erlbaum Associates.

McDonald, G. W. (1980). Family power: The assessment of a decade of theory and research. *Journal of Marriage and the Family, 42*, 111–124.

McGoldrick, M. (1993). Ethnicity, cultural diversity and normality. In F. Walsh (Ed.), *Normal family processes* (2nd ed., pp. 331–336). New York: Guilford.

McGuire, F., Boyd, R., & Barth, M. C. (1996). *Leisure and aging: Ulyssean living in later life.* Champaign, IL: Sagamon.

McKay, V. C., & Caverly, R. S. (1995). Relationships in later life: The nature of inter- and intragenerational ties among grandparents, grandchildren, and adult siblings. In J. F. Nussbaum & J. Coupland (Eds.), *Handbook of communication and aging research* (pp. 207–255). Mahwah, NJ: Lawrence Erlbaum Associates.

Messman, S. J., & Canary, D. J. (1998). Patterns of conflict in personal relationships. In B. H. Spitzberg & W. R. Cupach (Eds.), *The dark side of close relationships* (pp. 121–152). Mahwah, NJ: Lawrence Erlbaum Associates.

Metts, S., Sprecher, S., & Cupach, W. R. (1991). Retrospective self-reports. In B. M. Montgomery & S. Duck (Eds.), *Studying interpersonal interaction* (pp. 162–178). New York: Guilford.

Michalak, E. E., Wilkinson, C., Hood, K., Dowrick, C., & Wilkinson, G. (2003). Seasonality, negative life events and social support in a community sample. *British Journal of Psychiatry, 182*, 434–438.

Mickleson, K. D., & Kubzansky, L. D. (2003). Social distribution of social support: The mediating role of life events. *American Journal of Community Psychology, 32*, 265–281.

Miller, N. B., Smerglia, V. L., & Kitson, G. C. (1998). Stressful life events, social support, and the distress of widowed and divorced women: A counteractive model. *Journal of Family Issues, 19*, 181–193.

Miller, P. N., Miller, D. W., McKibbin, E. M., & Pettys, G. L. (1999). Stereotypes of the elderly in magazine advertisements 1956–1996. *International Journal of Aging and Human Development, 49*, 319–337.

Minuchin, P. (1992). Conflict and child maltreatment. In C. U. Shantz & W. W. Hartup (Eds.), *Conflict in child and adolescent development* (pp. 380–401). New York: Cambridge University Press.

Monsour, M. (2002). *Women and men as friends.* Mahwah, NJ: Lawrence Erlbaum Associates.

Moody, H. R. (1994). *Aging concepts and controversies.* Thousand Oaks, CA: Sage.

Morgan, D. L. (1988). Age differences in social network participation. *Journal of Gerontology, 43*, S129–S137.

Morgan, M. M., & Hummert, M. L. (2000). Perceptions of communicative control strategies in mother-daughter dyads across the life span. *Journal of Communication, 50*, 48–64.

Mosher, R. L., Youngman, D. J., & Day, J. M. (Eds.). (1999). *Human development across the life span: Educational and psychological applications.* New York: Praeger.

Nathanson, A. I. (2001). Mediation of children's television viewing: Working toward conceptual clarity and common understanding. In W. B. Gudykunst (Ed.), *Communication yearbook 25* (pp. 115–151). Mahwah, NJ: Lawrence Erlbaum Associates.

National Telecommunications and Information Administration. (2000). *Falling through the net: Toward digital inclusion.* Washington, D.C.: United States Commerce Department. Retrieved from http://www.search.ntia.doc.gov./pdf/fttnoo.pdf [Accessed June 18, 2002].

Nesselroade, J. R., & Reese, H. W. (1973). *Life-span developmental psychology: Methodological issues.* New York: Academic Press.

Neugarten, B. L., & Weinstein, K. K. (1964). The changing American grandparent. *Journal of Marriage and the Family, 26,* 199–204.

Ng, S. H., Liu, J. H., Weatherall, A., & Loong, C. S. F. (1997). Younger adults, communication experiences and contact with elders and peers. *Human Communication Research, 24,* 82–108.

Noller, P., Feeney, J. A., & Peterson, C. (2001). *Personal relationships across the lifespan.* East Sussex, UK: Psychology Press.

Noller, P., Feeney, J. A., Peterson, C. C., & Sheehan, G. (1995). Learning conflict patterns in the family: Links between marital, parental, and sibling relationships. In T. J. Socha & G. H. Stamp (Eds.), *Parents, children, and communication: Frontiers of theory and research* (pp. 273–298). Mahwah, NJ: Lawrence Erblaum Associates.

Noller, P., & Fitzpatrick, M. A. (1993). *Communication in family relationships.* Englewood Cliffs, NJ: Prentice-Hall.

Northcott, H. C. (1975). Too young, too old—Age in the world of television. *Gerontologist, 30,* 184–186.

Notman, M. T. (1982). The displaced homemaker: A crisis in later life—the midlife years and after. *Journal of Geriatric Psychiatry, 15,* 173–186.

Nunnally, J. C. (1973). Research strategies and measurement models for investigating human development. In J. R. Nesselroade & H. W. Reese (Eds.), *Life-span developmental psychology: Methodological issues* (pp. 87–110). New York: Academic Press.

Nussbaum, J. F. (1983). Relational closeness of elderly interaction: Implications for life satisfaction. *Western Journal of Speech Communication, 47,* 229–243.

Nussbaum, J. F. (1985). Successful aging: A communicative model. *Communication Quarterly, 33,* 262–269.

Nussbaum, J. F. (1989). *Life-span communication: Normative processes.* Hillsdale, NJ: Lawrence Erlbaum Associates.

Nussbaum, J. F. (1990). Communication within the nursing home: Survivability as a function of resident-staff affinity. In H. Giles, N. Coupland, & J. M. Wiemann (Eds.), *Communication, health and the elderly* (pp. 155–171). Manchester, UK: Manchester University Press.

Nussbaum, J. F. (1991). Communication, language and the institutionalised elderly. *Ageing and Society, 11,* 149–166.

Nussbaum, J. F. (1994). Friendship in older adulthood. In M. L. Hummert, J. M. Wiemann, & J. F. Nussbaum (Eds.), *Interpersonal communication in older adulthood* (pp. 209–225). Thousand Oaks, CA: Sage.

Nussbaum, J. F. (1998). Physician-older patient communication during the transition from independence to dependence. *The Journal of the Oklahoma State Medical Association, 91,* 1–5.

Nussbaum, J. F., & Bettini, L. (1994). Shared stories of the grandparent-grandchild relationship. *International Journal of Aging and Human Development, 39,* 67–80.

Nussbaum, J. F., Hummert, M. L., Williams, A., & Harwood, J. (1996). Communication and older adults. *Communication yearbook 19* (pp. 1–47). Thousand Oaks, CA: Sage.

Nussbaum, J. F., Pecchioni, L., Robinson, J. D., & Thompson, T. (2000). *Communication and aging* (2nd ed.). Mahwah, NJ: Lawrence Erlbaum Associates.

Nussbaum, J. F., Robinson, J. D., & Grew, D. J. (1985). Communicative behavior of long-term health care employees: Implications for the elderly resident. *Communication Research Reports, 2,* 16–22.

Nussbaum, J. F., Thompson, T., & Robinson, J. D. (1989). *Communication and aging.* New York: Harper & Row.

O'Bryant, S. L. (1994). Widowhood in later life: An opportunity to become androgynous. In M. R. Stevenson (Ed.), *Gender roles through the life span: A multidisciplinary perspective* (pp. 283–299). Muncie, IN: Ball State University.

O'Keefe, B. (1988). The logic of message design: Individual differences in reasoning about communication. *Communication Monographs, 55,* 80–103.

Olshansky, S. J., & Carnes, B. A. (2000). *The quest for immortality: Science at the frontiers of aging.* New York: Norton.

Ory, M. G., Abeles, R. P., & Lipman, P. (1992). *Aging, health, and behavior.* Newbury Park, CA: Sage.

Osborne, L. N., & Fincham, F. D. (1994). Conflict between parents and their children. In D. D. Cahn (Ed.), *Conflict in personal relationships* (pp. 117–141). Hillsdale, NJ: Lawrence Erlbaum Associates.

Paikoff, R. L., & Brooks-Gunn, J. (1991). Do parent-child relationships change during puberty? *Psychological Bulletin, 110,* 47–66.

Parrott, R. L. (1995). Motivation to attend to health messages: Presentation of content and linguistic considerations. In E. Mailbach & R. L. Parrott (Eds.), *Designing health messages: Approaches from communication theory and public health practice* (pp. 7–23). Thousand Oaks, CA: Sage.

Patterson, B. R. (1995). Communication network activity: Network attributes of the young and elderly. *Communication Quarterly, 43,* 155–166.

Patterson, B. R., & Bettini, L. A. (1993). Age, depression, and friendship: Development of a general friendship inventory. *Communication Research Reports, 10,* 161–170.

Patterson, B. R., Bettini, L., & Nussbaum, J. F. (1993). The meaning of friendship across the life-span: Two studies. *Communication Quarterly, 41,* 145–160.

Patterson, B. R., & Wright, K. B. (2001, November). *Macro-dynamics of friendship over the life span: The role of friendship style.* Paper presented at the annual meeting of the National Communication Association, Atlanta, GA.

Pawluch, D. (1986). Transitions in pediatrics: a segmental analysis. In P. Conrad & R. Kern (Eds.), *The sociology of health and illness: Critical perspectives* (pp. 155–171). New York: St. Martin's Press.

Pearce, W. B. (1976). The coordinated management of meaning: A rules based theory of interpersonal communication. In G. R. Miller (Ed.), *Explorations in interpersonal communication* (pp. 17–36). Beverly Hills, CA: Sage.

Pearce, W. B., & Cronen, V. (1980). *Communication, action, and meaning.* New York: Praeger.

Pearson, J. C. (1993). *Communication in the family: Seeking satisfaction in changing times* (2nd ed.). New York: HarperCollins.

Pecchioni, L. L., & Croghan, J. M. (2002). Young adults' stereotypes of the elderly with their grandparents as the targets. *Journal of Communication, 52,* 715–730.

Pecchioni, L. L., & Nussbaum, J. F. (2001). Mother-adult daughter discussions of caregiving prior to dependency: Exploring conflicts among European-American women. *Journal of Family Communication, 2,* 133–150.

Piaget, J. (1954). *The construction of reality in the child.* New York: Basic Books.

Piaget, J. (1959). *The language and thought of the child.* New York: Free Press.

Piaget, J. (1972). *The psychology of intelligence.* Totowa, NJ: Littlefield-Adams.

Powers, E. A., & Bultena, G. L. (1988). Sex differences in intimate friendships in old age. *Journal of Marriage and the Family, 26,* 738–747.

Prince, M. J., Harwood, R. H., & Mann, A. H. (1997). Social support deficits, loneliness and life events as risk factors for depression in old age. The Gospel Oak Project VI. *Psychological Medicine, 27,* 323–337.

Pritchett, L. M. (2000, June 21). New age of medicine. *Business first: The weekly business newspaper of greater Louisville.* Retrieved from http://louisville.bcentral.com/louisville/stories/2000/06/26/focus4.html [Accessed August 4, 2000].

Putnam, L. L., & Wilson, C. E. (1982). Communicative strategies in organizational conflicts: Reliability and validity of a measurement scale. In M. Burgoon (Ed.), *Communication yearbook 6* (pp. 629–652). New Brunswick, NJ: Transaction.

Rahim, M. A. (1983). A measure of styles of handling interpersonal conflict. *Academy of Management Journal, 26,* 368–376.

Rawlins, W. K. (1981). *Friendship as a communicative achievement: A theory and an interpretive analysis of verbal reports.* Unpublished doctoral dissertation. Temple University, Philadelphia, PA.

Rawlins, W. K. (1989). A dialectical analysis of the tensions, functions, and strategic challenges of communication in young adult friendships. In J. Anderson (Ed.), *Communication yearbook 12* (pp. 157–189). Newbury Park, CA: Sage.

Rawlins, W. K. (1992). *Friendship matters: Communication, dialectics, and the life course.* New York: de Gruyter.

Rawlins, W. K. (1995). Friendships in later life. In J. F. Nussbaum & J. Coupland (Eds.), *Handbook of communication and aging research* (pp. 227–257). Mahwah, NJ: Lawrence Erlbaum Associates.

Reed, S. K. (1988). *Cognition: Theory and applications* (2nd ed.). Monterey, CA: Brooks/Cole.

Richards, L. N., Bengston, V. L., & Miller, R. B. (1989). The generation in the middle: Perceptions of changes in adults' intergenerational relationships. In K. Kreppner & R. M. Lerner (Eds.), *Family systems and life-span development* (pp. 341–366). Hillsdale, NJ: Lawrence Erlbaum Associates.

Riggio, H. R. (2000). Measuring attitudes toward adult sibling relationships: The lifespan sibling relationship scale. *Journal of Social and Personal Relationships, 17,* 707–728.

Riggs, K. E. (1998). *Mature audiences: Television in the lives of elders.* Piscataway, NJ: Rutgers University Press.

Rimmerman, A., & Muraver, M. (2001). Experiencing undesired daily life events, instrumental functioning, social support and well-being of Israeli elderly women: Comparison
between caregivers/non-caregivers for adult children with mental retardation. *Journal
of Women and Aging, 13*, 57–70.

Roberts, S. D., & Zhou, N. (1997). The 50 and older characters in the advertisements of
Modern Maturity: Growing older, getting better? *The Journal of Applied Gerontology, 16*,
208–220.

Robinson, J., & Godbey, G. (1999). *Time for life: The surprising ways Americans use their
time*. University Park: Penn State Press.

Robinson, J. D., & Skill, T. (1995). Media usage patterns and portrayals of the elderly.
In J. F. Nussbaum & J. Coupland (Eds.), *Handbook of communication and aging research*
(pp. 359–391). Mahwah, NJ: Lawrence Erlbaum Associates.

Robinson, J. D., Skill, T., & Turner, J. W. (2004). Media usage and portrayals of the
elderly. In J. F. Nussbaum & J. Coupland (Eds.), *Handbook of communication and aging
research* 2nd ed., (pp. 423–446). Mahwah, NJ: Lawrence Erlbaum Associates.

Rogers, L. E. (1981). Symmetry and complementarity: Evolution and evaluation of an
idea. In C. Wilder-Mott & J. H. Weakland (Eds.), *Rigor and imagination: Essays from
the legacy of Gregory Bateson* (pp. 231–251). New York: Praeger.

Roloff, M. E. (1981). *Interpersonal communication: The social exchange approach*. Beverly
Hills, CA: Sage.

Rook, K. S. (1987). Social support versus companionship: Effects on life stress, loneliness,
and evaluations by others. *Journal of Personality and Social Psychology, 52*, 1132–
1147.

Rook, K. S. (1990). Stressful aspects of older adults' social relationships: Current theory
and research. In M. A. Stephens, J. H. Crowther, S. E. Hobfoll, & D. L. Tennenbaum (Eds.), *Stress and coping in later-life families* (pp. 173–192). Washington, DC:
Hemisphere.

Rook, K. S. (1995). Support, companionship, and control in older adults' social networks:
Implications for well-being. In J. F. Nussbaum & J. Coupland (Eds.), *Handbook of
communication and aging research* (pp. 437–463). Mahwah, NJ: Lawrence Erlbaum
Associates.

Ross, H. G., & Millgram, J. I. (1982). Important variables in adult sibling relationships:
A qualitative study. In M. E. Lamb & B. Sutton-Smith (Eds.), *Sibling relationships:
Their nature and significance across the lifespan* (pp. 225–249). Hillsdale, NJ: Lawrence
Erlbaum Associates.

Ross, C. E., & Mirowsky, J. (1990). The impact of the family on health: The decade in
review. *Journal of Marriage & the Family, 52*, 328–342.

Rowe, J. W., & Kahn, R. L. (1998). *Successful aging*. NY: Pantheon.

Roy, A., & Harwood, J. (1997). Underrepresented, positively portrayed: The representation of older adults in television commercials. *Journal of Applied Communication
Research, 25*, 39–56.

Roy, M. P., Steptoe, A., & Kirschbaum, C. (1998). Life events and social support as
moderators of individual differences in cardiovascular and Cortisol reactivity. *Journal
of Personality and Social Psychology, 75*, 1273.

Rudinger, G., & Rietz, C. (2001). Structural equation modeling in longitudinal research
on aging. In J. E. Birren & K. W. Schaie (Eds.), *Handbook of the psychology of aging*
(pp. 29–52). New York: Academic Press.

Rutter, M., & Rutter, M. (1993). *Developing minds: Challenges and continuity across the life span*. NY: HarperCollins.

Ryan, E. B. (1991). Normal aging and language. In R. Lubinski (Ed.), *Dementia and communcation: Clinical and research issues* (pp. 84–97). Toronto: Decker.

Ryan, E. B., Giles, H., Bartolucci, G., & Henwood, K. (1986). Psycholinguistic and social psychological components of communication by and with the elderly. *Language and Communication, 6*, 1–24.

Ryan, E. B., Hummert, M. L., & Boich, L. (1995). Communication predicaments of aging: Patronizing behavior toward older adults. *Journal of Language and Social Psychology, 13*, 144–166.

Saarni, C., Mumme, D. L., & Campos, J. J. (1998). Emotional development: Action, communication, and understanding. In W. Damon (Ed.), *Handbook of child psychology* (5th ed., Vol. 3). New York: Wiley.

Salomon, G. (1990). Cognitive effects with and of computer technology. *Communication Research, 17*, 26–44.

Salzman, C. (1995). Medication compliance in the elderly. *Journal of Clinical Psychiatry, 56*, 18–22.

Sanders, G. F., & Trygstad, D. W. (1993). Strengths in the grandparent-grandchild relationship. *Activities, Adaptation, and Aging, 17*, 43–50.

Sarason, B. R., Sarason, I. G., & Pierce, G. R. (1990). *Social support: An interactional view*. New York: Wiley.

Schaie, K. W. (1965). A general model for the study of developmental change. *Psychological Bulletin, 64*, 92–107.

Schaie, K. W. (1988). The impact of research methodology on theory building in the developmental sciences. In J. E. Birren & V. L. Bengtson (Eds.), *Emergent theories of aging* (pp. 41–57). New York: Springer.

Schaie, K. W. (1990). Intellectual development in adulthood. In J. E. Birren & K. W. Schaie (Eds.), *Handbook of the psychology of aging* (3rd ed., pp. 291–309). New York: Academic Press.

Schaie, K. W. (1996). *Intellectual development in adulthood: The Seattle longitudinal study*. New York: Cambridge University Press.

Schaie, K. W., & Baltes, P. B. (1975). On sequential strategies in developmental research. *Human Development, 18*, 384–390.

Schaie, K. W., & Hofer, S. M. (2001). Longitudinal studies in aging research. In J. E. Birren & K. W. Schaie (Eds.), *Handbook of the psychology of aging* (pp. 53–77). New York: Academic Press.

Schank, R., & Abelson, R. (1977). *Scripts, goals, and understanding*. Hillsdale, NJ: Lawrence Erlbaum Associates.

Scheflen, A. (1972). *Body language and the social order*. Englewood Cliffs, NJ: Prentice-Hall.

Scheflen, A. (1974). *How behavior means*. New York: Doubleday.

Schmidt, D. F., & Boland, S. M. (1986). Structure of perceptions of older adults: Evidence for multiple stereotypes. *Psychology and aging, 1*, 255–260.

Schwarzer, R., & Leppin, A. (1991). Social support and health: A theoretical and empirical overview. *Journal of Social and Personal Relationships, 8*, 99–127.

Schwebel, J., Maher, C. A., & Fagley, N. S. (Eds.). (1990). *Promoting cognitive growth over the life span*. Hillsdale, NJ: Lawrence Erlbaum Associates.

Selman, R. (1980). Development of the concept of intention. In W. A. Collins (Ed.), *Minnesota symposium on child psychology* (Vol. 13, pp. 92–104). New York: Academic Press.

Selman, R. (1981). The child as friendship philosopher. In S. R. Asher & J. M. Gottman (Eds.), *The development of children's friendships* (pp. 242–272). Cambridge, UK: Cambridge University Press.

SeniorNet (2000). SeniorNet survey about the Internet, April 2000. Retrieved from http://www.seniornet.org/php/default.php?PageID=5472&Version=0&Font=0 [Accessed June 20, 2001].

Shantz, C. U. (1993). Children's conflicts: Representations and lessons learned. In R. R. Cocking & K. A. Renninger (Eds.), *The development and meaning of psychological distance* (pp. 185–202). Hillsdale, NJ: Lawrence Erlbaum Associates.

Shantz, C. U., & Hartup, W. W. (1992). Conflict and development: An introduction. In C. U. Shantz & W. W. Hartup (Eds.), *Conflict in child and adolescent development* (pp. 1–11). New York: Cambridge University Press.

Sherry, J. L. (2001). The effects of violent video games on aggression: A meta-analysis. *Human Communication Research, 27,* 409–431.

Sillars, A. L. (1980). Attributions and communication in roommate conflicts. *Communication Monographs, 47,* 180–200.

Sillars, A. L. (1991). Behavioral observation. In B. M. Montgomery & S. Duck (Eds.), *Studying interpersonal interaction* (pp. 197–218). New York: Guilford.

Sillars, A. L. (1995). Communication and family culture. In M. A. Fitzpatrick & A. L. Vangelisti (Eds.), *Explaining family interactions* (pp. 375–399). Thousand Oaks, CA: Sage.

Sillars, A. L., Coletti, S. F., Parry, D., & Rogers, M. A. (1982). Coding verbal conflict tactics: Nonverbal and perceptual correlates of the "avoidance-distributive-integrative" distinction. *Human Communication Research, 9,* 83–95.

Sillars, A. L., & Weisberg, J. (1987). Conflict as a social skill. In M. E. Roloff & G. R. Miller (Eds.), *Interpersonal processes: New directions in communication research* (pp. 140–171). Newbury Park, CA: Sage.

Sillars, A. L., & Wilmot, W. W. (1989). Marital communication across the life span. In J. F. Nussbaum (Ed.), *Life-span communication: Normative processes* (pp. 163–190). Hillsdale, NJ: Lawrence Erlbaum Associates.

Silvern, S. B., & Williamson, P. A. (1987). The effects of video game play on young children's aggression, fantasy, and prosocial behavior. *Journal of Applied Developmental Psychology, 8,* 453–462.

Simmons Market Research Bureau. (1991). *The 1990 study of media and markets.* New York: Author.

Singh, B. R., & Williams, J. S. (1982). Childlessness and family satisfaction. *Research on Aging, 3,* 218–227.

Singh, M. A. F. (2002). Exercise comes of age: Rationale and recommendations for a geriatric exercise prescription. *Journal of Gerontology: Medical Sciences, 57A,* M262–M282.

Smith, A. D. (1996). Memory. In J. E. Birren & K. W. Schaie (Eds.), *Handbook of the psychology of aging* (4th ed., pp. 236–250). New York: Academic Press.

Smith, J., & Baltes, P. B. (1990). A life-span perspective on thinking and problem-solving. In M. Schwebel, C. A. Maher, & N. S. Fagley (Eds.), *Promoting cognitive growth over the life span* (pp. 47–69). Hillsdale, NJ: Lawrence Erlbaum Associates.

Smith, S. L., & Boyson, A. R. (2002). Violence in music videos: Examining the prevalence and context of physical aggression. *Journal of Communication, 52*, 61–83.

Sommerville, R. (2001). Demographic research on newspaper readership: How demographics affect decisions in print journalism. *Generations, 25*, 24–30.

Sparks, G. G. (2002). *Media effects research: A basic overview.* Belmont, CA: Wadsworth.

Sprecher, S., & Felmlee, D. (1993). Conflict, love and other relationship dimensions for individuals in dissolving, stable, and growing premarital relationships. *Free Inquiry in Creative Sociology, 21*(2), 1–12.

Staton, A. Q. (1990). *Communication and student socialization.* Norwood, NJ: Ablex.

Stephens, M. A. P. (1990). Social relationships as coping resources in later-life families. In M. A. P. Stephens, J. H. Crowther, S. E. Hobfoll, & D. L. Tennenbaum (Eds.), *Stress and coping in later-life families* (pp. 1–20). New York: Hemisphere.

Sterns, H. I., & Huyck, M. H. (2001). The role of work in midlife. In M. E. Lachman (Ed.), *Handbook of midlife development* (pp. 447–486). New York: Wiley.

Stevenson, M. R. (Ed.). (1994). *Gender roles through the life span: A multidisciplinary perspective.* Muncie, IN: Ball State University.

Stevenson, M. R., Paludi, M. A., Black, K. N., & Whitley, B. E., Jr. (1994). Gender roles: A multidisciplinary life-span perspective. In M. R. Stevenson (Ed.), *Gender roles through the life span: A multidisciplinary perspective* (pp. ix–xxxi). Muncie, IN: Ball State University.

Stocker, C., Dunn, J., & Plomin, R. (1989). Sibling relationships: Links with child temperament, maternal behavior, and family structure. *Child Development, 60*, 715–727.

Stroebe, M. S., Hansson, R. O., Stroebe, W., & Shut, H. (2001). *Handbook of bereavement research: Consequences, coping, and care.* Washington, DC: American Psychological Association.

Suls, J. (1982). Social support, interpersonal relations, and health: Benefits and liabilities. In G. S. Sanders & J. Suls (Eds.), *Social psychology of health and illness* (pp. 255–277). Hillsdale, NJ: Lawrence Erlbaum Associates.

Swayne, L. E., & Greco, A. J. (1987). The portrayal of older Americans in television commercials. *Journal of Advertising, 16*, 47–54.

Sypher, B. D., & Zorn, T. (1986). Communication-related abilities and upward mobility: A longitudinal investigation. *Human Communication Research, 12*, 420–431.

Szinovacz, M., & Ekerdt, D. J. (1994). Families and retirement. In R. Blieszner & V. Bedford (Eds.), *Aging and the family: Theory and research* (pp. 375–400). New York: Praeger.

Thibaut, J., & Kelly, H. (1959). *The social psychology of groups.* New York: Wiley.

Thomas, K. W., & Kilmann, R. H. (1974). *Conflict mode instrument.* Tuxedo, NY: XICOM.

Thomas, V., & Wolfe, D. B. (1995, May). Why won't television grow up? *American Demographics*, 24–29.

Thompson, L. W., Breckenridge, J. N., Gallagher, D., & Peterson, J. (1984). Effects of bereavement on self-perceptions of physical health in elderly widows and widowers. *Journal of Gerontology, 39*, 309–314.

Thompson, T., Robinson, J. R., & Beisecker, A. E. (2004). The older patient-physician interaction. In J. F. Nussbaum & J. Coupland (Eds.), *Handbook of communication and aging research* (2nd ed.) (pp. 451–477). Mahwah, NJ: Lawrence Erlbaum Associates.

Troll, L. E. (1982). *Continuations: Adult development and aging.* Monterey, CA: Brooks/Cole.

Troll, L. E. (1983). Grandparents: The family watchdogs. In T. H. Brubaker (Ed.), *Family relationships in later life* (pp. 63–74). Beverly Hills, CA: Sage.

Troll, L. E. (1987). Mother-daughter relationships through the life span. In S. Oskamp (Ed.), *Family processes and problems: Social psychological aspects* (pp. 284–305). Newbury Park, CA: Sage.

Umberson, D. (1987). Family status and health behaviors: Social control as a dimension of social integration. *Journal of Health and Social Behavior, 28,* 306–319.

Umberson, D. (1993). Relationships between adult children and their parents: Psychological consequences for both generations. *Journal of Marriage and the Family, 54,* 664–674.

U.S. Bureau of the Census. (1991). *Current population reports: Population profile of the United States: 1991* (Series p-23, No. 173). Washington, DC: U.S. Government Printing Office.

U.S. Census Bureau. (2000). *Marital status of the population 65 years and over by citizenship status: March 2000.* Retrieved January 17, 2003, from http://www.census.gov/population/socdemo/foreign/ppl-151/tab02.pdf

U.S. News & World Report. (2001, June 4). Shaping up under a watchful eye: Hospital-based gyms offer medical expertise, 71.

U.S. News & World Report. (2002, May 27). Working out with grandpa, 38.

Utz, R. L., Carr, D., Nesse, R., & Wortman, C. B. (2002). The effect of widowhood on older adults' social participation: An evaluation of activity, disengagement, and continuity theories. *The Gerontologist, 42,* 522–537.

Vandell, D. L., & Bailey, M. D. (1992). Conflicts between siblings. In C. U. Shantz & W. W. Hartup (Eds.), *Conflict in child and adolescent development* (pp. 242–269). Cambridge, UK: Cambridge University Press.

Van der Voort, T. A. (1986). *Television violence: A child's eye view.* New York: North-Holland.

Van Erva, J. P. (1998). *Television and child development* (2nd ed.). Mahwah, NJ: Lawrence Erlbaum Associates.

Van Maanen, J. (1976). Breaking in: Socialization to work. In R. Dubin (Ed.), *Handbook of work, organization, and society* (pp. 67–130). Chicago: Rand McNally.

Vaux, A. (1988). *Social support: Theory, research, intervention.* New York: Praeger.

Wade, T. D., & Kendler, K. S. (2000). Absence of interactions between social support and stressful life events in the prediction of major depression and depressive symptomology in women. *Psychological Medicine, 30,* 965–972.

Waldrop, M. M. (1992). *Complexity: The emerging science at the edge of chaos.* New York: Simon & Schuster.

Walker, A. J., & Allen, K. R. (1991). Relationships between caregiving daughters and their elderly mothers. *The Gerontologist, 31,* 389–396.

Walsh, F. (1988). The family in later life. In B. Carter & M. McGoldrick (Eds.), *The changing family life cycle: A framework for family therapy* (pp. 311–332). New York: Gardner.

Ward, C. R., & Smith, T. (1997, Fall). Forging intergenerational communities through information technology: A conscious effort is required. *Generations,* 38–41.

White, H., McConnel, E., Clipp, E., Bymum, L., Teague, C., Navas, L., Craven, S., & Halbrecht, H. (1999). Surfing the Net in later life: A review of the literature and pilot study of computer use and quality of life. *Journal of Applied Gerontology, 18,* 358–378.

Williams, A., & Nussbaum, J. F. (2001). *Intergenerational communication across the life span.* Mahwah, NJ: Lawrence Erlbaum Associates.

Willis, S. L. (1996). Everyday problem solving. In J. E. Birren & K. W. Schaie (Eds.), *Handbook of the psychology of aging* (4th ed., pp. 286–307). New York: Academic Press.

Wilmot, W. W., & Sillars, A. L. (1989). Developmental issues in personal relationships. In J. F. Nussbaum (Ed.), *Life-span communication: Normative processes* (pp. 119–132). Hillsdale, NJ: Lawrence Erlbaum Associates.

Wilson, B. J., Smith, S. L., Potter, W. J., Kunkel, D., Linz, D., Colvin, C. M., & Donnerstein, E. (2002). Violence in children's television programming: Assessing the risks. *Journal of Communication, 52,* 5–35.

Wood, J. T. (1982). Communication and relational culture: Bases for the study of human relationships. *Communication Quarterly, 30,* 75–84.

World Almanac and Book of Facts. (2001). Mahwah, NJ: World Almanac Books.

Wright, K. B. (2000a). The communication of social support within an on-line community for older adults: A qualitative analysis of the SeniorNet community. *Qualitative Research Reports in Communication, 1,* 33–43.

Wright, K. B. (2000b). Computer-mediated social support, older adults, and coping. *Journal of Communication, 50,* 100–118.

Wright, K. B., & Query, J. L. (2004). On-line support and older adults: A theoretical examination of benefits and limitations of computer-mediated support networks for older adults and possible health outcomes. In J. F. Nussbaum & J. Coupland (Eds.), *Handbook of communication and aging* (2nd ed., pp. 499–519). Mahwah, NJ: Lawrence Erlbaum Associates.

Xu, Z.-n. (2001). Relationship between postpartum depression, life events and social support. *Chinese Journal of Clinical Psychology, 9,* 130–136.

Ylanne-McEwen, V. (2000). Golden times for golden agers: Selling holidays as lifestyles for the over 50s. *Journal of Communication, 50,* 83–99.

Zietlow, P. H., & Sillars, A. L. (1988). Life-stage differences in communication during marital conflicts. *Journal of Social and Personal Relationships, 5,* 223–245.

Author Index

Subject Index

A

Acquisitive friendship style, 102
Active mediation, 217
Adaptability, 64–65
Adolescents. *See also* Children
conflict and, 79, 146–147, 149, 152, 153, 157
exercise and, 206
friendship and, 111–112, 159–160
gender roles in, 127
health messages for, 180
Internet use by, 200–201
role changes in, 74–75
siblings and, 157
social support for, 172
work role socialization in, 134–135
Adult children
as caregivers for elderly parents, 83–85, 130–131
departure of, 80–83
relationship between elderly parents and, 91–95
Adults. *See* Middle-age individuals; Older adults; Young adults
African Americans, 236
Age
health communication and, 190–191
marital conflict and, 164–165
mental health and, 34, 38
sibling conflict and, 156–157
stereotypes and, 34–35, 113, 201, 235–238

Aggressive behavior
environmental and trait influences on, 220–221
role of media in, 219–224
violent media content and, 221–222
Aging. *See also* Older adults; Older parents
cognitive processes and, 34, 36–39
elements of variability and, 7
gender roles and, 129
perceptions of, 95–96
stereotypes of, 34–35
American Association for Retired Persons (AARP), 231, 234
Anticipatory socialization, 134
Attachment theory, 58
Authoritarian parenting, 67, 68
Authoritative parenting, 67, 68

B

Baby Boomer Bistro, 199
Birth order, 69–70
Brain development, 28
Buffering model, 170–171

C

Caregivers
for elderly parents, 83–85, 130–131
mothers as primary, 151
siblings as, 158
CAT perspective, 258, 259
Chaos theory, 18